TIBET AND ITS HISTORY

His Holiness The Dalai Lama

TIBET AND ITS HISTORY

Second Edition, Revised and Updated

HUGH E. RICHARDSON

SHAMBHALA
Boston & London
1984

SHAMBHALA PUBLICATIONS, INC.
314 DARTMOUTH STREET
BOSTON, MASSACHUSETTS 02116

© 1962 BY H. E. RICHARDSON
NEW MATERIAL © 1984 BY H. E. RICHARDSON
ALL RIGHTS RESERVED
9 8 7 6 5 4 3 2
FIRST PAPERBACK EDITION

DISTRIBUTED IN THE UNITED STATES BY RANDOM HOUSE
AND IN CANADA BY RANDOM HOUSE OF CANADA LTD.

PRINTED IN THE UNITED STATES OF AMERICA

LIBRARY OF CONGRESS CATALOGING-IN-PUBLICATION DATA

RICHARDSON, HUGH EDWARD, 1905–
TIBET AND ITS HISTORY.

REV. ED. OF: A SHORT HISTORY
OF TIBET. 1962.
BIBLIOGRAPHY: P.
INCLUDES INDEX.
1. TIBET (CHINA)—HISTORY.
I. RICHARDSON, HUGH
EDWARD, 1905– .
SHORT HISTORY OF TIBET.
II. TITLE.
DS786.R5 1986   951'.5   86-11836
ISBN 0-87773-376-7 (PBK.)

CONTENTS

ILLUSTRATIONS

PREFACE

Listening to the debate on Tibet at the 14th session of the General Assembly of the United Nations in October 1959 I was struck by the need for a guide to Tibetan history which had regard not only to its continuous development over thirteen centuries but also to the Tibetan background and character and to the Tibetan point of view. That is what I try to offer in this book. It is meant for the general reader and is, therefore, not weighted with footnotes and detailed references but I hope that anyone who wants to check the evidence for statements in it will find no difficulty in doing so from the bibliography at the end.

Conditions and institutions in Tibet are described as I saw them before the end of 1950. The use of the past tense has been imposed by the Chinese Communist invasion and occupation of the country which introduced sweeping changes and culminated in the tragic events of March 1959 and the abolition of the long-established form of government.

Tibetan words and names are rendered phonetically. Transliteration of the original spelling should be unnecessary for students of Tibetan and would only confuse the general reader.

I have enjoyed the help of several Tibetan friends in many matters and I am also grateful to Sir Olaf Caroe, K.C.S.I., K.C.I.E., a former Foreign Secretary to the Government of India, and Mr. Marco Pallis, author of *Peaks and Lamas* and an expert on Tibetan life and religion, who were kind enough to read the manuscript and who gave me valuable advice. Many of their suggestions have been embodied in the book; such mistakes as there may be are my own.

November, 1961.   H.E.R.

TIBET AND ITS HISTORY

I

THE TIBETAN BACKGROUND

There is no general agreement about the territorial limits of Tibet; only part of the country has been surveyed and there has never been a properly conducted census. Figures of area, population, etc. are therefore approximations and the considerable variations in different sources are due to the different assumptions on which their calculations are based.

Sir Charles Bell, the best-known British authority, has differentiated between 'political' and 'ethnographic' Tibet; and in the map on page 2 of this work an attempt is made to follow that distinction. The shaded area is 'political' Tibet. There Tibetan governments have ruled continuously from the earliest times down to 1951. The region beyond that to the north and east, enclosed in a broken line, is its 'ethnographic' extension which people of Tibetan race once inhabited exclusively and where they are still in the majority. In that wider area 'political' Tibet exercised jurisdiction only in certain places and at irregular intervals; for the most part, local lay or monastic chiefs were in control of districts of varying size. From the eighteenth century onwards the region was subject to sporadic Chinese infiltration. But in whatever hands actual authority might lie, the religious influence of Lhasa was a long-standing and all-pervading force and large donations of money and valuable goods were annually sent to the Dalai Lama. Loyalty to the spiritual supremacy of the Dalai Lama united the outlying monasteries with those of central Tibet and enhanced the feeling of kinship among people of Tibetan stock wherever they might be.

Radiating lines on the map at p. 2 show that for a few centuries 'political' Tibet's authority spread far beyond its ethnographic borders; but that period ended in the tenth century.

In the text which follows Tibet means 'political' Tibet except

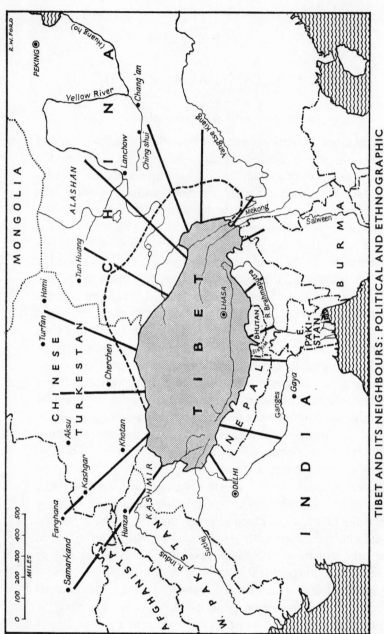

TIBET AND ITS NEIGHBOURS: POLITICAL AND ETHNOGRAPHIC

Shaded area: **Political Tibet**
Broken line: **Limits of Ethnographic Tibet**
Radiating lines: **Extent of Tibetan influence in 6th to 10th centuries**

where otherwise stated or where a different interpretation is
obvious from the context.

GEOGRAPHY

Political Tibet lies roughly between the 28th and 36th parallels
of north latitude and the 79th and 99th of east longitude. The land
falls from west to east and from north to south. It is shaped like
a clenched right fist with the wrist towards the east, and is
enclosed on three sides by mountain ranges. On the north are the
Kuen Lun and Tang La ranges; on the west the massif of the
Karakoram and Ladakh mountains; and on the south for 1,500
miles the majestic sweep of the Himalaya. Only to the east is
there a gap in the mountain ramparts. The Yangtse, Mekong, and
Salween rising in the northern part of that area flow first through
a stretch of comparatively open upland before they turn southwards and cleave three deep parallel gorges which make almost
as formidable a barrier as the mountain ranges.

The area enclosed in those impressive boundaries is about
500,000 square miles. Of that, the greater part—perhaps three-
quarters—is a high, tangled wilderness of mountain ranges and
plains, all of 16,000 feet or over, uninhabited or sparsely scattered
with nomads. The southern quarter of the country contains the
valleys of many great rivers and their tributaries where, from an
elevation of some 15,000 feet down to 9,000 feet, lies the main
cultivated area of Tibet.

A very early poem, a kind of national hymn, of the ninth
century or even earlier, describes Tibet as 'The centre of high
snow mountains; the source of great rivers; a lofty country, a
pure land'. That is a true description, for the mountains which
ring it round are the highest in the world and in the lofty upland
enclosed by them lie the sources of some of the greatest rivers of
Asia. In the south-west, within a distance of about 80 miles, both
the Indus and the Brahmaputra (which is known as the Tsang-po
in Tibet and the Dihang in north-east Assam) rise and take their
divergent courses westward and eastward, breaking through the
mountain barrier at points a thousand miles apart. In the same

small stretch of country are the sources of the Sutlej and Karnali which also force their way through the Himalaya. Going eastward, there are still more rivers which rise in Tibet and penetrate that seemingly impenetrable barrier—the Trisuli, Arun, Manas, and Subansiri—but the gorges which these rivers carve through the Himalaya are so sheer that they do not give easy access to the Indian side; the mountain range has to be crossed by passes of 15,000 to 18,000 feet, most of which lie to the north of the high crest of the Himalaya and are in general comparatively easy of approach from Tibet but steep and laborious on the southern side.

The great rivers which rise in the north-east—the Yangtse, Mekong, and Salween (the Huang Ho rises in ethnographic, not in political, Tibet)—wander for a great distance through rugged upland, marshy plain and grassy valleys before launching their swift southward course, close together, down the eastern borders of Tibet. It is the gap in the north-east corner of this region, between the mountain barrier and the river gorges, that provides the least difficult approach to Tibet; but it is like the entrance to a great fish-trap for, once in, there is no easy way out of the wide encirclement of mountains. Tibet has, therefore, never been a through route for migratory peoples or world-conquering armies and the absence of easy communications has tended to preserve not only the seclusion and conservatism, but also the independence and the national homogeneity of the Tibetans.

Apart from Nepal, only India and China had frontiers with Tibet. India, quite near to the centre of Tibetan life, was restricted by the mountain barrier to small-scale, but constant, exchanges of holy men, pilgrims, and traders. Towards China, until the recent development of motor traffic, the comparatively open access from the north-east, which made larger-scale movements feasible, was counterbalanced by the great distances, stern climate, and the bare, rugged country with scanty grazing and supplies covering the 800 miles between Lhasa and the remote north-west frontier of China near the Kokonor.

RACE

The racial origins of the Tibetans are little known. Systematic study has been restricted by the inaccessibility of the country, the dislike of many Tibetans visiting India to submit to anthropometric examination, the lack of ancient skeletal material due to the virtual impossibility of conducting archaeological excavation and of more recent skeletal material because of the funeral custom of disposing of the dead by cutting up the body, crushing the bones, and feeding the fragments to dogs and vultures.

Ethnologists—whose interpretations disagree widely—have observed two principal strains in the Tibetan population: one tall, long-limbed, often with aquiline features, and long-headed; the other shorter in stature, with high cheekbones, flat noses, and round heads. The former type which is found mainly among the nomads of the north and east and also in the aristocratic families may be related to what Buxton describes as a tall dolicocephalous race of great antiquity quite distinct from what he calls 'Yellow Man'. The ancient Turkic race and the true Mongols may also be traced to that stock. The second type is predominant in the cultivated valleys of central Tibet and in the west. This may be an offshoot in the remote past of the same parent stock, known to Buxton as 'Yellow Man' and to others as Proto-Chinese or Pareoean, from which the modern Chinese, the Burmese, and the Thai are also descended. Possibly the round-headed type formed the original stratum of the population and were later invaded and dominated by the long-headed. There may also be a considerable admixture with neighbouring peoples on all sides by absorption of refugees and outcasts, capture, intermarriage, etc. The subject is one for specialists but it is evident that the Tibetans cannot, with scientific accuracy, be described as a 'Chinese' people; and, indeed, the Chinese have for 2,000 years or more looked on them as a separate race.

LANGUAGE

Tibetan is defined as a Tibeto-Burman language and is quite distinct from the Sino-Thai group although it may have a common origin as remote as the common stock from which the different races descended. It has a monosyllabic basis and the word order is subject (in agentive case): object: verb (verbal noun). Many experts describe it as a tonal language; but although there are, naturally, variations in pitch and stress, there is nothing comparable to the system of fixed tones in Chinese.

Tibetan writing, too, has always been entirely different from the Chinese and has never employed ideograms. The Tibetan script was, traditionally, borrowed from India in the seventh century and resembles the northern Gupta script of that period. There are thirty consonants and four vowel signs. The form of the letters and orthography are virtually unchanged since their introduction. The oldest surviving inscriptions and manuscripts dating from the eighth century can be read easily by present-day Tibetans and, allowing for some obsolete words and constructions, can be generally understood.

POPULATION

Estimates vary widely. An early census by the Mongols in the thirteenth century, which cannot have been more than selective, showed only 300,000 people. Father Orazio Della Penna in the eighteenth century goes to the other extreme with a figure of 33,000,000. The Chinese Communists have recently published the figure of 1,274,969. The previous official Chinese estimate in 1951 was three and three-quarter millions. It is not clear how the subsequent census was conducted nor whether it relates to the whole of 'political' Tibet. Without further information it is not possible to accept the figure, which is considerably less than that of most recent Western writers whose estimates range from 5,000,000 (Klaproth) to between 2,000,000 and 3,000,000—a figure favoured by myself.

It is generally assumed on the evidence of land lying un-cultivated that the population has been declining and the blame is assigned to the custom of adelphic polyandry, by which several brothers share one wife, and the neutralization of a large part of the male population by the heavy drain of the celibate monasteries.

Plate 1

(a) Lhasa city from the south

(b) Western gateway to Lhasa

(c) Lhasa from the east

Plate 2

(*a*) Incarnate Lamas of the older sects

(*b*) Abbots of Drepung

Although such arguments sound plausible they are not yet supported by any reliable and systematic evidence.

OCCUPATIONS

The greater part of the population are farmers and herdsmen; but every Tibetan—noble, monk, villager, nomad, or muleteer—is at heart a trader and this propensity combined with the custom of going on leisurely pilgrimage to the distant holy places of India did much to reduce the mental isolation of the people. A scattering of professional trading firms in the towns provided the nucleus of a small, prosperous middle class in which might be included the stewards who managed the estates of the great landlords, the lower ranks of the administrative service of the government, and the senior warrant officers of the army. There was also the less reputable occupation of brigandage practised by bands of robbers who haunted the wilds of northern Tibet from which they descended to attack caravans on the routes across those lonely desert highlands. In such country their activities were beyond control by the limited resources of the district officials and were regarded as one of the normal risks against which traders had to guard by joining in strong caravans for the dangerous parts of the journey. Some of the brigands had a regular subsidiary occupation in the collection of salt from the upland lakes and its sale in outlying markets or even in Lhasa itself.

TOWNS

There are few towns of any size. Lhasa, the capital, is the largest with a population before the Chinese occupation in 1952 of some 25,000–30,000—about 45,000–50,000 if the population of the great monasteries on its outskirts be included. Shigatse and Gyantse—quite close to one another and within 120 miles of Lhasa—come next in size and had populations of perhaps 12,000 and 8,000 respectively.

COMMUNICATIONS

Before the Communist invasion no wheeled vehicles were

used. Transport was by riding and pack animals. Roads were, in general, rough, narrow tracks. There were no bridges over major rivers. The rivers are navigable only for short stretches and the only kind of boat—apart from large wooden ferry barges—was the yak-skin coracle which could not be used except for journeys downstream.

Since 1952 the Chinese Communists have built many hundreds of miles of motorable road. Lhasa is linked with China by two main roads, each following roughly an old pack route, the southern running from Tachienlu through Chamdo and the northern from Lanchow through Sining and Nagchukha. From Lhasa a road extends to Gartok and Rudok in the west and joins up with Sinkiang by the route across the Aksai Chin in the northeast of Ladakh which has recently caused serious disagreement between the governments of India and China. Many subsidiary roads exist including one from Shigatse through the Chumbi valley to the borders of Sikkim and another from Taklakot to the Lipu Lekh pass on the western border of Nepal. Probably the greatest of many remarkable engineering feats is the road from Tachienlu which crosses four great river gorges as well as much mountainous country.

Near Lhasa the Kyi Chu River has been bridged but up to 1960 there were no reports of bridges having been made over the Tsang-po; and traffic from Lhasa to Shigatse must still cross by ferry.

Airfields have been made near Lhasa and in the west of Tibet.

CLIMATE, VEGETATION, ETC.

In a country of such extent, lying between the dry plains in Turkestan and the moisture-laden Himalaya and ranging in elevation from 2,000 feet in the deep gorges of the Dihang to the summit of Mt. Everest at 29,000 feet, there is great variety of climate, rainfall, and vegetation. For example, Lhasa in the Kyi Chu valley at a height of 12,000 feet has temperatures up to 80° F. in summer and rarely falling below 5° F. in winter. The rainfall is about 18 inches. On the upland plateau at elevations of 17,000 feet very much lower temperatures are recorded—maximum 45° to 65°F and minimum down to − 27° F.—together with strong cold winds. Rainfall is considerably less, only about 6–8 inches.

On the uplands there is little vegetation except grasses, but in the river valleys good crops of barley, wheat, peas, beans, and buckwheat are grown; while willow, poplar, walnut, and apricot are the most common trees.

It is probable that more land than is already in use could be brought under cultivation and that the existing outturn could be considerably increased by improved farming methods. As it is, the annual yield is reported to be generally greater than current needs; and I was informed, before the Chinese invasion, that there was a reserve of grain sufficient for three years. There were also large flocks of sheep, goats, and yaks.

ECONOMY

Although the Tibetan peasant or herdsman, with his thick homespun clothes and usually unkempt appearance, may not have given an impression of material prosperity, want, destitution, or starvation were very rare in Tibet. The people were notably sturdy and enduring; and the standard of living of a Tibetan peasant, although stern and comfortless, could reasonably be claimed to be higher than that in many other parts of Asia.

On a wider scale, Tibet as a whole lived in economic balance with its neighbours. Tibetans produced their staple food and wove woollen cloth to wear. Requirements from outside were principally brick-tea, porcelain, and silk from China; iron, copper, cotton textiles, broadcloth, rice, sugar, and miscellaneous household goods mainly from India. Tibetan exports of wool, skins, borax, etc., to the value of perhaps £250,000, brought more than enough foreign exchange to pay for the imports.

The mineral resources of Tibet, although sometimes assumed to be great, were never properly surveyed nor was any attempt made to exploit them before the Communist invasion. Gold was mined rather haphazardly in west Tibet and was also produced by washing the sands of several rivers of the east; it is known that small quantities of coal, iron, and copper were present but mining was considered to offend Tibetan religious principles and to impair the essence of the soil. The results of Chinese prospecting since 1952 are not known.

CHARACTER AND SOCIAL CUSTOMS

Western visitors so diverse in personality and objective as the Jesuit Fathers Francisco d'Azvedo in the seventeenth century and Ippolito Desideri in the eighteenth, the British emissaries George Bogle and Samuel Turner also in the eighteenth century, the Indian Civil Servant Sir Charles Bell and the mountaineer and explorer Heinrich Harrer in the twentieth century, all agree in describing the Tibetans as kind, gentle, honest, open, and cheerful. They are humorous, able to enjoy leisure, intelligent, and self-reliant; and they accord a high position to women. They have inborn good manners: servants and peasants behave with a deference and politeness which does not exclude the expression of an independent opinion; among the nobles and gentry one finds an easy courtesy from which the panache and flattery of some other Asian countries are absent. The good treatment by the Tibetans of their domestic animals has impressed many travellers.

These pleasant and engaging qualities do not exclude a streak of hardness which shows in the severe punishment of offenders but which is not allied to cruelty or to pleasure in inflicting pain; it reflects, rather, the simplicity and lack of luxury in their existence and the austerity of their surroundings. There is also a latent excitability which breaks out occasionally, but rarely, in fierce explosions of emotion and violence.

Those generalizations are based on the people with whom the visitor to Tibet comes most frequently into contact—the settled villagers of western and central Tibet and the Lhasa nobility. Just as there are differences of dress and dialect in so wide a country, so there are differences in the proportion in which the various characteristics are shown. Compared with the settled farmer, the nomad herdsman appears not only almost incredibly hardy but also shy, wary, and slow-thinking. But an even wider contrast in temperament is that which, following generally the division of political from ethnographic Tibet, distinguishes the central Tibetans from their kinsmen to the north-east and east. The best-known groups there are the Amdowas of the region roughly between Jyekundo and the Kokonor and the Khampas who live between the upper Yangtse and the Chinese border. They are in general livelier, more demonstrative, quick-tempered, and less peaceable than the central Tibetans. They have a reputation for fierce and carefree bravery—which may degenerate into truculence; and, especially the Khampas, were much divided into clans which waged long-standing, bitter, and violent feuds with one another. These are the people of whom much has recently been heard as leaders of resistance to the Chinese.

RELIGION

The one aspect of the national character that has most influenced their past and their present is the devotion to religion which dominates the thoughts and actions of every Tibetan.

The religion is a specialized development of Mahayana Buddhism of which the seeds were planted during the seventh century by teachers from Nepal, India, and China. The first chapels and temples were built at that time, in the reign of King Song-tsen Gampo. Buddhism gradually displaced the former animist religion, called Bön, and in doing so absorbed, or at least made subservient to itself, some Bön practices. The history which follows will show the vicissitudes through which the Tibetan Buddhist church acquired in 1642, a thousand years after its foundation, the absolute dominance in temporal affairs which has been, since then, the most striking characteristic of Tibetan life. From that time Church and State were almost interchangeable terms and all political matters were looked on as subordinate to the needs and interests of religion.

The best-known aspects of Tibetan religion were the number and size of the monasteries throughout the country; the system of reincarnating Lamas, which has been operative since the twelfth century and of which the Dalai Lama is the chief exemplar; the method by which the reincarnation of the Dalai Lama is discovered; ritual dances, miscalled 'Devil Dances'; oracles; and ascetics. Less is heard about the considerable number of quiet devout priests who spent their lives in study, meditation, and teaching, and of the no less devout monastic men of affairs who administered the discipline and the property of the numerous monasteries. In lay life, too, much sincere and unspectacular piety existed in the daily religious observances and the not infrequent retreats for meditation which formed a great part of the life of every family.

Almost every family in Tibet contributed at least one member to the religious order with the result that the population of the monasteries was proportionately very large. Bell estimates the figure at between a quarter and half a million. The title Lama, which means 'exalted' or 'superior', is given only to the higher orders of the priesthood and should not be applied indiscriminately to every member of the main body of monks and novices who inhabit the monasteries. Women are also admitted to the religious life, but the number of nuns was a very small fraction of the number of monks.

The power of religion in Tibet spread outside its own frontiers where it influenced the policies of its immediate neighbours. In the domestic affairs of Tibet itself, it had the significant result of creating an eager and unquestioning acceptance by the whole people both of the practice of their faith and of the philosophy of life that it inculcated. Criticism was hardly known except from a few religious teachers. There was no Piers Plowman in Tibet.

The depth of Tibetan faith is attested by the Jesuit Father Ippolito Desideri who lived at Lhasa between 1716 and 1721 and acquired great proficiency in the language. Indeed, he compares enviously the devotion of the Tibetans to their religion and priesthood with the behaviour of Christians.

Whether, as is sometimes said, the Tibetans were deliberately tamed by the introduction of Buddhism or whether they welcomed a faith which suited their national character, the rule of religion led to a determined conservatism and a dislike of change of any sort. The Tibetans consciously feel themselves to be 'inside' a special organization, and they have consistently resented foreign interference in their affairs; but their nature, although not immune from superstition, has kept them free from intolerance or fanaticism and they have always been ready to judge other people—those 'outside'—by their works.

CULTURE

Tibetan conservatism is reflected in all aspects of their culture. Although a high degree of skill and craftsmanship is attained in painting, wood-carving, and metal work, the products are on traditional lines, almost entirely of a religious nature, and conscious invention is not much in evidence. In architecture too, although the technique is skilful and the design often majestically impressive, there is little development. Similarly in literature, the scope is restricted to religious works and, while much ingenuity and thought are devoted to elaborating and expounding the philosophical ideas of the doctrine, there is little opportunity for the secular imagination. Apart from some pleasing folk-verses and the admixture of homely and earthy aphorism with the spiritual in the sublime hymns of the eleventh-century Tibetan saint, Mila-repa, poetry on worldly themes is limited to one writer of love lyrics and he, surprisingly, was a Dalai Lama.

Each of the neighbouring civilizations, in China and India, of course had its effect on Tibetan life. That of China can be seen in external features such as food and dress and, to some extent, in the organization of government; that of India in religious and moral ideas and literary models. Both countries and Nepal contributed influences on the art, design, and decoration of Tibet; but whatever was borrowed from outside was adapted to suit local conditions and the native Tibetan character and mentality, with a result that remains strikingly original and homogeneous.

EDUCATION

The ability to read and write is fairly widespread. Every monk, and they constituted perhaps an eighth of the population, received that much education; but it cannot be said that all of them carried their studies very far beyond that point. All the children of a noble family, boys and girls alike, learned to read and write as a matter of course and could spend their leisure reading Tibetan history, the lives of holy men, and so on. A selection of the young nobles went on to the official school at which the principal emphasis, as in all Tibetan schools, was on acquiring a good hand. Other studies were the learning of passages from religious books by heart, becoming acquainted with the formal style of official correspondence, and with the rudiments of calculation. Tibetan ideas of mathematics are of the simplest; and government accounts were kept by a primitive form of abacus using sticks, stones, etc. of different kinds in a tray divided into compartments.

Similar studies were taught in the school for monk officials but monks in the monasteries had a much more intensive course of education, starting with years of memorizing religious books and moral precepts and progressing to the study of philosophy, logic, and debating—all, of course, within the limits of the religious canon.

In the towns there were schools which any child might attend whose parents could pay a small fee; and it is probable that a considerable proportion of townspeople acquired a modicum of literacy. In the country a landowner usually set up a school for his own children; and there the children of his servants and of the village headman and substantial peasants in the neighbourhood could also learn to read and write and to memorize some prayers —sufficient knowledge to enable them to keep rough accounts, write a letter, and read, although not always understand, the sacred books.

SOCIAL ORGANIZATION

Although the power of a Church which inculcated such conservatism has never been challenged or even questioned by Tibetans, it has been viewed with dislike by every foreign power which has had designs of changing the course of events in Tibet.

Recently, since the uprising of March 1959, violent criticism of the whole Tibetan system has been persistently voiced by the Chinese Communists. For obvious propaganda reasons they have concentrated on the results of conservatism rather than its causes and they have stigmatized Tibetan society as being based on the feudal oppression of serfs by a handful of upper-strata reactionaries.

Society in Tibet was divided strictly into upper and lower classes, nobles and ordinary men, by a clearly defined gradation in which everybody knew his proper place. Similar distinctions existed also in the religious hierarchy. By present-day standards such a system may appear outdated but that does not necessarily mean that it was oppressive. It should be judged by its results.

In theory all land in Tibet belonged to the state from which the noble landowners and great monasteries held large estates. In return the nobles paid revenues to the state, largely in produce of various kinds and also by service—it being their duty to act as officials of the government. Estates could be, and not infrequently were, resumed; but, generally, once a great family was established in certain properties it acquired a hereditary right to them. They also held certain properties which they had obtained from other landholders. The monasteries, which owned even larger estates than the nobility, made their return by prayers and rites for the welfare of the state.

On those great estates the peasants, who held a stretch of land free of rent, had to cultivate the rest of the landlord's farmland and also provide various services—free transport, work on roads, a member of the family to serve in the army, and so on. In addition to the peasants on the big estates there were many smallholders who held land directly from the government.

Tibetan economy was not based on cash and a very small proportion of the dues from the peasants to the landlord or the landlord to the government were money payments. Even Communist writers have had to admit that there was no great difference between rich and poor in Tibet. The richest Tibetan noble would cut a poor figure, in terms of wealth, compared with a moderately well-to-do businessman in Calcutta or Bombay.

The landowner was a kind of patriarchal head of a household and, in spite of the customary deference shown him by his subordinates, there was no gulf fixed between them. In such a society the idea of payment by service was normal; and the services, like all other relations between government and landlord and landlord and peasant, were governed by custom. The guardian of custom was the Dalai Lama to whom every Tibetan had the right of appeal. But it can be understood that the difficulty and expense of exercising that right, especially by someone who might live several weeks' journey from the capital, allowed the landlord considerable latitude. Still, there was another factor which prevented him from exceeding the dictates of custom. A constant shortage of labour gave the peasant the ultimate sanction of running away. Conditions of work were by all appearances easy. The Tibetan, although certainly not an idler, did not give the impression of being overburdened with work or with care.

LAW AND PUNISHMENT

A further line of attack by Communist critics has been the allegation of brutally inhuman punishments inflicted by landlords, both monk and lay, on their peasants.

There was no all-embracing code of laws in Tibet. Tibetans are still proud to look back to the seventh-century King Song-tsen Gampo as the author of their law. His code consists, in fact, of sixteen general moral principles. There is also a code of thirteen rules of procedure and punishment drawn up by the first prince of the Pagmotrupa family, which ruled Tibet in the fourteenth to fifteenth centuries, and revised by the Vth Dalai Lama in the seventeenth century; a further revision and some additions were made by a Regent in the nineteenth century. But the administration of justice was guided rather by custom and usage, for which Tibetans have the profoundest regard. Formerly, lawful punishments included mutilations such as the cutting off of a hand or foot and putting out the eyes. Such penalties were never lightly inflicted but were decreed only in instances of repeated crime. Flogging was the principal punishment. The most spectacular and gruesome punishments of which there is record in Tibet were those inflicted with all the refinements of torture at public executions by the Chinese when they 'restored order' in 1728 and 1751. Even in the nineteenth century although the power to inflict mutilation existed in theory it was only rarely put into effect; and in 1898 all such penalties were forbidden by a decree of the XIIIth Dalai Lama except for the crime of treason. It is possible that in the more remote districts mutilation and torture were occasionally and illegally inflicted by district officials or by landlords, who enjoyed magisterial powers over their peasants; but the climate of Tibetan opinion, which was always advancing even though its progress might appear slow, had become increasingly averse from punishments of that sort.

ARMY AND POLICE

Army. The army in normal times numbered about 10,000 to 12,000. The greater part was stationed on the eastern border and there were about 1,500 men at Lhasa, including the Dalai Lama's bodyguard, with smaller detachments at Shigatse and other important places in the west and north. It was armed principally with rifles, but had in addition a few old-fashioned mountain guns and a small number of machine guns and Lewis guns. Western training was given on a small scale in 1922 but was discontinued after about four years, since when the lessons of that period continued to be handed down by Tibetan instructors. Service in the army was mainly in the nature of a tax owed in return for holding land. The men were paid in grain, tea, and butter, with a small sum of cash each month. What might be described as the equivalent of warrant officers were drawn from the same stratum of society as stewards of estates or by promotion of able ordinary soldiers. They were the backbone of the army because the higher-ranking officers were appointed from among the lay officials of the noble class who often had no military experience.

Police. A small police force was planned for Lhasa in 1922 but never became fully effective and after a few years dwindled into a handful of untrained watchmen. The tracking of offenders was done by a body of couriers, a purely Tibetan organization of long standing.

THE GOVERNMENT

The structure of the Tibetan Government before the Communist domination has never been very satisfactorily described. A somewhat extended outline of it is, therefore, attempted here.

Two separate fields of authority converged in the hands of the Dalai Lama: direction of the church, of which he is head; and the regular administration of the country. To carry out his instructions and keep him informed of the course of events the Dalai Lama commanded what amounted to two separate civil services of 175 specially trained monks and an equal number of hereditary lay nobles, known respectively as Tse-trung and Trung-khor. The nobles were a remnant of the ancient aristocratic system of government, and the monk officials the instrument of the religious ascendancy established by the Dalai Lamas after the seventeenth century. They were, in a sense, a projection of his dual nature as temporal and spiritual ruler and their activities extended, beyond what might be thought their proper element, into almost every sphere of government, including that of district administration, so that there was a dualistic arrangement by which a monk was to be found in almost every government office as colleague of one or more laymen.

The parallelism between the religious and the civil administrations and a rather complicated arrangement of checks and balances may be made clearer by the diagram on page 19 and the explanatory comments which follow.

The Dalai Lama. On assuming power at the age of about 18, a Dalai Lama becomes supreme temporal and spiritual ruler of Tibet—a position which, in the minds of his people, can be altered by nothing but his departure from this world. Being deemed the reincarnation of an aspect of the Buddha, he has an aura of divinity; but the awe and religious devotion in which he

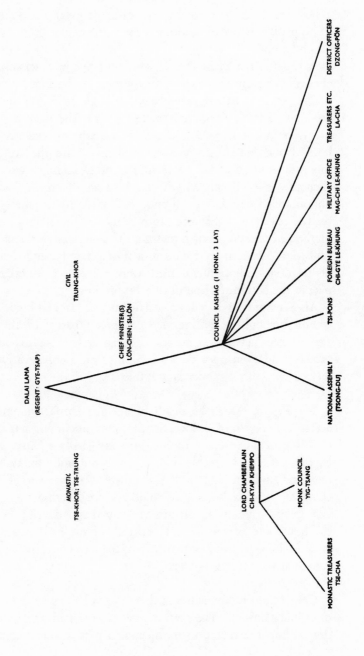

THE TIBETAN GOVERNMENT

GRADATION AND CHANNELS OF RESPONSIBILITY

DALAI LAMA
(REGENT: GYÉ-TSAP)

MONASTIC
TSE-KHOR; TSE-TRUNG

CIVIL
TRUNG-KHOR

CHIEF MINISTER(S)
LÖN-CHEN; SI-LÖN

LORD CHAMBERLAIN
CHI-KYAP KHENPO

MONK COUNCIL
YIG-TSANG

MONASTIC TREASURERS
TSE-CHA

COUNCIL KASHAG (1 MONK. 3 LAY)

NATIONAL ASSEMBLY
(TSONG-DU)

TSI-PÖNS

FOREIGN BUREAU
CHI-GYÉ LE-KHUNG

MILITARY OFFICE
MAG-CHI LE-KHUNG

TREASURERS ETC.
LA-CHA

DISTRICT OFFICERS
DZONG-PÖN

is held are given warmth by the complete loyalty and affection of his people, many of whom have seen their ruler grow up from his childhood.

A Dalai Lama is, in theory, absolute; but in practice certain checks have ensured that he shall conform to the ancient customs of the country. In the first place, although he is the apex and the glory of the religious system, it is to the system that he owes his position. A Dalai Lama is brought up exclusively by learned and influential monks and Lamas, and the weight of monastic opinion was so powerful that no Dalai Lama would risk alienating it too deeply and driving it to find the means, which it undoubtedly could have found, of stultifying his designs. A further check was that the office cannot be hereditary and the method of selection is such that the child—at least in the past two centuries—was usually found in a simple family, and thereafter his relations, although ennobled, were excluded from taking any part in the administration during his lifetime.

Also, it was necessary for a Dalai Lama to conduct his administration through a civil service composed partly of the most experienced hereditary nobles and partly of specially trained monks; and even on a determined autocrat a conservative civil service can exert a moderating influence.

The Regent. After the death of a Dalai Lama and until the accession to power of his successor the government was in the hands of a Regent who was in recent times invariably a Lama, chosen by the National Assembly. No Regent could enjoy the unlimited devotion and prestige of a Dalai Lama but a man of strong character in so exalted a post could acquire a commanding position in the country. In practice, rivalry might develop between the household of the Regent and that of the Dalai Lama who were looking forward impatiently to the day when their protégé should assume ruling power.

Chief Minister. Next in rank there might be one or more Chief or Prime Ministers. The position was always held by a senior lay official but it was not an indispensable part of the system. The post, which has its prototype in remote antiquity, was apparently revived by the XIIIth Dalai Lama, who ruled Tibet from 1895 to 1933, to serve as a link between himself and the lay Council. Chief Ministers did not sit with the Council, but passed on its recommendations to the Dalai Lama, with a note of their own opinion.

The Council. Called in Tibetan the Kashag, the Council was the principal executive body of the Tibetan government. It usually consisted of three lay nobles and one high-ranking monk who was treated as the senior member. It was not a cabinet in which each member had a special portfolio but all the Councillors, known as Shap-pé (Lotus-foot) or Kalon (Minister of Council), had corporate responsibility. All government business including comparatively petty issues of every sort came to the Council for consideration and their view was forwarded to the Dalai Lama (or Regent) for decision. The Council was also a Court of Justice whose findings similarly went to the Dalai Lama for judgment. An arrangement of that kind was only possible in a country where there was little litigiousness and where —partly owing to the small numbers of the civil service—the volume of government business was very small.

The Executive. Next below the Council came the whole range of specialized administrative offices in a fixed order of precedence. Traditionally, the highest of these was that of Tsi-pön, of whom there were four. This ancient office can be traced back to the eighth century; and the duties of the Tsi-pöns were the maintenance of revenue records, the assessment and assignment of revenue, and the training of the lay officials. They also acted as presiding officers and official spokesmen in the National Assembly.

Although they held the senior post, the Tsi-pöns might be outranked in personal precedence by other lay officials who had been awarded high titles of honour such as Dzasa or Théji. For example, a new Bureau of Foreign Affairs was established in 1942 and in view of its importance two senior officials, one monk the other lay, with the rank of Dzasa, were put in charge of it. Similarly the heads of the Military Department, sometimes known as the Commanders-in-Chief, were also Dzasas—one monk and one lay. These officials took personal precedence over the Tsi-pöns who were not usually awarded the title of Dzasa or Théji. There was an elaborate and strictly observed order of rank running through the whole official hierarchy, but it would serve no useful purpose to record here which rank usually went with which office.

In addition to the superior ranks of nobles and specially selected monk officials, there was a small service of clerks and petty officials of similar standing to the stewards and head servants in a great household. The majority of the senior officials of the Tibetan Government were concentrated at Lhasa. Exceptions were the high-ranking officers who held posts which might be described as the Governorship of a Province. There were four of these, the most important being the Governor of East Tibet (Do-mé Chi-Kyap) who usually had the rank of a Councillor, followed by the two Governors (both lay) of Western Tibet (Gar-pöns).

District Administration. There were about 100 districts in Tibet most of which were administered by two officials known as Dzong-pön, of whom, in most of the more important districts, one was usually a layman and the other a monk. That duplication meant that each acted as a check on the other and that the church was able to keep an eye on the secular branch. Although the district officials were under the general supervision of the Provincial Governor they were directly responsible to the Council. They led a comparatively independent existence and had wide powers in their own jurisdiction, being guided by a general and traditional set of rules rather than by frequent instructions from the capital on points of detail.

Payment of Officials. Before turning to the other side of the administration it should be noticed that no official received anything but a nominal salary. Their services were, as has been said, given in return for the estates they held. It was the established

Plate 3

At the New Year Ceremony, Lhasa

Plate 4

A Lhasa ceremony—driving out evil

system that persons who were suitably qualified by rank frequently secured their appointments by what can only be described as bribery but which in Tibet carried no moral stigma. Once appointed, the official expected to recover his costs in similar bribes and presents from persons seeking his favour. The district administration was, as it were, let out on a contract basis with a certain fixed sum to be paid to the treasury from each district. The officer in a good district might well have paid a high sum for his posting and he sought to make good his expenses and clear some profit over and above the sum he had to pay in revenue to the Treasury.

Although such a system would be condemned by western standards, it had long been accepted in Tibet and the exactions of officials were, like everything else there, limited by the dictates of custom and by public opinion. In particular, fear of being called to account by the Dalai Lama was a strong deterrent from excess.

The Monastic Administration

The highest monastic or religious official below the Dalai Lama was the *Chi-Kyap Khempo*, or Lord Chamberlain. He was the head of the Dalai Lama's personal household which used to contain a number of high monk officials; and he was also in charge of two treasuries, the personal treasury of the Dalai Lama and an official treasury in the Potala. He ranked next after the Members of the Council.

Monastic Council. Below the Lord Chamberlain was a Council of four monks, who were known as Trung-yik Chem-po. This was of lower rank than the Council (Kashag) and was rather the counterpart of the Tsi-pöns: those two being the only official bodies exclusively composed of monks and laymen respectively. The duties of the Monastic Council—or Yik-tsang—were to supervise the administration of the monasteries—except for the three great monasteries of Lhasa. They were also, with the Tsi-pöns, presiding officers of the National Assembly and official spokesmen there. The selection, training, and discipline of the monk civil service was their responsibility. The monk civil service was thus almost completely separated from the lay service for, although monk officials served in every branch of the administration and were answerable together with their lay colleagues for their reports and their actions, the Council had no power to appoint or discipline them. In practice they were in a special sense the Dalai Lama's personal service and used to attend his daily levée from which the mass of the lay officials were excused.

Monastic Treasurers. On a slightly lower level than the monk council and, like it, responsible to the Dalai Lama through the Lord Chamberlain, was a body of four Treasurers, three monks and one layman who were the counterpart of, and senior to, the lay Treasurers of the civil administration, of whom there were three laymen and one monk.

Titles. Just as there were honorific titles among the lay officials so there were for the monks, e.g. Ta Lama, Khenchen, Khenchung.

General. The monk officials were a peculiar phenomenon. Some were recruited directly from the younger sons of noble houses who looked for a career in the Church but many were young men from ordinary families whose ability had secured them a place in the special training school. By taking part in the duties of government, monk officials separated themselves from the daily routine and to some extent from the spirit of life in the monasteries; and although they acted as the watchdogs of the Church in the civil administration they seemed to fall between two stools and were often viewed with some suspicion by the main body of monks.

The National Assembly. In the plan of the government, the National Assembly has been shown in an indeterminate position between the two branches of the administration. It was not a permanent body but met only when summoned by the Council to debate and give its opinion on specified matters of particular moment. Its views were reported to the Council which submitted them to the Dalai Lama or Regent. An Assembly was part of the Tibetan Government in the earliest days. Then, it was probably composed of the higher orders of officials; and in recent times the National Assembly had the same sort of appearance but with an important difference. In general its meetings were attended by a selection of the higher officials, excluding the Members of Council who by custom were never permitted to attend; but its main significance was that at its meetings the voice of the great monasteries of Lhasa, with their 20,000 monks, was heard through their abbots. In times of great crisis it was customary to summon a full Assembly which included representatives of every class and occupation of Tibetan society—soldiers, boatmen, shopkeepers, farmers, and so on. As already mentioned, the Monk Council and the Tsi-pöns acted as official spokesmen in the Assembly and reported its views to the Council. It was also its duty to appoint a Regent to act during the minority of a Dalai Lama. The National Assembly was always the mouthpiece of Tibetan conservatism and independence; more particularly it was noted for its constant opposition to Chinese pretensions.

Public Opinion. In spite of their ready acceptance of the rule of religion, the Tibetan people have never acquiesced with spineless timidity in everything that was done by their government. Public opinion always and everywhere was deeply concerned with the strict observance of custom and, if any officials seemed to the people to transgress the bounds of what was usual, by deeds of injustice or rapacity or even by foolishness and eccentricity, criticism was voiced in a typically Tibetan way. There were no newspapers, cartoons, or broadsheets but the women whose daily task it was to carry water from the river to their masters' houses would, loudly and merrily, sing lampoons on the acts of their rulers. The songs were often witty, allusive, and pointed. By tradition the women enjoyed complete immunity and did not hesitate to sing even in the presence of the object of their attacks. In this way what the people were thinking soon became known all over the city. Sometimes criticism was expressed in anonymous posters stuck up in prominent places in the towns. Knowledge of popular grievances published by these means usually had its effect.

Conduct of Official Business. In the conduct of official business there was rarely any appearance of urgency. Discussions were long, calm, and deliberate. It was essential for officials to be completely and fully seized of any subject before reporting with their recommendations to the Dalai Lama, for once a decision was taken by him it was well-nigh irrevocable. Government records, of a voluminous and inconveniently bulky nature, were very carefully kept. There appeared to be less accuracy and detail in the accounts of the Treasuries and there was no sure and simple way for the government to ascertain exactly what its resources were. Traditional and ancient civil and religious rites were just as much part of the business of government as the regular duties of administration. Whole days were devoted to such ceremonies, attendance at which was a duty. They were far from being mere pageantry and were considered a vital necessity for the welfare of the state. Official holidays were also the occasion of some ceremony but without so much formality. For a week or more in the autumn all government business was interrupted and the population of Lhasa repaired to the parks surrounding the city where each department of the government in turn gave an all-day party, while the ordinary folk held their own merrymaking under the trees.

It will have been seen that there was, in theory, an elaborate balance between monk and lay in the Tibetan government. The highest posts below the Dalai Lama or Regent were held by lay officials; but that was little more than a sop to the pride of the nobility. The infiltration of monk officials in almost every department, the voice of the abbots in the National Assembly, and the absolute authority of the Dalai Lama gave preponderant influence to the Church. But the nobles were not mere ciphers. They were the traditional support of the Church; they were persons of substance and of inherited experience and they often produced men of character with powers of leadership. Although there was nothing like a division into political parties in Tibet there was, of course, competition for influence and a variety of rivalries and jealousies between the great families, between monasteries, and between colleges in the same monastery. Personality counted for a great deal and a layman or a monk of unusual ability could make an important impact on the direction of affairs, whatever post in the government he happened to occupy.

Inevitably, English phraseology is used about the organs and activities of the Tibetan Government; but it should be appreciated that the words are out of character and do not have the same meaning in the Tibetan political environment.

To the outside world Tibetan life may appear from the foregoing picture to be rugged and backward and the Tibetan Government may seem to have been a repository of curiously slow-moving and archaic customs; but a civilization and a government deserve to be seen in proper perspective and judged by their results. Simplicity and deliberateness are not the same as stupidity and inefficiency nor are ancient customs and institutions necessarily bad. Western travellers, from the earliest pioneers in the seventeenth century onwards, have described the Tibetans as easy-going, kindly, cheerful, and contented. It is impossible to reconcile the unanimity of that evidence with current allegations that the people were downtrodden, oppressed, and exploited; and it should be added that in thirteen centuries of recorded history, although there have sometimes been complaints and even insubordination against certain rapacious officials, there has been no instance of general agrarian discontent—let alone anything like a popular rising against the government. It must be concluded that the Tibetans accepted their long-established way of life and their social inequalities not merely with passivity but with active contentment. That may seem surprising, even reprehensible, to those who are unable to value or tolerate the ideas and standards of other people and who long to level out all variety by the diffusion of material benefits which they take to be synonymous with progress; but the sincerity of Tibetan feelings was seen when recent foreign attempts to introduce change and an alien conception of social justice were so strongly resisted that they could only be carried through by force. That does not mean that the Tibetans were opposed to changes of every sort but that they valued the right, enjoyed in other countries, to progress in their own way and were determined to resist attempts to impose changes on them from outside.

THE RELIGIOUS KINGS TO THE RULE
OF THE DALAI LAMAS: 630–1642

THE KINGS OF TIBET AND THE T'ANG DYNASTY OF CHINA

As early as the second century B.C. and at intervals down to the third century A.D. nomad tribes of Tibetan stock, known as the Ch'iang, harried the borders of north-west China, but the Tibetans as a separate people do not figure in history until the seventh century A.D. when they suddenly emerge as a formidable military power fighting their way into the confines of China and demanding a Chinese princess in marriage for their king.

Great powers do not spring up overnight; the Tibetan Kingdom was the fruit of centuries of growth and consolidation. In both Tibetan and Chinese histories there are hints from which a credible outline of Tibetan history can be carried back at least to the early fifth century; and, if archaeological excavations should ever be permitted in Tibet, it might be possible to establish evidence of even greater antiquity.

Before Tibet forced itself on the attention of its Chinese neighbours as a unified country it had been parcelled out among a number of clans each headed by its chief. Early in the sixth century several of these chiefs combined to support the head of one clan as their leader; and other clans were gradually brought under his sway. This unity released a great store of energy which was directed first against the nomadic and semi-settled tribes of Tibetan and Turkic stock which lay between Tibet and China. Most of the leaders of the Tibetan clans may well have come originally from those areas and their natural field for expansion was in that direction.

Once they had imposed their authority on the intervening tribes the Tibetans pressed on into China itself and in 635 their young king, Song-tsen Gampo, demanded and eventually received a Chinese princess as his bride. Song-tsen Gampo is one of the famous names in Tibetan tradition. To him are attributed not only the creation of Tibetan military greatness, but also the introduction of writing and of the Buddhist faith. His Chinese contemporary was the Emperor T'ai Tsung, founder of the T'ang dynasty, renowned for his energy and ability; and Tibetan achievements should be viewed in the light of the strength and greatness of the Chinese Empire of the day.

Although Chinese records—as is their manner towards non-Chinese peoples—speak rather patronizingly of the customs of the Tibetans, the latter were not merely a barbaric nomad tribe. By the seventh century they already had walled towns and small castles surrounded by farmland; they were also skilled workers in metal, making highly serviceable armour and weapons as well as fine decorative gold mail for ceremonial use, and elaborate golden utensils. Such crafts suggest several centuries of development.

After their first invasion of China the Tibetans extended their warlike activities in all directions with remarkable vigour. We find them conducting an expedition into India in 648. In 670 they annihilated the Tu-yu-hun people of the Koko Nor area; and by capturing the four main Chinese strongholds in Chinese Turkestan they cut Chinese communications with the west and laid the foundations of a Tibetan Empire in Central Asia.

In the west they occupied Hunza and they may have penetrated as far as Swat with which country they had a religious connection. They were in contact with the Arab conquerors of Transoxiana and we hear of Tibetan operations so far west as Farghana and Samarkand. For the most part relations with the Arabs were friendly but Harun ar-Rashid, the Caliph of Baghdad of the *Thousand and One Nights*, allied himself for a short time with the Chinese against the Tibetans who were growing too powerful for his comfort.

In the north and north-east the Tibetans marched with the Uighurs and with the Western Turks (Tou-Kiue). They frequently made common cause with the latter against China.

In the south they dominated the kingdom of Nepal and the hill tribes on the Indian side of the Himalaya. Their activities spread also into Upper Burma.

To China itself the Tibetans were a constant source of trouble. Their armies pushed farther and farther into the territory of the T'ang Empire. Tibetan generals and ministers occupied and administered almost the whole of Kansu and the greater part of Szechwan and northern Yunnan. To win respite the Chinese had to pay a yearly tribute of 50,000 rolls of silk and in 763, when a new Emperor provoked their resentment by withholding this peace-offering, the Tibetans even captured the Chinese capital which was then at Chang'an (Sian) and set up, for a short time, the brother of the preceding Tibetan king's Chinese wife as Emperor of China.

Tibet and China, it is clear, were then two powers on an equal footing. In fact, the Tibetans were regularly the aggressors and, in general, had the upper hand. This was hitherto admitted even by the most hardened Chinese champions of their country's claims on Tibet; but recently the Communists have stated that in the T'ang period Tibet paid tribute to China. Study of the T'ang Annals themselves shows that this is a falsification of history and it can be briefly disproved by reference to two inscriptions—one of the T'ang and the other of the Manchu Ch'ing dynasty. The first is a treaty concluded between China and Tibet in A.D. 821 (Appendix, p. 244). It is recorded in Chinese and Tibetan on a stone pillar in Lhasa and witnessed by leading ministers of state on either side. It is beyond question a treaty between equals. The other inscription is also in Chinese and Tibetan. It was set up at Lhasa in 1794 by the Chinese Representative, Ho Lin, and it is recorded also in histories of the Ch'ing dynasty. In it there is the statement that 'in the T'ang and Sung dynasties there were friendly relations between China and Tibet but Tibet was not then numbered among the vassals of China'.

In later times Tibetans looked back to those early days as the heroic age of the Chö-gye—The Religious Kings. There is no doubt that Tibetan historians, themselves Lamas and writing when Buddhism was in the ascendant, exaggerated the extent and power of religion at that time. There is, equally, no doubt that many of the early kings were, in fact, patrons and supporters of Buddhism. What they did might be compared with the part played by Ethelbert and Edwin, about the same time, in the early days of the Christian Church in Saxon England. The religious foundations of Song-tsen Gampo and his immediate successors were quite modest chapels and Buddhist influence probably reached only a small number of the people. The first exponents of the faith were priests from India and China and cannot have had much contact with the mass of the people. Their presence, especially that of the Chinese, might also have had a political colour. At all events, after about 150 years, contention arose between Chinese and Indian religious teachers. The former, perhaps influenced by Taoist quietism, preached that enlightenment could be attained instantaneously, by complete inactivity; the latter, holding the traditional view, argued that it was a gradual process requiring activity extending over a long series of lives. A great debate was held c. 792 which resulted in triumph for the Indian doctrine and the banishment of the Chinese teachers.

Shortly before those events enough progress had been made for the Tibetans to have the first of their own monasteries—Samyé, founded c. 779—and to be admitted to the priesthood. Their scholars became indefatigable and meticulous translators of religious works from Sanskrit and Chinese originals. At this stage, it seems that some elements of the older Bön religion were incorporated into, or at least made subservient to, the new faith. The great figures connected with these developments were the Indian Tantric Master, Padmasambhava; the Indian scholars Santarakshita and Kamalashila; and the Tibetan king Tri Song De-tsen.

It is remarkable that in the seventh to ninth centuries the Tibetans were able to keep up such widespread military activity for so long. Perhaps the population of Tibet was larger than it is now; and it is clear that the Tibetans used as soldiery the peoples on whom they imposed their domination. Nevertheless, even with such help, the strain of maintaining so extensive an empire, which had no obvious bond of cohesion, must have been considerable. But shortage of manpower was not to blame for the collapse of Tibetan greatness. That came about through dissension among the nobles whose union had made such greatness possible. In particular there was constant rivalry between the heads of the noble families from which the kings took their wives, each in turn seeking to establish a dominant influence at court. Religion, also, played a part in these divisions, serving the ends of faction probably almost as much as those of faith. The recently introduced Buddhist teachings, which were supported actively by some of the kings and less so by others, met with opposition from many nobles who held to the older Bön beliefs. Unless the king himself was a forceful character—and the majority of the Tibetan kings died comparatively young and usually by violence—there was no central authority strong enough to hold the nobles together for long. It was easy also for a general commanding an army in the border provinces of China, far from Lhasa, to disregard the authority of the king. Eventually the rivalries of the nobles led to a split in the royal family itself. Lang Darma, the last of Song-tsen Gampo's line to rule over all Tibet, died in 842 after a brief reign during which he persecuted Buddhism almost to extinction. On his death two young children were set up as claimants to the throne, each with support from a different party among the nobility. The Tibetan Kingdom then broke up into a number of disunited princedoms and, for the most part, temporarily deserted the Buddhist faith. One branch of the royal family migrated to the west and established new and prosperous kingdoms there; others were dispersed, with diminished estate, in many places throughout the east and centre of Tibet; while, on the eastern border, a powerful general continued almost on his own, and for his own ends, the ancient struggle against China.

By then the T'ang dynasty also, which had grown up together with the Tibetan Kingdom, had entered on its decline; but it outlived the Tibetan kingship by about a generation and was able in that time to recover almost all the Chinese territory which the Tibetans had occupied. The end came in 905 when the dynasty collapsed and there was no central government in China strong enough to maintain control over the border provinces. So Tibet and China drew apart, leaving a sort of no-man's-land between them. The Tibetans retreated from their Central Asian and South Himalayan empire into their mountainous carapace bounded by the Karakoram, the Kuen Lun, and the Himalayan ranges; and they never again stuck their heads outside those limits.

There is confusion in Tibetan histories about the chronology immediately after the fall of the Kingdom and little definite can be gathered about political or religious conditions in Tibet for about two centuries after that time. Light begins to enter with the arrival in 1042 of the great Indian teacher Atisha (Dipankara Srijñana) to whom is attributed the restoration of the Buddhist faith. Within thirty years there were founded some of the earliest of a succession of famous monasteries whose influence, wealth, and power were destined to shape the course of Tibetan history.

As for relations with China, for more than three centuries after the fall of the T'ang dynasty in 905 the only dealings the Chinese had with the Tibetans were courtesies or skirmishes with border tribesmen of Szechwan and Yunnan in the time of the Five Dynasties and of the Sung Emperors. There were no exchanges at all between a Chinese government and any rulers of Tibet proper.

TIBET AND THE YUAN AND MING DYNASTIES

The connection between Tibet and China was eventually reestablished through the conquest of both countries by another Central Asian people—the Mongols.

In 1207, when Chingis Khan was on his way to assail the Tangut state of Si-hia, the leading nobles and abbots of Tibet, fearing that their turn would come next, sent a delegation to him with an offer of submission. This formal acknowledgement of his overlordship satisfied Chingis for the time and, while he lived, there was no Mongol interference in Tibet. Later, Ogodai's second son Godan, then governor of the Kansu region, was responsible for the first authenticated foreign invasion of Tibet when, in 1240, he sent a raiding force which penetrated almost to Lhasa, looting and killing. There was no attempt at that time to take over the administration; and Mongol overlordship was not put on a regular basis until 1249 when Godan having summoned the most eminent Tibetan Lama of the day, the Sakya Pandita, made him Viceregent in Tibet.

In 1251 both Godan and the Sakya Pandita died and, soon after, Tibet came within the orbit of Kublai Khan who had not then become supreme ruler of the Mongols but was merely governor, on behalf of his brother Mangu (Mongka), of the border region between China and Tibet. In 1253 a nephew of the Sakya Pandita, called Phagpa, who had earlier visited Mongolia in attendance on his uncle, presented himself at Kublai's court. His personality and religious teaching were so inspiring that Kublai made him his chaplain, gave him authority over all Tibet from the far west to the Koko Nor and established him as his Viceregent for that country, with the title of Tisri (Ti shih).

Phagpa, whose position was still further enhanced when Kublai became ruler of all the Mongols in 1260, was entrusted with the duty of reorganizing the Tibetan administration and revenue system. When he died in 1274 another Lama of Sakya was appointed Tisri. Thus the Mongols were effective overlords of Tibet, in a relationship with a pronounced religious character, before their conquest of China which was not complete until 1279. After that, Kublai, as Emperor of China, and his successors of the Yuan dynasty continued to conduct their relations with Tibet through a series of Tisris—all Lamas and almost all from Sakya—who had to spend much of their time at the imperial court.

In spite of their titular authority, the Tisris were far from being accepted in Tibet as unquestioned masters of the country. Rivalry between them and the lay nobility and between the Sakya sect, to which most of the Tisris belonged, and other monasteries was held in check only by the shadow of the imperial power; and when, about the middle of the fourteenth century, the institution of Tisri grew feeble together with the authority of its creators and patrons, the Mongol emperors, it was replaced in Tibet by a lay hegemony.

The collapse of the Yuan dynasty was hastened by the rapid degeneration of the Mongol stock when transplanted from the hardy life of the steppe to the luxury of the Chinese court. In China, Kublai's successors were hated as foreign conquerors and they added to their unpopularity by exaggerated adulation of the Buddhist priesthood in which were included many Tibetans. Within less than a century the native fire and energy of the Mongols were extinguished and in 1368 the Chinese, in what was hailed as a national revival, found strength to overthrow their alien rulers and to establish the native Ming dynasty.

In Tibet, where Mongol overlordship was, perhaps, resented less because it was exercised indirectly, the decline of the Yuan dynasty had become evident even earlier. A Tibetan national revival had taken place some time before the eviction of the Mongols from China. It was led by Chang-chub Gyaltsen, a monk of the noble family of Pagmotru who lived in the valley of the Tsang-po some 75 miles south-east of Lhasa. His political career, which began in 1338 at the age of about 36, was at first directed at making use of existing factions and rivalries in Tibet to increase his personal authority. Other noble families and the great monasteries they patronized were jealous of the supremacy of Sakya which had the favour of the Yuan dynasty and was maintained by a Tibetan armed force under the command of a Sakya general. The Pagmotru family was closely connected with the rival Kargyupa sect and by winning the support of discontented noblemen and monastic leaders, Chang-chub Gyaltsen was able to take over influential positions in complete disregard of the Emperor's representatives in Tibet and the authority of Sakya. By 1350 he had established himself as actual master of all Tibet, deliberately fostering a feeling of national unity and reviving the traditions and glories of the early kings. The enfeebled Yuan Emperor could do nothing but accept the *fait accompli* and regularize the position by the grant of a title to Chang-chub Gyaltsen. There was no open breach and a connection between Tibet and the imperial court was maintained by frequent visits from Lamas of several sects; but the temporal bond was a mere formality and by 1358 the office of Tisri had ceased to exist. What link there was consisted in a nominal expression of allegiance by the ruler of Tibet to the person of the Mongol Emperor; and a diplomatic connection with the Mongols was kept up even after the fall of the Yuan dynasty and its eviction from China. The appearance of a new dynasty in China meant nothing to the Tibetans.

From the foregoing, it may be seen that there is no substance in the claim of some Chinese writers that Tibet was in unbroken subordination to China from the time of the Yuan dynasty. The link between Peking and Tibet came into being only through the conquest of China by a foreign power which had already been accepted by the Tibetans as their overlord. Even before their expulsion from China the later Mongol emperors enjoyed no more than a purely formal and personal relationship with Tibet; and although the Chinese recovered their own territory from the erstwhile foreign conqueror they did not take possession of that of the Mongols, nor did they exercise or attempt to exercise any authority in Tibet. China and Tibet had each recovered its independence of the Mongols in its own way and at different times.

The Ming dynasty almost at once established a connection with the Tibetan Church by inviting prominent Lamas of the different sects to visit China. But although the influence of the Lamas was considerable, Tibet was not then governed by them. Its rulers were the princes first of Pagmotru and then, from about 1481, those of Rimpung and after that, from about 1565, the princes or kings of Tsang. There is no evidence that any of them made an act of submission, even of the most formal nature, to the Ming emperors.

The frequent visits by Tibetan monks are described in the annals of the Ming dynasty as 'tribute missions'. Such missions were an important part of the Chinese diplomatic and commercial system. In foreign affairs they provided for regular contact with other peoples and established a flexible link which might, if opportunity offered, be developed into something more rigid. Their commercial aspect was apparently of less consequence and the missions were generally a concession by which the Chinese paid for the useful and flattering political connections. In return for 'tribute' of products of their own country the foreign envoys received consignments of such desirable goods as silk, tea, and porcelain to a much greater value. Indeed, in the Ming period this commerce, which was largely in the hands of the eunuchs who dominated the court, became such a costly nuisance that imperial edicts had to be promulgated restricting the frequency of the missions and the number of persons of whom they should consist.

To conform to the lofty disdain with which the Chinese regarded the outside world, the practical uses of the tribute system were sublimated into elements in the mystique of imperial state-craft. China was viewed as the centre of the world and 'barbarians' from outside came there, dazzled by its greatness, to acknowledge its supremacy. In return, the Emperor had the duty of extending his gracious benevolence. The idea of political relationships on an equal footing had no place in such a framework and the absurdi-ties to which that led can be seen in the well-known letter of the Emperor Ch'ien Lung to King George III at the time of Lord Macartney's mission to China in 1793. The Emperor addressed the King as a humble and devout suppliant and exhorted him reverently to obey the imperial instructions. In the same vein, the Pope appears in a list of tributaries of the Ch'ing dynasty together with Holland, Portugal, and Russia.

Without doubt, other nations of Asia were impressed by the ancient prestige of Chinese civilization and the grandeur of the court with its ceremonial carefully stage-managed to enhance the awfulness of the imperial presence. But that does not mean that every foreign visitor who made the kotow to the Emperor was a vassal acknowledging Chinese overlordship of his country. The facts need to be looked at from both sides and the circumstances of the various missions examined.

Stripped of the fanciful embroidery of Chinese protocol the missions from Tibet can be seen to have consisted mainly of Lamas and monks from the leading monasteries whose visits were supposed to be limited to intervals of three years, and of tribal chieftains of the borderland who might, in some cases, send a mission every year. These were corporate or personal business ventures having no connection with the ruler of Tibet and cer-tainly not acting as his official representatives. Visits to China by various Lamas during the Ming dynasty are mentioned in Tibetan records of the fifteenth to seventeenth centuries but there is no hint that the question of Tibet being subordinate to China ever occurred to Tibetan historians of that time. It is significant that, whereas letters from Emperors of the Yuan dynasty to Tibetan Lamas sometimes contain instructions on monastic administration, those of the Ming Emperors are purely complimentary.

Over the lay rulers of Tibet the Ming dynasty exercised neither authority nor influence. Distant diplomatic relations existed. In 1488 the Emperor Ch'eng Hwa sent an honorific seal to a prince of Pagmotru. But, by then, ruling power had passed to the Rimpung family and neither they nor the Tsang princes, who succeeded them c. 1566, appear to have had dealings with the Ming court. There are, therefore, no grounds for claiming that Tibet was in any real sense tributary to China during the Ming period; and that claim is denied in Ho Lin's inscription (p. 30 above) which regards Tibet as a vassal only from the beginning of the Ch'ing regime.

The establishment of actual Chinese overlordship over Tibet in the Ch'ing period will be described in a later chapter. Inscriptions of that time leave no doubt that there took place a complete change in the nature of the relationship between the Imperial Court and Tibet from that which had subsisted in the time of the preceding Ming dynasty. Recent Chinese arguments that the Ming emperors inherited from their Mongol predecessors any claims on Tibet or that there was any recognition by the Tibetans of Chinese supremacy can therefore be dismissed as mere pretence.

THE ORIGIN OF THE DALAI LAMAS AND THEIR RULE

The spiritual and temporal ascendancy of the Dalai Lama, which in recent times has been the most striking feature of the Tibetan state, was the culmination of a long process of adjustment between the Buddhist hierarchy and the lay nobility.

Buddhism, when it first appeared in Tibet in the seventh century, was a foreign introduction restricted probably to a few noble families, including that of the king, and ignored or resisted by the many followers of the old animist religion known as Bön. A small number of Buddhist priests from India and China ministered to the new faith until the later part of the eighth century when Tibetans themselves were ordained as priests and the first Tibetan monastery—as distinct from the temples which were built earlier—was founded at Samyé. After that, Buddhism made rapid advances and by the end of the eighth century Tibetan priests of noble family were holding the highest offices in the administration.

A strong reaction marked the closing years of the Tibetan kingship under the apostate Lang Darma, after whose death in about 842 there is something of a Dark Age in Tibetan Buddhism. But, in the words of the religious historians, 'the embers were kept alive'; and in 1042 a new blaze of faith was kindled by the arrival of the great Indian missionary, Pandit Atisha. He had been invited by the ruler of Western Tibet, a descendant of the early kings. From the west, Atisha's activities extended into Central Tibet and, under his inspiration, ruling nobles all over the country fostered a revival of Buddhism. From then onwards the faith prospered greatly and the political importance of religious leaders increased correspondingly. New and richly-endowed monasteries sprang up and by the time of the Mongol connection with Tibet several religious hierarchs held positions of influence. Sakya, Drikhung, Tshal, and Tshurpu were among the greatest of these. Each had its powerful lay supporters and a private army commanded often by a reliable member of the family of the original religious founder and head of the monastery. This was the least admirable aspect of the growth of the monasteries; and the rivalry and bitter fighting between them is a blot on the Tibetan Middle Ages. Yet it was also a time of intense literary activity in the service of religion and it produced many saints, scholars, and teachers of legendary fame and piety.

By making the Sakya Pandita his Viceregent in Tibet—as described above—Godan established the temporal supremacy of a religious figure there for the first time. But in doing so he was giving authority to the head of one sect only, not to the head of a united Church. The power of the Sakya hierarchs was viewed with jealousy just as much by the Lamas of other sects as by the lay nobility of Tibet, and when Chang-chub Gyaltsen supplanted Sakya rule after it had lasted about a century he did so with the support of Sakya's monastic rivals. There is no sign of any sharp division between churchmen and laymen as such, but Chang-chub Gyaltsen's glorification of the Tibetan monarchs of the sixth to ninth centuries as 'The Religious Kings' suggests that, in his policy of creating a spirit of nationalism, he was underlining the thesis that the function of the Church should be to support the Ruler who would, in return, be its Protector.

Chang-chub Gyaltsen himself and his lineal successors relied on the support of the Kargyupa sect. The Rimpung princes, who eventually ousted the Pagmotru dynasty, had the backing of the Karmapa sect—a powerful offshoot of the Kargyupa—of which they were patrons. And the influence of the Karmapa hierarchs was important also to the success of the Tsang kings who, in due course, followed the Rimpung family.

On to this scene the Dalai Lamas made a comparatively late entry. They owed their appearance to the great religious teacher known as Tsong Khapa (1357-1419), the founder of a new sect, the Gelugpa, popularly called the Yellow Hats. Tsong Khapa, so named from his birthplace, the district of Tsong-kha near the Koko Nor, was a monk of exceptional intellectual attainments, religious devotion, and proselytizing ability. His aim was a reform of monastic discipline, a return to greater austerity and spirituality, and, perhaps, ultimately the ending of divisions and rivalries in the Tibetan Church.

One of Tsong Khapa's leading disciples was his nephew, a monk called Gedün Truppa, whose learning and vigorous propagation of the Master's doctrine won many followers for the new sect. He founded one of the greatest Gelugpa monasteries at Tashilhunpo near Shigatse, and he was its abbot at the time of his death in 1475. Some years later it was recognized that his spirit had undergone reincarnation in a young monk named Gedün Gyatso, and he too, in due course, was similarly succeeded by a child, Sonam Gyatso, who was recognized as the third incarnation of Gedün Truppa. Sonam Gyatso was a brilliant scholar and a zealous missionary. He visited Mongolia and in 1578 converted the leading prince, Altan Khan of the Tumed, together with large numbers of his followers. The Khan gave Sonam Gyatso the title of Talé (Dalai), meaning 'Ocean', and that title was later applied retrospectively to his two predecessors.

Other Tibetan Lamas had their followers in Mongolia but they do not appear to have shown the proselytizing energy of the new sect which in a very short time commanded the spiritual allegiance of almost all the rival tribes of Mongolia. That had important results. It laid the foundations on which the supremacy of the Dalai Lamas was eventually to rest and, even more important, it created what might well become a rallying point for the consolidation of disunited Mongol tribes into another great Mongol Empire. This was a disturbing prospect for the Chinese and so, when eventually the Gelugpa sect, which commanded the loyalty of most of the Mongols, also became the ruling power in Tibet, it was expedient for the rulers of China to secure control over the high priest of this spiritual unity. At the time of Sonam Gyatso, however, the Gelugpas had no temporal influence in Tibet but the austerity, discipline, and spiritual quality of its Lamas attracted a growing number of followers including some influential nobles. In that way, through its lay supporters, the new sect gradually became involved in the political contentions of the day, and was soon the principal rival of the dominant Karmapas.

So long as the ruling dynasty, the kings of Tsang, had the physical power to maintain their supremacy in Tibet the position of the Karmapa, as their religious advisers and supporters, was safe. But in 1642 Gusri Khan, a Mongol prince of the Qośot tribe, supported by other Mongol followers of the Gelugpa sect, invaded Tibet, defeated and killed the King, displaced the Karmapa Lamas from their high estate, and set up the Dalai Lama of the day—he was the fifth and his name was Ngawang Lobzang Gyatso—as religious head of the country.

At first, the Dalai Lama's authority was under the protection of Gusri Khan who assumed the title of King of Tibet which he transmitted to his descendants. The relationship between the two is an example of the purely Central Asian concept of Patron and Priest in which the temporal support of the lay power is given in return for the spiritual support of the religious power. That had been the formal description of the bond between the Mongol Emperors of China and their Lama Viceregents for Tibet. It is an elastic and flexible idea and not to be rendered in the cut-and-dried terms of modern western politics. There is in it no precise definition of the supremacy of one or the subordination of the other; and the practical meaning of the relationship can only be interpreted in the light of the facts of the moment. Gusri himself, although maintaining most friendly and respectful relations, was to some extent a check on the supremacy of his religious colleague, the Dalai Lama. But he died in 1655 and his successors showed little interest in the administration of Tibet. They lived either in the upland hunting-grounds three days' journey north of Lhasa or in their native Koko Nor country. To begin with they appointed a Regent to speak for their interests at Lhasa, but gradually the Vth Dalai Lama, who was a man of great determination and force of character, drew all power into his own hands, including that of appointing the Regent. The office and title of King remained with Gusri's lineal successors until 1717 but, except for a final burst of activity which will be described below, its holders were completely indifferent to what went on in Tibet and made no effort to influence the Dalai Lama's government of the country.

MANCHU PROTECTORATE IN TIBET

1720–1792

THE RISE OF THE CH'ING DYNASTY

While the Qośot Mongols and the Vth Dalai Lama were working out a new pattern for Tibet, the Chinese Ming dynasty, which had never had more than a distant interest in Tibet, was completely distracted by its own decadence and by a mounting threat from the north-east. There, the various tribal and family divisions of the Manchu people had been overcome towards the end of the sixteenth century by the vigour and determination of Nurhachi. At first he maintained amicable relations with the Ming court but in 1618, once his authority at home and his military preparations were complete, he sent an invading army into China. The Manchus continued to encroach farther and farther upon Chinese territory and in 1636, although he had not by then attempted to possess himself of the capital at Peking, Nurhachi's son and successor, Abahai, assumed the title of Emperor of China and named his dynasty the Ch'ing.

The Manchus, although of a different stock, had a close mental affinity with the Mongols, and both Nurhachi and Abahai cultivated relations with them, largely by marriage alliances. Through the strength and authority resulting from the new unity of the Manchu tribes, Abahai was able to take advantage of the Mongols' disastrous tendency to faction and so to establish a superior position in relation to them. With the overwhelming energy resulting from that process of unification and consolidation, the Manchus soon succeeded in capturing Peking and in securing Chinese acceptance of their new dynasty. That was in 1644, and it is something of a fiction to represent the Ch'ing dynasty as beginning at an earlier date. Abahai himself, in spite of his assumption of the title of Emperor in 1636 and although he was posthumously honoured as the Emperor T'ai Tsung Wên, never ruled at Peking.

It was while the Manchus were imposing their domination on China that Gusri Khan conquered the King of Tibet and set up the Dalai Lama as religious sovereign. Recent Chinese arguments about their 'overlordship' of Tibet assert that Gusri was at that time a vassal of 'China' and that, accordingly, the Dalai Lama was in a similar position. This tendentious presentation of the facts is suggested in an official Chinese Edict of 1720—of which more will be said later—where there is the obvious motive of justifying action then taken in Tibet.

Abahai succeeded in establishing his superiority over many of the Mongol tribes who were his immediate neighbours but that did not include the Qośot Mongols of the Koko Nor of whom Gusri Khan was the chief. It is evident that Gusri had diplomatic relations with the Manchus, but there is nothing to suggest that he was their vassal. In 1642, when the success of his invasion of Tibet was in the balance, he and the Dalai Lama sent envoys to the Manchus and so did the King of Tsang and the Karmapa Lama whom Gusri was attacking. Both sides were trying to win the support of what was then clearly the most effective power in East Asia even though at the time the Manchus were not yet masters of China. Abahai's reply to the overtures from the rival parties was vague and temporizing. There is no tone of authority; and that correspondence is an entirely insufficient foundation for a claim to Manchu overlordship of Tibet—let alone Chinese overlordship. In the event, the issue was decided in favour of Gusri and the Dalai Lama without any intervention by the Manchus who had been careful to commit themselves to neither side.

So long as Gusri was alive, the Vth Dalai Lama had to defer to Mongol advice to some extent. It is probable that Gusri was responsible for the acceptance by the Dalai Lama of repeated invitations from the Manchu Emperor Shun-chih that he should visit Peking. This visit has been interpreted in different ways. Recent Chinese writers claim that the Dalai Lama went as a vassal. Western writers, even before the fall of the Manchu dynasty, say that he went as an independent ruler. It is beyond doubt that he was treated with extraordinary respect. Even Li

Tieh-tseng, a zealous champion of Chinese supremacy who makes the most of every scrap of evidence, can say no more than that 'the ceremony does not bear full evidence that the Dalai Lama was treated as an independent Monarch'. The only suggestion that Li can produce of any treatment of the Dalai Lama as a vassal is that it is reported in Chinese records that he bent the knee at his reception by the Emperor. On such points one may have doubts of the veracity of Chinese reporting. I have personal knowledge of similar unfounded claims in regard to the ceremony at the enthronement of the present Dalai Lama. In the case of the Vth Dalai Lama it should be remembered that the Emperor was not only a newcomer from the robust and informal Manchu court to the ancient ceremony and make-believe of the Chinese court; he was also an ardent Buddhist and there are stories that he resigned the throne and ended his life as a Buddhist monk. It is probable that his reception of the Dalai Lama was so sincerely effusive that his Chinese court annalists, with an eye to their rigid and artificial conventions, were compelled to add some favourable embroidery to the facts.

It is difficult to see any reason for rejecting the view put forward in 1910 by the American scholar Rockhill, without any apparent *arrière pensée*, that the Dalai Lama was treated as an independent ruler. However that may be, the issue should be judged not on the basis of a single disputed ceremonial, but on the facts of the previous and subsequent relationship between the Manchus and Tibet.

When Gusri Khan died in 1655, the Dalai Lama became sole arbiter of Tibetan affairs. His influence was also exerted outside Tibet among the Mongols and among the Tibetan-speaking tribes of the Chinese border provinces. His policy there sometimes coincided and sometimes conflicted with that of the Manchu emperors. He interested himself, to their concern, in rebellions against them in Yunnan in 1675 and 1680; on the other hand, his influence among the Mongols was mainly directed at restraining the warlike propensities of the Dzungars of the Ili district. His motive was to protect the Qośot and Khalka tribes, with whom he had close connections, but in doing so he was also warding off a threat to China, for the energy and ambition of the Dzungars had created in Central Asia a powerful and aggressive rival to the Ch'ing dynasty.

The Dalai Lama's skill in foreign affairs is only one aspect of his dominant and energetic character. The title—The Great Fifth —by which he is generally known, rests even more on his powers of organization and leadership; on the blend of forceful measures and conciliation by which he brought peace and unity to Tibet and combined, for the first time, temporal and spiritual rule in one person; on his strict supervision of religious discipline and on the literary works for which he himself found time and in which he encouraged others. He was also a vigorous builder and the soaring majesty of the vast palace-monastery he caused to be raised on the Potala hill at Lhasa is a noble memorial of his greatness.

The Dalai Lama's death in 1682 set in train a series of events which finally brought about Chinese intervention in Tibet. In his later years he had been assisted by Sangyé Gyatso, widely believed to have been his natural son, whom he appointed Regent and in whom he had full confidence. There is a story from Chinese sources that Sangyé Gyatso ingeniously concealed the death of the Dalai Lama in order to keep power in his own hands. It is said that he acted with such intolerable tyranny that he was killed by Lhabzang Khan, the descendant of Gusri and successor to the titular position of king. This led to an invasion by the Dzungar Mongols with whom Sangyé Gyatso had been intriguing and who were hostile to Lhabzang. The Emperor, therefore, sent an army to help Lhabzang and to defend Tibet. That is a disingenuous oversimplification intended to show the Manchu Emperor's actions in the most favourable light and to justify in retrospect his position in Tibet after 1720.

Let us look at the sequence of events from the Tibetan point of view. It has been maintained above that there was no relationship of subordination which would make it incumbent on the Tibetans to report the death of a Dalai Lama to the Emperor of China or to consult him about a successor. The new Dalai Lama was actually discovered, in the usual manner, within a few years of his predecessor's death; he was trained near Lhasa and enthroned in 1696. The death of the Fifth Dalai Lama was concealed for fourteen years and although the Chinese Emperor suspected he was being deceived, he was not officially informed until the new Dalai Lama had been enthroned. This gave grave offence; but what was worse in Chinese eyes was the abandonment by Sangye Gyatso of the restraining policy of the late Dalai Lama and the cultivation with Galdan Khan, the restless chief of the Dzungar Mongols, of relations which amounted to almost open hostility towards the Emperor. The Ch'ing dynasty did not need to worry greatly so long as the influence of Lhasa was used for peaceful ends in Mongolia but once that influence became implicated in a policy which might lead to the reunification of Mongolia under the banner of religion, imperial control of Tibetan policy became an urgent necessity.

The manner in which this aim was achieved reflects the greatness of the Emperor K'ang Hsi (1661–1722). He was not only a resolute ruler—at least in his prime—and a skilful diplomat, but being himself a Central Asian, he possessed a sympathetic understanding of the minds of his Central Asian neighbours. He also enjoyed some exceptional good luck.

It happened that the titular King of Tibet, Lhabzang Khan, was not willing to follow the line of feeble indifference adopted by the earlier successors of Gusri. He planned to restore the real influence of the kingship. For a number of reasons, his family had lost touch and sympathy with their Mongol kinsmen in the Koko Nor area. Lhabzang, therefore, turned for help to the Emperor. This suited K'ang Hsi well. He himself was able to remain in the background while he egged on Lhabzang to remove Sangyé Gyatso. A brief war in 1705 achieved that result. The next step was to remove the VIth Dalai Lama. Tsangyang Gyatso, the child who had been selected and enthroned by Sangyé Gyatso, turned out, to all appearances, quite unsuitable as a Dalai Lama. He was a libertine and a poet; in fact, the only writer of lyrical verse that Tibet has produced. Lhabzang and the Emperor were not unaware of the possible repercussions of interference in Tibetan religious affairs but they seem to have thought that in view of the Dalai Lama's notorious behaviour he could be displaced without difficulty, perhaps even with Tibetan approval. Lhabzang therefore arrested him and sent him under escort towards China. It at once appeared that he had misunderstood the Tibetan attitude to their Dalai Lama. The apparent shortcomings of Tsangyang Gyatso did not at all diminish Tibetan devotion to his person or their fury that any foreigner should interfere in their religious institutions. Only the intervention of the Dalai Lama himself averted a serious riot when he was arrested; but not long after, when it was known that he had died—murdered perhaps—on the way to China, Tibetan indignation was intense. Great anger was also stirred up among the Dzungars and the Mongols of the Koko Nor. Lhabzang, whose nature it was to plunge on stubbornly, declared that Tsangyang Gyatso had not been the true incarnation of his predecessor; and he appointed as Dalai Lama a 25-year-old monk, reputed to be his own natural son. K'ang Hsi perceived that Lhabzang had made a serious mistake in attempting to thrust his nominee on the Tibetans and he delayed announcing formal approval of the new appointment. At the same time he sent an adviser to help Lhabzang in his difficulties. The Emperor showed his hard-headed political acumen by securing from Lhabzang, in return for imperial support, the promise of the regular payment of tribute. That was the first occasion on which tribute had been paid to the Manchus by the Mongol King of Tibet and the first acknowledgement of Manchu supremacy. It was the doing not of the Tibetan government but of Lhabzang himself.

The Emperor's political sense was rewarded. The Tibetans would have nothing to do with Lhabzang's nominee but soon chose for themselves a child born soon after the death of Tsangyang Gyatso in Litang, a place where the late Lama, in a delightful poem, had indicated that he would be born again: 'White crane lend me your wings. I shall not go far away, only a visit to Litang; then I'll come home again.'

Everything pointed to trouble; and it was not long in coming. In 1717 the Dzungars launched an invasion of Tibet declaring that they came to put down Lhabzang and to restore the rightful

Dalai Lama. Militarily they were very successful. They stormed Lhasa and killed Lhabzang; they also deposed the so-called Dalai Lama whom he had appointed. In all this they had the sympathy of the greater part of the Tibetan people; but there was something lacking. The Emperor had outmanœuvred them and had forestalled their plan to get possession of the child from Litang whom the Tibetans looked on as their new Dalai Lama. By a stroke of luck, K'ang Hsi managed to get hold of the child himself. When the Tibetans found that the Dzungars were not bringing the child with them they began to feel disillusioned, and that feeling turned to hatred when the Dzungars began looting the holy places of Lhasa and oppressing the populace. The Tibetans rose against the now intolerable intruders and waited hopefully for help from China, which Lhabzang had summoned before his defeat. The field was thus open for the Emperor. In 1718 he dispatched a military expedition to Tibet. It was annihilated by the Dzungars not far from Lhasa. In angry determination the Emperor sent another and greater force which made its way to Lhasa in the autumn of 1720, drove the Dzungars out of Tibet, and escorted back to Lhasa the longed-for Dalai Lama.

The Emperor had played his hand with masterly ability. Although he had not been able to save his rather obtuse friend Lhabzang, he had repelled a dangerous bid by the most powerful and hostile section of the Mongol race to secure control of Lhasa and its religious influence. His army was welcomed at Lhasa as the saviour of the Tibetans, the restorer of peace, and the bringer of the Dalai Lama.

There was one small error of judgment. The beloved libertine Tsangyang Gyatso was treated as though he had not been a true incarnation; the stop-gap appointed by Lhabzang was conveniently forgotten; and the child from Litang was enthroned as the VIth Dalai Lama. But to the Tibetans, then and now, Tsangyang Gyatso was the VIth Dalai Lama, and the child, Kesang Gyatso, the VIIth; and eventually the Manchu emperors had to fall in line with Tibetan opinion on that matter.

At all events, K'ang Hsi had secured his object—a footing in Lhasa and the key to religious control over Mongolia. This was the foundation of nearly two centuries of Manchu overlordship of Tibet and it should be observed that it was brought about not by conquest of the Tibetans but by skilful opportunism, and that once again it was a non-Chinese Emperor of China who had established a connection with Tibet.

An account of those events is contained in an Edict of 1720 by the Emperor K'ang Hsi of which a copy in four languages is inscribed on a stone pillar at Lhasa. The Edict, which is a magnificent example of Chinese skill in the art of specious propaganda, is aimed at explaining and justifying the Emperor's actions in Tibet. It is so worded as to imply, rather than claiming openly, that ever since 1640, some eighty years before, the Manchu emperors had enjoyed a special position in regard to Tibet. The Emperor refers to envoys being sent from Tibet to T'ai Tsung—who was not then, nor ever became, acknowledged Emperor of China—and it describes the relationship which followed that exchange in the specific terms of Patron and Priest. Then it slides almost imperceptibly into the assumption that the Emperor was in some way the overlord of Lhabzang Khan; but it is all left vague and indeterminate and there is no definite claim, such as appears in inscriptions of two generations later, that Tibet was 'counted among the vassals' from the time of the Emperor T'ai Tsung.

ESTABLISHMENT OF CHINESE INFLUENCE AT LHASA

The nature of Chinese influence in Tibet underwent several changes during its existence of nearly two centuries between 1720 and 1912. The position at the outset has aptly been described as a Protectorate by Professor L. Petech whose work *China and Tibet in the Early XVIII Century*, is the *locus classicus* for the period. It was imposed, as has been seen, without any Tibetan opposition— even amicably. There was no treaty or exchange of letters. In the confusion following the Dzungar terror, the Manchu generals simply took control, restored peace, and helped to organize a new government to take the place of the old. Traditional Tibetan forms were preserved and the most important administrative body was a Council of Ministers to advise the Dalai Lama. The principal change was the disappearance of the King and the abolition of the office of the Regent, who had been technically the representative of the King. Thereafter there would only be regents of a different kind, acting for the Dalai Lama when he was a minor. The administrative responsibilities of the Tibetan government extended from Western Tibet to the Upper Yangtse; but over and above the Tibetan administration there was now imposed a Manchu Military Governor with a garrison of some 2,000 troops.

As soon as the new Tibetan government was in running order, it began to find Manchu supremacy irksome. In particular, Tibetan revenues had to pay for the maintenance of the Manchu garrison. That was a trouble which was to recur frequently in the relations between China and Tibet. The presence of foreign troops at Lhasa was always followed by shortage of supplies and a sharp rise in prices. The public invariably complained and demanded the withdrawal of the troops. Such a position immediately confronted the Emperor Yung Ch'êng when he succeeded to the throne in 1722 on the death of his father K'ang Hsi. The new Emperor decided that the Manchu troops should be withdrawn and that instead of a military governor there should be a civil adviser at Lhasa. The change, which took place in 1723, marks the end of the first short phase of Manchu overlordship in Tibet.

Unfortunately for Tibet, the withdrawal was followed very soon by an outbreak of civil strife. The principal Minister had been unpopular with his colleagues and was able to maintain his position only through the support of the Manchu military governor. The imperial representative appointed in 1723 was powerless, without the backing of an army, to control the Tibetan officials or to restrain their rivalries. Intrigues culminated in a civil war which lasted from 1727 to 1728. This is not the place to describe its course. Its effect was to throw Tibet once more into a state of confusion which roused Chinese fears of further Dzungar intervention in Tibet, for the Dzungars were still a power with whom they had to reckon. As both parties in Tibet appealed to the Emperor for help, he decided to send an army to restore order. By the time the army reached Tibet one of the contestants had already established his supremacy and there was no necessity for any military action. So, for a second time foreign troops arrived at Lhasa with Tibetan consent.

The Emperor had learned by experience that he would have to station an armed force at Lhasa if he wanted to retain his influence in Tibet and ensure orderly government there. He set about devising a new arrangement to secure that object. The Tibetan Council was reconstituted under the leadership of Phola Teji who was the victor in the civil war and who had previously been a supporter of Lhabzang Khan; and, to represent the Emperor, two civil officers were appointed—the Ambans as they are known in Tibet—with an armed garrison under a military commander to ensure respect for their position. They were, in effect, little more than observers with the duty of reporting to Peking on events in Lhasa. It was not their function to take part in the actual government of Tibet but their presence, in command of a substantial armed escort, provided the Emperor with some assurance that if ever his advice on matters of administration or policy should become necessary, it would be respected.

One incidental result of the reorganization was to diminish the temporal power of the Dalai Lama, which had been built up in the time of the Vth Incarnation, and to restore much more influence and authority to the lay ministers. During the Manchu Protectorate of 1720–1723 and during the civil war of 1727–1728 the VIIth Dalai Lama was a minor; but his father and court officials were rightly considered by the Emperor to have been largely responsible for the intrigues which brought about the civil war. It was therefore decided to remove the Dalai Lama from Lhasa and in 1728 he was invited to visit Peking. He set out on the journey but was taken no further than Litang where he stayed for seven years, after which he was allowed to return to Lhasa on the strict condition that he refrained from political activity.

Tibetans have long memories; and thoughts of this invitation and the removal of the Dalai Lama in 1728 may well have influenced their fears when the present Dalai Lama was similarly invited to Peking in 1959.

Although the removal of the Dalai Lama left the lay ministers a fairly free hand, they still had to pay regard to the strength of monastic opinion. It happened that Phola, the head of the new administration, was a great man and could take advantage of the opportunity to govern in such a way as to restore peace and confidence in Tibet and avoid offending any section of the community. He was careful never to oppose the Chinese contumaciously; but by his ability and tact in dealing with them, he reduced Manchu supremacy to a matter of form only. The Emperor was able to rely on Phola to such an extent that he did not need to worry about the internal affairs of Tibet. Phola was in effect ruler of the country and in 1740 as a reward for his great services he was given a title which honoured him as 'Prince' or 'King' of Tibet. Although there is a tendency among present-day Tibetans to regard him as a traitor because he did not openly oppose Chinese overlordship of Tibet, there can be no doubt that Phola was one of the best rulers Tibet has had and that for some eighteen years he gave his country prosperous and peaceful government.

DALAI LAMA AND PANCHEN LAMA

At the same time that they engineered the removal of the Dalai Lama in 1728, the Manchus took steps to build up a priestly rival to him on whose co-operation they might hope to rely, and who might perhaps act as a counterweight to the immense religious prestige of the Dalai Lama. They chose the obvious candidate, the second Lama in the Gelugpa church, known as the Panchen, to whom in 1728 they offered the sovereignty of wide areas in North-Central and Western Tibet. The Lama declined the greater part of the offer and accepted it only so far as it related to districts near his monastery at Tashilhunpo. That was the beginning of a long policy of playing off the one Lama against the other. The offer of temporal power was made solely by the Chinese. The Tibetan government was not a party to it, and the status it professed to confer on the Panchen Lama has never been recognized by Lhasa. In Tibetan theory, the Panchen Lama's rights over the districts concerned were never more than those which the Tibetan feudal nobility and the great monasteries exercised over their large estates. The Chinese, on the other hand, found it in their interest to keep alive the rivalry between Lhasa and Tashilhunpo and to build up the position of their favoured Lama by large claims on his behalf to temporal authority over parts of Tibet and also to spiritual superiority over the Dalai Lama.

To understand the relationship between the two Lamas it is necessary to examine briefly the relevant religious ideas of the Tibetans.

The Buddhist goal is to escape from the wheel of cause and effect which drags all creatures, now up and now down, through a series of rebirths in the material world until, by gaining enlightenment, the vicious circle of 'becoming' is broken and the right to cease being reborn is won. Beings who have attained that perfected state but choose to return to the world in human bodies to help others on the way to deliverance are known as Bodhisattvas. For the Tibetans such beings embody the supreme ideal of the spiritual life. A number of Bodhisattvas as well as other celestial entities are held to manifest themselves through various lines of Lamas among whom the Dalai and Panchen Lamas are the most famous although by no means the most ancient since they can trace their spiritual lineage no further back than the fifteenth century. They both belong to the now dominant Gelugpa sect but there are Lamas of the older Kargyupa and Karmapa sects who can count eighteen or more previous incarnations extending in an unbroken succession over eight and a half centuries.

Mahayana Buddhism believes in a sort of primordial Buddha—the 'idea' of a Buddha one might say—which is known as Adi Buddha. That idea projects itself into the plane of spiritual meditation in five other forms, or ideas, known as Dhyani Buddhas; and the Dhyani Buddhas are further projected into the material sphere in the form of five Bodhisattvas. In the theology of the Gelugpa sect the Dalai Lama incarnates an aspect of one of those Bodhisattvas—the Compassionate Avalokiteswara, known in Tibet as Chenrezi.

The Vth Dalai Lama had a venerable and learned teacher named Lobzang Chökyi Gyaltsen whom he appointed Abbot of Tashilhunpo. He also pronounced that Lobzang Chökyi Gyaltsen was an incarnation of the Dhyani Buddha Amitabha (Öpame in

Tibetan) and that he would continue to undergo reincarnation, with the title of Panchen Lama. Amitabha is the Dhyani Buddha in the meditative sphere whose projection into the sphere of the practical world is the Bodhisattva Avalokiteswara of whom, it will be remembered, the Dalai Lama is an incarnation. It was natural that the Dalai Lama should honour his teacher by seeing in him an incarnation of the meditative, intellectual force of which he himself was the incarnation in the world of practical affairs.

A Dhyani Buddha is an idea of the purely spiritual plane and to that extent it is arguable that the Panchen Lama is 'more spiritual' than the Dalai Lama; but he can only be true to his nature if he remains in spiritual contemplation and abstains from all contact with the temporal world. The Dalai Lama, on the other hand, is true to his nature when he influences the practical world. The argument of the spiritual superiority of the Panchen Lama, therefore, logically debars him from having any temporal power or political interests. If he does so, the validity of his incarnation may be called in question. At all events, no Panchen Lama has ever acted as Regent of Tibet except for a brief spell of eight months in 1844.

There was another way in which champions of the Panchen Lama tried to build up his stature in order to put him more on a level with the Dalai Lama. It is the habit of Chinese writers to describe the late Panchen Lama as the IXth. To the mass of Tibetans it is beyond question that he was the VIth in succession from Lobzang Chökyi Gyaltsen, the teacher whom the Vth Dalai Lama created Ist Panchen Lama. The higher numbering is the result of calculating that two Abbots of Tashilhunpo, before Lobzang Chökyi Gyaltsen, and one of Tsongkapa's disciples were all earlier incarnations of the Panchen Lama. Tibetan records show that none of these persons was considered in his lifetime to be an incarnation of any holy person.

Metaphysical hair-splitting and pious fiction, such as the above, have small practical weight and, when it comes to the test of the actual relationship between the two Lamas, although by a natural convention whichever is the elder is the tutor of the other, there is no doubt which is the effective superior. In the neighbourhood of Tashilhunpo many people looked on the Panchen Lama as in a special sense their spiritual leader as well as their feudal lord, but there was no question even there that the Dalai Lama was supreme, both spiritually and temporally, over all Tibet.

CHANGING TIDES: 1750–1792

Phola died in 1747 and was succeeded in the office of King, smoothly and without question, by his younger son Gyurmé Namgyal who had been trained for the succession in preference to the elder son who was a retiring, devout, and rather sickly person. Gyurmé Namgyal was a very different character from his father and, in him, there came out the latent Tibetan dislike of that foreign rule which Phola had been content to accept and reduce to a formality: Gyurmé soon began to intrigue with the Dzungars whose restless ambitions in Mongolia were still a lively threat to the peace of China. Outwardly he maintained an appearance of friendliness towards the imperial representatives— the Ambans—at Lhasa but he quickly succeeded in weakening their position and in moving one step nearer a break with China by persuading the Emperor to reduce the strength of the Manchu garrison at Lhasa to so little as one hundred men. The Emperor, forgetful of what happened after 1723 when Yung Ch'êng withdrew his garrison, agreed to the request.

Gyurmé's behaviour gradually became more arrogant and unrestrained. He brought unpopularity on himself by ruthlessly removing possible competition from his elder brother and his nephews by having them put to death or driven into exile. From many signs it appeared to the Ambans that he was planning open rebellion; but the Emperor—it was by then Ch'ien Lung (1735–1796)—refused to take their suspicions seriously. Eventually, in 1750, the Ambans decided to take action on their own responsibility. They invited Gyurmé to their residence and there murdered him out of hand. Gyurmé was disliked by the Dalai Lama and the old nobility, and it is probable that his removal might have passed off without much trouble if it had not been that one of his attendants was able to escape from the scene of the murder and immediately to raise a mob against the Ambans. Tibetan hatred of foreign interference would be cause enough for such a sudden outbreak even if there was no great love for Gyurmé Namgyal.

As soon as he heard of the disturbance the Dalai Lama sent orders that no one was to harm the Ambans. Leading Tibetan ministers also tried to calm the crowd; but it had by then worked itself into such a state of hysterical excitement that, defying even the orders of the Dalai Lama, it attacked and set on fire the residence of the Ambans. Since the withdrawal of the garrison there was no adequate force to protect the place, and both Ambans were killed with most of their officers and men.

Within a very short time the Dalai Lama, who showed his ability and firmness once he had the opportunity of exercising them, had succeeded in restoring order. He appointed a senior minister to carry on the government and he sent a report to the Emperor of what had happened. Before that letter reached him, Ch'ien Lung received news of the outbreak from one of the survivors. He had brought the trouble on himself by ignoring the warnings of his representatives; now, perhaps, he thought that he had to deal with a full-scale rebellion against his authority. A military expedition was immediately dispatched.

A regular cycle in the affairs of Tibet and China was beginning to become apparent. A military expedition followed by a reorganization of the government at Lhasa; then a decline in the imperial interest and influence there, leading to an internal crisis calling for another expedition and another reorganization—and so on once more.

On this occasion, as in 1720 and 1728, there was no need for the Manchu troops to do any fighting. There had been no rising against the Emperor, only an act of mob violence against his Ambans who had grossly exceeded their authority. There had been no important persons involved. Order had long since been restored and offenders punished. The only thing left to do was to reorganize the government again.

This time the obvious step was taken of abolishing the kingship. The Council of Ministers was restored to the position of importance which it had lost during the ascendancy of Phola; and the

Dalai Lama, who had proved his ability and his readiness to co-operate with the Emperor, was given back much of the power that had been exercised by his predecessor, the Great Vth Dalai Lama. The Ambans were now made responsible for general supervision of the Tibetan government and for giving it advice if that appeared necessary.

In their effect on the internal balance of Tibet, the changes amounted to the resurgence of religious supremacy as against that of the lay nobility. Under Phola the executive power of the civil branch had in effect taken first place, and the Dalai Lama had been thrust into the background so far as practical measures of government were concerned. But Phola, although a noble, was not a member of one of the oldest families and was regarded as a 'new man'. It needed all his talent for conciliation and arrangement to keep the support of his noble colleagues behind him. He also had difficulties with the Church; for tolerant and generous and tactful though he was, it could not be forgotten by the priesthood that he was borrowing the temporal authority of the Dalai Lama. It is a mark of his greatness that he succeeded so long in maintaining a united and successful government without either an open display of autocracy or the need to call in outside support. Gyurmé Namgyal had neither the temperament nor the skill for a balancing act of that sort. It is hard to see what he thought was to be gained from taking action against the Emperor—if such were indeed his thoughts—and one may guess that he suffered from mental instability and a sort of *folie de grandeur*. At all events his short, tempestuous reign convinced the Emperor that a hereditary kingship did not provide a solid foundation for peaceful government in Tibet. The reforms of 1750 put the temporal supremacy of the religious hierarchy on a lasting basis which was never afterwards challenged.

Religious supremacy did not, in effect, mean that the Dalai Lama himself always exercised supreme power; but it did mean that the nobility took second place as administrative and advisory officials of the religious ruler.

The VIIth Dalai Lama Kesang Gyatso had apparently accepted his eclipse by Phola without resentment, perhaps because he could see that the country was being properly administered. But his character had been maturing and by the time of Phola's death he was 27. The overbearing behaviour and bad administration of Gyurmé Namgyal stirred the Dalai Lama to more determined political activity and when matters came to a crisis he proved that he was well able to act as ruler. After the reorganization of 1750 he continued an uneventful administration with the help of his Council until his death in 1757. That was followed by a different sort of régime which was to last for over a century—government by regent.

The old office of Regent for the Mongol King was abolished in 1720 but once the Dalai Lama had been reinstated as ruler it was obvious that someone would have to act for him in his minority; and the custom grew up that this post of Regent should be held by a Lama. It happened that the taste for power so affected the Regents that during a period of about 120 years from the death of Dalai Lama Kesang Gyatso until the accession of the XIIIth Dalai Lama actual authority was exercised by the Lama himself for only seven years. The VIIIth Dalai Lama was the only one of the five in that period to reach a mature age. He was a mild and contemplative person with no great interest in temporal affairs and, although he lived to be 45, for most of his life he was content to let a Regent conduct the administration. After him, the IXth and Xth Dalai Lamas died before attaining their majority: one of them is credibly stated to have been murdered and strong suspicion attaches to the death of the other. The XIth and XIIth were each enthroned but died soon after being invested with power. For 113 years, therefore, supreme authority in Tibet was in the hands of a Lama Regent, except for about two years when a lay noble held office and for the short periods of nominal rule by the XIth and XIIth Dalai Lamas.

It has been sometimes suggested that this state of affairs was brought about by the Ambans—the Imperial Residents in Tibet—because it would be easier to control Tibet through a Regent than when a Dalai Lama, with his absolute power, was at the head of the government. That is not true. The regular ebb and flow of events followed its set course. The Imperial Residents in Tibet, after the first short flush of zeal in 1750, grew less and less interested and efficient. Tibet was, to them, exile from the urbanity and culture of Peking; and so far from dominating the Regents, the Ambans allowed themselves to be dominated. It was the ambition and greed for power of Tibetans that led to five successive Dalai Lamas being subjected to continuous tutelage.

Nevertheless, even in those conditions, Tibetan affairs ran smoothly enough to cause no uneasiness at Peking and it was not for over forty years that the pattern repeated itself and a new crisis in 1792 called forth yet another imperial intervention in Tibet.

IV

TIBET'S DOORS CLOSE: 1792

TIBET AND THE WESTERN WORLD

Drawing aside for a moment from the mainstream of relations between China and Tibet, we may consider shortly the contact with the western world which affected Tibet during the Ch'ing period in China.

The fascinating glimpses of Tibetans in the accounts of medieval Christian missionaries to the Mongol court—such as Odoric of Pordenone and William of Rubruck—and of the incomparable Marco Polo reveal little more than that the Tibetans had a reputation in neighbouring countries for strange ways and rare magical powers.

Foreign contact with Tibet itself began with the journey in about 1600 of a Portuguese merchant, d'Almeida, who succeeded in entering Ladakh. He imagined he had discovered there a long-lost Christian community and his reports aroused the Jesuit College to an interest in Tibet as a new mission field. In 1624 Father Antonio d'Andrade, sent from Goa, surmounted the dangers and hardship of a journey through the Himalaya and succeeded in laying the foundations of a mission in Tsaparang, capital of the West Tibetan Kingdom of Gugé. The mission continued there with varying fortunes, ministered to by a succession of devoted Fathers, until strife between Gugé and Ladakh and growing opposition to the work of the mission brought it to an end in about 1640.

Inspired by information acquired by the Fathers at Tsaparang two other Jesuits, Stephen Cacella and John Cabral, set out from Bengal in 1627 and, travelling through Bhutan, found their way to Shigatse. There they were welcomed by the King—a ruler of the Tsang dynasty—but owing to the death of Cacella in 1630 they were not able to found a permanent mission. In 1661 two Jesuit Fathers, John Grueber and Albert d'Orville, travelling from

China to India by way of Tibet and Nepal, stayed about two
months at Lhasa but it was not their task to attempt to found a
mission there; and they have left tantalizingly little by way of
an account of what they saw.

Eventually, in 1707, a mission of Capuchin Fathers, headed
by Fathers Giuseppe d'Ascoli and Francois de Tours, reached
Lhasa and established a firm footing there. The mission continued
until 1745 when lack of funds and pressure from the Tibetan
monks and Lamas brought about its closure. Among the names
connected with it are those of Fathers Domenico da Fano and
Orazio della Penna; but the figure who commands the greatest
affection and renown is the Jesuit Ippolito Desideri who arrived
at Lhasa in 1716 after the long, hard journey from Leh, to find
the Capuchins already entrenched there. He was kindly received,
but the Capuchins were determined to keep the Lhasa mission
field to themselves. Nevertheless, while protracted correspondence
with Rome was going on, Desideri was able to stay for five years
in Lhasa. He was a missionary in the great tradition of Fathers
Matteo Ricci in China and Roberto de Nobili in India who
devoted themselves to the life and thought of the country in
which they were working, studying the language, religion, and
customs with an absorption and thoroughness which has perhaps
never been equalled. Desideri, too, although he had a shorter time
than they, made a most careful study of the religion and manners
of Tibet and he succeeded in learning Tibetan so well that he was
able to write in that language an attempted refutation of the
Buddhist teachings. This had a great reception in Lhasa where it
was read with attention and admiration, but without changing
any convictions.

Desideri's comments on Tibetan history and contemporary
events are of special value because he was in Lhasa at the time of
the Dzungar invasion and the Chinese expedition. He enjoyed
the friendship and protection of Lhabzang Khan and records his
death with grief. Desideri's *Account of Tibet* reveals also his affection for the Tibetans; and his testimony to the strength of their
religious faith, even though he was bound to condemn what he
believed to be its fallacy, deserves to be remembered: 'I confess

that I blamed myself and was ashamed to have a heart so hard
that I did not honour, love and serve Jesus, sole Master, sole and
true Redeemer, as this people did a traitor, their deceiver.'

After the closure of the Capuchin Mission in 1745 there were
never any more Christian missionaries at Lhasa and nothing
remains of the Faith they tried to teach except one moving re-
minder. From the ceiling of a narrow passage which leads into
the Jo-khang of Lhasa—the holiest place in all Tibet—hangs a
shapely bell on which is inscribed in bold letters 'Te Deum
Laudamus'.

The absence of opposition to foreign travellers entering Tibet
in the seventeenth and early eighteenth centuries gives a different
picture from the traditional one of Tibet as a closed country.
Civilians, too, might go there if they could face the difficulties of
the journey, for there is an account of a wealthy and adventurous
Dutch merchant, Samuel Van der Putte, who travelled, between
1725 and 1735, from India to China and back again to India. On
both journeys he passed through Lhasa where he is said to have
stayed a long time; but he was one of those reticent travellers
who will not publish their journals. He died young and before his
death ordered the destruction of all his notes on his travels.

It is probable that those early visitors to Tibet, especially the
missionaries, accustomed the Tibetans, to some extent, to different
ideas and somewhat widened their horizon; but in general the
Fathers were careful to avoid political issues and it was not for
nearly twenty-five years after the closing of the Capuchin
mission at Lhasa that the world of western diplomacy and state-
craft began to impinge on Tibet.

The expansion of British influence in India spread inevitably
to the stable barrier of the Himalaya. First it touched on Nepal
where as early as 1769 a small and abortive mission under Captain
Kinloch attempted to stay the progress of the Gurkha conquest
over the previous Newar rulers of the country. Soon after, the
Bhutanese, perhaps infected by the unrest and violence in Nepal,
invaded Cooch Behar in the plains of Bengal and a near neighbour
of the British Government of India. At the request of the Raja
of Cooch Behar, Warren Hastings sent an armed force which

drove the Bhutanese out of the plains and entered the foothills of Bhutan itself. A rapid and probably unexpected consequence was a letter from the Panchen Lama to Warren Hastings. This first diplomatic contact between Tibet and Britain was conducted in dignified but friendly language. The Panchen Lama, describing himself as concerned only with religion and peace, explained that the Bhutanese, who were a rude and ignorant people, were subjects of the Dalai Lama. He admitted that they had given provocation by their raids but urged that now they had been well beaten it would be better to leave them alone and not to provoke further strife by invading their country.

To claim the Bhutanese as subjects of the Dalai Lama was an exaggeration. The link was another of those loose and variable Central Asian relationships. The Bhutanese respected the Dalai Lama as a great religious figure and honoured him as a powerful neighbouring ruler. But the Gelugpa domination had not extended to Bhutan and there were closer bonds with the Tibetan hierarchs of the older sects. Attempts by Lhasa to impose its jurisdiction on Bhutan by war had been fiercely resisted and had had only temporary effect; but in a crisis with the non-Tibetan world it was natural for the Bhutanese to turn for help, as they did now, to their neighbours and kinsmen in Tibet.

Hastings eagerly responded to the Panchen Lama's overture. The idea of closer contact with a strange and little-known country on his border was certain to appeal to his lively intellectual curiosity and wide-ranging interest in commercial prospects. Trade between India and Tibet was no new thing. It had been carried on freely through Nepal before the peace of that country was upset by the Gurkha conquest in 1769. It is mentioned by Ralph Fitch in 1583. There was also a religious and commercial connection between Tashilhunpo and Benares and it was an agent of the Raja of Benares who brought the letter from the Panchen Lama to Hastings. The possibility of encouraging trade with Tibet, especially as a source of supply of gold and silver, had been tentatively examined by officers of the East India Company even before the appointment of Hastings as Governor-General of Bengal in 1772; and the idea that Tibet might provide

a route to China had also been in their minds, but no such
opportunity had presented itself before.

Hastings decided to send an envoy to express his friendly
feelings for the Tibetans and also to find out about the products
of the country and its trading needs. He chose a young Scot,
George Bogle, who set out on his mission in 1774. Bogle was a
good choice. He resolutely and gaily found his way through
Bhutan, overcoming all sorts of difficulties by patience and good
humour. In 1775 he reached Tashilhunpo and, before long, had
won the friendship of the IIIrd Panchen Lama and had cultivated
a close intimacy with his family. He married a Tibetan lady,
described as a sister of the Panchen Lama, by whom he had two
daughters. The girls were later educated at Bogle's ancestral
home in Lanarkshire and there each married a Scottish husband.
All reference to Bogle's Tibetan wife seems to have been suppressed when his papers were edited for publication; but his
descendants, of whom several survive in Britain, now look back
to that ancestry with pride.

Bogle's *Narrative*, delightful in itself, throws a good deal of
light on the condition of Tibet in the eighteenth century as well as
on the objects of Hastings's policy there. The IIIrd Panchen Lama,
Lobsang Palden Yeshé (1738–1780), was one of the great figures
of the day. The VIIth Dalai Lama died when the Panchen was
about 20 and the VIIIth Dalai Lama was slow to develop and by
comparison undistinguished. No Regent could rival the prestige
of a Panchen Lama and the Lama was also, at Tashilhunpo, free
from interference by the Emperor's representatives. But above
all the IIIrd Panchen Lama was a man of remarkable character,
learning, and ability; added to which, as we see from Bogle,
he had an affable and friendly nature. The Regents at Lhasa may
well have felt overshadowed by a figure of such stature and that
feeling of jealousy kept alive the rivalry between Lhasa and
Tashilhunpo which was so convenient for the imperial interests;
but, this time, it was a question of playing Lhasa off against
Tashilhunpo rather than the other way round. The Emperor
Ch'ien Lung showed great regard for the Panchen Lama and
consulted him frequently, but from Bogle's account it can be

seen that the Panchen could justifiably be accounted the real champion of the rights of Tibet and of the Dalai Lama. The impression gained by Bogle was that, although the supremacy of the Emperor had to be acknowledged, that was done grudgingly and its external expression was strictly confined to Lhasa. The Panchen Lama had considerable freedom of action in his own jurisdiction and considerable influence—but not authority—all over Tibet. The intervention on behalf of Bhutan appears to have been entirely on his own initiative; and its upshot in the visit of Bogle was clearly not welcomed at Lhasa, for the Panchen Lama was unable to arrange for Bogle to go there.

Suspicion of the foreigner combined with jealousy of Tashilhunpo probably united the Regent and the Ambans in refusing to allow Bogle to proceed to Lhasa. The Panchen Lama could not overcome that objection but he was able to send his own recommendation to Tibetan traders all over the country, including Lhasa itself, that they should resort to the markets which Hastings proposed to establish in India for Tibetan trade. Both the Lama and Bogle appreciated that in the existing circumstances the best way to move Lhasa was to approach the Emperor direct; and they made plans for a visit to China by Bogle.

The achievements of Bogle's mission to Shigatse, although materially not very great, were important in that relations between the British in India and Tibet got off to an auspicious start with excellent personal connections of a most valuable nature having been established. Bogle also secured a trading agreement with Bhutan and he arranged with the Panchen Lama that a Buddhist temple should be built at Calcutta. It will be noticed that at no time did any suggestion of territorial aims in Tibet enter into Hastings's policy.

Hastings was well pleased by what Bogle had achieved and in 1779 he entrusted him with a further mission to Tibet, this time with specific instructions to seek a means of communication with China; but news that the Panchen Lama was about to leave for Peking caused the plan to be postponed. In 1780 Hastings's policy in Tibet suffered a blow when the Panchen Lama died at Peking, and Bogle himself died in India in the following year. Nevertheless, the good effects of Bogle's visit continued. The authorities at Tashilhunpo considered that they had a particular association with the British in India, and in 1782 the brother of the late Panchen Lama, who was acting as Regent in the interim, sent to inform Hastings that the new incarnation had been found. This sign of friendship was quickly followed up by Hastings with the dispatch to Tibet of Capt. Samuel Turner. Turner was, it appears, more reserved than Bogle but was certainly as able an observer and as patient and equable a diplomatist. Like Bogle, he got no farther than Tashilhunpo, nor did he gain any new commercial concessions. That is not surprising. The Panchen Lama was an infant and the Dalai Lama much under the thumb of his Regent. Regencies in Tibet are, moreover, traditionally a time for maintaining the *status quo*.

Without so authoritative a figure as the IIIrd Panchen Lama to provide a standard, Turner attributes more actual authority to the Chinese than did Bogle; but he, perhaps, mistook for Chinese obstruction to his hopes what was in fact obstruction by the Regent at Lhasa who was a powerful figure, completely dominating the Ambans and not well-disposed towards the regime at Tashilhunpo under whose patronage Turner's visit took place. At all events, Turner reinforces Bogle's view of the Tibetan attitude towards China by the clear statement in his report that the Tibetans always avoided admitting complete dependency on the Chinese Emperor.

The driving force behind British policy towards Tibet was removed, soon after the end of Turner's mission, when Hastings departed from India. There were no further British envoys to Tibet; but trade began to quicken and contact was maintained through the remarkable Indian agent, Purangir Gosain. No account of early British dealings with Tibet would be complete without mention of him, for he played a constructive part in Tibet's relations with both India and China. He accompanied both Bogle and Turner to Tashilhunpo. His association with the Panchen Lama was just as close as with the British. It was Purangir who brought the Panchen Lama's letter to Hastings in 1774 and he accompanied the Panchen Lama on his visit to Peking. Purangir reported that at an interview with the Emperor the Panchen Lama—as he had promised Bogle—spoke in favour of the British in India. This has been questioned by Professor Cammann on no better ground than that he does not think it likely; but that is inadequate reason for rejecting Purangir's clear and circumstantial report, which the Panchen's brother and Chief Steward also supported, and it may be safely said that Bogle, Turner, and Purangir Gosain gave a promising start to relations between British India and Tibet.

THE GURKHA WAR

The death of the IIIrd Panchen Lama in 1780 may have lightened the Emperor's mind of some slight uneasiness; but the root cause of anxiety about Tibet and the practical reason for Chinese interest in that country had been removed some time earlier when the defeat of the Dzungars in 1757 had dissipated the last threat of a new Mongol Empire in the steppes. The Patron no longer, it seemed, had to worry about protecting his Priest; and so long as there was neither danger from outside nor disturbance within, the scantest imperial attention was bestowed on Tibet. Persons sent there as Ambans, after the reforms of 1750, were of poor quality and character and made no attempt to stand up to the Regents at Lhasa. On their part, the Tibetans, not being affected by the uncompromising Western attitude to nationalism, were content to continue what had become a habit—the formal recognition of a link with, but not ultimate dependence on, the Emperor together with the practical freedom to do as they pleased in their own country. For the best part of a century they had not needed imperial protection; but neither they nor the Chinese court seem to have appreciated the danger which was building up in Nepal.

The Mallas who had ruled Nepal before the Gurkha conquest in 1769 were peaceful by nature and of strong Buddhist sympathies. They maintained a friendly and very profitable connection with the trade and currency arrangements of Tibet. The

Gurkhas were aggressively Hindu and disposed to be contemptuous of the Tibetans. It was not long before troubles boiled up over
frontier disputes and details of commercial and monetary affairs.
Gurkha tempers and cupidity were sharpened by the instigation
of the VIIIth Sha-mar (Red Hat) Karmapa Lama, a renegade
member of the late Panchen Lama's family; but they did not
need much persuasion to lay hands on the riches of Tashilhunpo,
especially as they might reflect that the Panchen Lama's encouragement of British trade with Tibet had done some damage
to their own commercial interests. The Gurkhas wasted little
time over finding excuses and in 1788 they sent an army into
Tibet. It occupied a number of frontier districts and withdrew
only when bought off with a promise of tribute. That dubious
arrangement was negotiated by the Chinese military commanders
who had been specially appointed to repel the invasion. A
Tibetan Minister from Lhasa also took part in the agreement, and
it was connived at by the imperial representative in Tibet who
sent a false report to the Emperor on the strength of which
Ch'ien Lung later described this pitiful bargain as one of the Ten
Victories of his reign.

One instalment of the tribute money was paid in 1759; but in
the following year the Dalai Lama refused to allow it because he
had not approved the original agreement. The Gurkhas, in fury,
invaded Tibet again and rapidly penetrated as far as Shigatse
and the glittering spoils of the great monastery of Tashilhunpo.
The facts could no longer be kept from the Emperor who, with
equal anger, dispatched a vast and well-organized army which,
with striking efficiency and success, threw the Gurkhas out of
Tibet and, crossing the great Himalayan range, reached Nawakot
within twenty miles of the Nepalese capital, Kathmandu. The
Gurkhas had humbly to bind themselves to offer tribute every
five years in allegiance to the Emperor, to return what they had
looted from Tashilhunpo, and to abstain in future from any
breach of peace with Tibet.

For the fourth time in nearly 75 years an imperial army had
had to be sent to Tibet. Ch'ien Lung was, understandably,
annoyed at the trouble and expense of so large an undertaking, as

well as at the affront to his dignity. After inflicting punishment on the officials who had misled him, he set about examining how such a situation had arisen and how it might be prevented from recurring. The poor quality of his Ambans was, he believed, largely to blame for what had happened and he decided that better men should be sent in future and that they should exercise stricter control over the Tibetan authorities.˙ A number of measures were decreed to bring this about, to remove the difficulties which had arisen over monetary and commercial problems, and to regulate the system of taxation, the administrative organization and so on. Two other reforms have attracted considerable attention. One was a device for the selection of High Lamas by lot, making use, for that purpose, of a golden urn presented by the Emperor; the other, the control of all Tibetan communications with foreign countries, sometimes described as the closing of the frontiers.

Those changes have been interpreted as the imposition of full Chinese sovereignty on Tibet and on paper they look something like that. But the element of fiction and artificiality in Chinese relations with Tibet and the one-sided character of most versions of Sino-Tibetan history need to be taken into account. Looked at with an eye to their practical effect, the reforms will be seen to have brought about no greater or more lasting a degree of imperial authority than had been exercised under the previous arrangements. Perhaps, too, the infection of dynastic decline, the seeds of which can be detected even at that peak of Manchu success, inspired, as a feverish reaction at Peking, the feeling that it was necessary to assert a closer control over Tibet.

At all events, the pattern already made familiar by past history was followed again in the new circumstances. For a few years there were active, well-chosen Ambans at Lhasa, notably Ho Lin the brother of Ch'ien Lung's favourite and evil genius Ho Shen. He made a busy display of supervision and set up several inscriptions to testify to his zeal. But by the test of actual exercise of authority it can be seen that quite soon after 1793 the ebb tide set in strongly. In 1804 one Amban had to be removed for misconduct. In 1818 another was found to be colluding in an attempt to evade the Emperor's orders. In 1823 another inefficient Amban was dismissed. At the same time the influence of the Tibetan Regents rose to even greater heights than before; and from 1819 until 1844 one of the most powerful and most oppressive Regents in Tibet's history was able to exert well-nigh absolute rule without any interference from the Ambans.

The decree purporting to regulate the selection of the Dalai Lama by lot is well known and is sometimes cited as evidence of Chinese control over Tibet; but in 1808 on the very first occasion on which it should have been employed the Tibetans completely disregarded it and the Emperor had to accept the *fait accompli*. Again in 1818, when the Xth Dalai Lama was being sought for, another attempt to ignore the Decree was detected by the Emperor in time to insist on the prescribed procedure being followed; but it can hardly have been mere coincidence that the child whom the Tibetans had already put forward as the new Dalai Lama was the one chosen subsequently by the formality of the lot.

The one provision in the reforms of 1793 which did have lasting effect was the exclusion of foreigners. There was an unfounded suspicion encouraged by the Chinese, who certainly held it themselves, that the British in India had helped the Nepalese in the war of 1792. Even if the Tibetans did not believe that there had been active British support for the Gurkhas, they had reason to feel disappointed and disillusioned because the Panchen Lama himself had appealed to the British Government for help and had got nothing more than vague offers of mediation. After that, a general fear, which had been in Tibetan minds as early as the time of Bogle's visit, was progressively confirmed by the extension of British ascendancy all along the Himalayan foothills in areas where the influence of Lhasa, even if not sovereign, had long been respected. There was also an attack on Tibetan religious beliefs in the activity of the Christian missionaries who began to settle on the Indian and Chinese borders of Tibet from about the middle of the nineteenth century. And so, whether in accordance with Chinese policy or not, Tibet after 1792 deliberately closed its doors to foreigners. Nevertheless, a few succeeded in breaking through the embargo. Thomas Manning in 1811, so sketchily disguised that the Tibetans can have had no doubt that he was English, was received by them without hostility. He has left confirmation of the bad quality and conduct of the imperial representatives at Lhasa. Moorcroft's mysterious stay at Lhasa from 1826 to 1838 must be dismissed as legend; but the Lazarist Fathers Huc and Gabet arriving from China in 1846 were treated amiably by the Tibetan Regent and rather less so by the Amban. Their account contains useful information about Tibetan suspicions of the British and about the status of the Chinese at that time: they regarded the Amban as a mere ambassador sent to watch what the Tibetans did.

The evidence therefore shows that, whatever the intention of the 1793 reforms, the substance of Chinese authority in Tibet was in practice no greater than it had been before. Indeed, in one very important respect the foundation of the connection between the two countries was weakened. The encroachments of the West in China itself, leading to the Anglo-Chinese war of 1840, left the Emperor with no strength to fulfil the function of Protector as had been done in 1792. A Dogra invasion of West Tibet in 1841 was repelled by a force which was purely Tibetan, although it has sometimes been wrongly described as 'Chinese'. In 1855 the Gurkhas, without regard for the oath they had taken to the Emperor in 1792, again invaded Tibet. This time there was no imperial army to protect the Tibetans. They were defeated and had to make a humiliating treaty (Appendix, p. 247). It is interesting that in the treaty both parties affirm that they will continue to regard the Emperor of China 'with respect'. Although they both had full freedom of action in their own affairs and although the Nepalese had just shown open disrespect by violating the agreement of 1792, they still acknowledged the politico-mystical aura of the Empire and—after all—what would they have gained by an open breach? That is another example of the need to look at the affairs of Tibet, not only with a sense of period, but also with a sense of the Central Asian ambience.

V

THE WEST BREAKS IN

BRITISH OVERTURES

Consolidation of their power in India drew the British continually nearer to the Himalaya—a stable frontier dividing the Indian world from that of Central Asia. Relations with Nepal were settled in 1816 by the Treaty of Segauli which also gave the British direct control of the Himalayan districts of Kumaon and part of Garhwal. At the same time, a group of Hill States from Tehri to the borders of Ladakh was taken under British protection. In 1846 when Kashmir was made over to Maharaja Gulab Singh, Spiti and Lahul were detached from Ladakh and incorporated in the administered district of Kangra. Ladakh itself, as a dependency of Kashmir, came indirectly under British influence. To the east of Nepal, the Darjeeling district was acquired from the Raja of Sikkim in 1835 and, after several vicissitudes, satisfactory settlements were reached with Sikkim in 1861 and Bhutan in 1865. As part of the latter, the Kalimpong area was attached to British India. Further east, a series of agreements, beginning in 1844, with the chiefs of the little-known hill tribes living between the plains of Assam and the crest of the Himalaya, assured the security of the Brahmaputra valley.

In this way there emerged a Himalayan frontier of India cushioned off from Tibet for almost its whole length by states and peoples in varying degrees of dependency on the Indian Government. With most of those states and peoples the Tibetans, too, had their own particular relationships, in general customary and undefined, depending either on the bond of religious allegiance to the Dalai Lama or on long-established local trade or grazing connections. The Government of the Dalai Lama did not exercise direct authority in Ladakh, Sikkim, Bhutan, or any area south of the Himalaya except for the Chumbi valley, nor was it represented in those countries by permanent envoys; but the ties of religious homage, trade, racial affinity, and a degree of common interest had given Lhasa a special position and influence. The Chinese Emperor, as nominal overlord and protector of the Dalai Lama, might also claim an interest there, though one far more shadowy and indeterminate than his interest in Tibet.

There were, therefore, along the frontier not a few anomalies and ambiguities, unsuspected at the time because the Tibetan policy of exclusion obscured the significance and effect of those links of race, religion, and custom between the cis-Himalayan regions and Tibet.

An attraction and challenge lay in that secretive hinterland from which descended into India a trickle of pilgrims and petty traders but to which the return traffic was so jealously restricted. From 1846 onwards there was a ceaseless quest for information. The pioneer journeys of the Stracheys and Cunningham in West Tibet were followed by half a century of adventurous exploration by British, Russian, French, Scandinavian, and American travellers. A special, though less spectacular, contribution was made by the courage and determination of the Indian and Sikkimese Pundits of the Survey of India. British officers stationed in the frontier districts were for ever seeking ways to open communications and trade with Tibet. Missionaries on the border, also, were often acute observers and informants.

A substantial body of knowledge was built up from these tireless explorations and inquiries; but its scope was limited. Most of the Western travellers could penetrate only thinly populated regions remote from Lhasa. Indian Government officers met only Tibetans of quite low rank who, while usually affable enough, could not be relied on to transmit messages to Lhasa. There was no opportunity for close and friendly acquaintance with persons of real importance such as there had been in the time of Bogle and Turner. Reports from the missionaries were sometimes coloured by prejudice and professional optimism. The Pundits, suffering from the limitations of disguise and the need to move principally among the lower orders of society, produced more valuable reports on topography and communications than on social, economic, and political conditions in Tibet.

The development of trade was still the principal object of the Indian Government's interest in Tibet and that interest was stimulated by inquiries from business organizations in Britain and China as well as in India. From the information it was able to acquire the Indian Government concluded that the Tibetans themselves were ready to accept—perhaps even to welcome— closer relations and would admit British visitors if only the objections of the Chinese Government could be overcome. On this premise and in the hope of renewing the friendship which existed in the days of Warren Hastings and of arranging a fair basis for trade, including that in Indian tea—on which a complete embargo prevailed—proposals were repeatedly put forward that the Chinese Government should be approached through the British Legation at Peking to grant an order of admittance to Tibet.

British diplomatists in China took an entirely different view of the real obstacle to intercourse with Tibet, and one which proved to be nearer the truth than that prevailing in India. They believed that the Chinese Government would never willingly grant permission for a British visit to Tibet partly because it did not want to see its own position there endangered and partly because it was improbable that, even if permission were granted, the Tibetans would honour it. The latter argument was supported by at least one instance when a foreign traveller secured a passport for Tibet from a Chinese governor on the eastern border only to find it rejected by the Tibetans.

Nevertheless, pressure from India could not always be resisted and in 1846 a specific but fruitless overture was made at Peking, linked with the proposal that the boundary of Ladakh should be demarcated by a joint Anglo-Chinese commission. Informal soundings were made on several subsequent occasions but the cause was not one very close to the heart of the British Legation and it was, in each case, deemed to be either useless or inexpedient to put the matter to an official test. At last, in 1876, the negotiation of the Chefoo Convention offered a suitable opportunity for including a separate article, which the Chinese were in no position to resist, agreeing to provide facilities for a British mission

of exploration across Tibet from India to China or in the reverse
direction (Appendix, p. 249).

It was not until 1885 that the Government of India decided to
test the value of this Chinese concession. Permission was secured
through the British Legation at Peking for Colman Macaulay of
the Bengal Government to lead a mission to Lhasa. Everything
was ready when it became known that difficulties had arisen; and
the expedition was abandoned. The reason, given as 'international
considerations', was, rather strangely, written into the Anglo-
Chinese Convention of 1886 regarding Burma in a clause modifying the special article of the Chefoo Convention (Appendix,
p. 249).

What had happened was that the Tibetans had flatly refused to
accept the proposed mission and the Chinese were quite unable
to compel them. This cannot have caused much surprise to the
British Legation in China but the belief that the Chinese exercised
actual authority in Tibet died hard elsewhere and standard English
works on history reflect the view that it was only about 1898 that
'the control of the Ambans was visibly weakening'. In fact,
although the last rags of influence and prestige were stripped from
the imperial representatives at Lhasa in 1895 by the assumption
of power by the XIIIth Dalai Lama and by the disaster to Chinese
morale in the Sino-Japanese war of 1894–95, there had been no
real Chinese control in Tibet in the previous thirty years. Even
when that came to be appreciated in India it took some time more
to appreciate the depth of distrust which made the Tibetans prefer
the light yoke of their ineffectual overlord to the dangers inherent
in official relations with their pushing British neighbours.

The proposed British Mission of 1885, assembled near the
Tibetan frontier with a small military escort, seemed like the
spearhead of invasion and to forestall or delay it the Tibetans,
early in 1886 before orders for the abandonment of the expedition
were known, had collected an armed force in the Chumbi valley
whence they sent a detachment across the Himalaya to occupy
a position near Natong, inside the borders of Sikkim. The
Tibetans had never accepted the right of the British to any connection with Sikkim, and there were arguable uncertainties about

the exact limits of Sikkimese territory; but Natong was well south of the mountain passes forming the natural frontier and had for at least twenty years been treated by the British as part of Sikkim. The Tibetan advance, therefore, appeared to be an attack on Sikkim; but the Raja of Sikkim, who was at the time in somewhat equivocal relations with the Tibetans, was an uncertain factor.

No immediate military action was taken to repel the intruders. The approach through Peking was tried first and the Chinese Government was asked to compel the Tibetans to withdraw, an ample time limit of one year being allowed. Nothing happened; and there is no evidence that the Chinese even attempted to influence the Tibetans. At last, in 1888, after an ultimatum to the Tibetan commander and a letter to the Dalai Lama, both of which were ignored, a British force was sent to the Sikkim frontier. The Tibetans withdrew but later made a surprise attack and were promptly driven out of Sikkim and pursued into the Chumbi valley, whence the British retired.

This was the first armed conflict between Britain and Tibet and, although the Tibetans had good reason to resent the extension of British authority into what had long been a Tibetan sphere of influence, they had made no attempt to put their case in discussion and had invaded territory where they had never exercised active jurisdiction.

The clash and the brief British pursuit across the border alarmed Peking where it was feared that a direct settlement between Britain and Tibet might follow. The Chinese rapidly opened negotiations in India to define the status of Sikkim and provide for trade between India and Tibet. Discussion dragged on until 1890 when an Anglo-Chinese Convention was concluded (Appendix, p. 250). But that was only the first stage. Three more years were needed before a set of Tibetan Trade Regulations could be signed in 1893 (Appendix, p. 251). It was almost all wasted labour. No Tibetan representative was party to either agreement and the farce of Chefoo was re-enacted on a larger scale. The Tibetans actively obstructed the operation of a treaty which affected their interests but to which they had not given their consent. The Chinese had been chiefly concerned with saving appearances and, even if they were genuinely anxious to do so, were quite incapable of compelling the Tibetans to accept what had been signed on their behalf. Stalemate, which lasted for five years, was eventually broken in 1899 by the arrival of Lord Curzon as Viceroy.

The Tibetan question came to life again early in the new Viceroyalty. The Trade Regulations of 1893 had fallen due for revision in 1898 and little had been done to put them into effect, nor had there been any progress in attempts to demarcate the frontier of Sikkim. Curzon made one more effort to exert pressure through the Ambans but he soon came to the conclusion that this was useless and that Chinese authority in Tibet was no more than a fiction. The only hope of a solution lay, in his opinion, in direct communication with the Tibetans themselves. Two letters were, therefore, addressed to the Dalai Lama and transmitted, with difficulty, through different channels. The Tibetans were quite prepared to shelter behind the Emperor when it suited them. The letters were returned unopened with the indirect and evasive reply that it would displease the Chinese if the Dalai Lama were to correspond with the British.

RUSSIA AND TIBET

The Tibetan policy of Lord Curzon was so closely concerned with Russian expansion in Asia that, before continuing the main theme, a short discursion on that subject may be worth while.

The interest of the Russians in Asia had its springs in their idea of Russia as heir by reversion to the dominions of her former Mongol conquerors, an idea which was not particularly strange to later Mongols, many of whom looked on the Czar as the Tsagan Khan—the ruler of the White Horde. The eastward flow may be said to have begun with the annexation of the Khanates of Kazan and Astrakhan in the mid-sixteenth century and was encouraged in a northerly direction by the peaceful acquisition of Siberia towards the end of the same century. Steadily pushing on, in a blend of trade and adventure, by the middle of the seventeenth century Russians had reached the Amur river where their progress was eventually halted by the Manchu rulers of China—then at the height of their vigour—in the Treaty of Nerchinsk of 1689.

By the foundation of Orenburg in 1732 a wide new field towards the south and east was opened to Russian energies. Although the plans of Czar Paul and of Napoleon and Czar Alexander for an overland invasion of India may have been little more than bravado on a grand scale, from the middle of the nineteenth century the tide of Russian deployment, advancing over the plains and plateaux of the Oxus and Jaxartes basin, gave point to those earlier threats and presented a serious challenge to the defence and foreign policy of the British Government in India. There was the Russian scare at the time of the First Afghan War; and the progressive occupation of territories between Chinese Turkestan and the Caspian brought the flood of expansion ever nearer the mountain barriers of Persia, Afghanistan, and India: Ili in 1854—though this was later returned to China; Tashkent in 1865; Samarkand in 1868; Bokhara in 1869; Khiva in 1873 and Khokand in 1876; Turkmenistan in 1881; Merv in 1884; Penjdeh in 1885; the Pamirs in 1895. There was an element of inevitability in all this as Prince Gorchakov explained in a famous memorandum of November 1864. Russia was seeking a stable frontier in much the same way as the British in India had been drawn on to the Himalaya.

As these two powers converged, Tibet, whose horizon had for long been bounded loosely by Asian neighbours with similar minds and similar policies, was caught in the pincers; and, although still remaining withdrawn in spirit, in the matter of its frontiers and its political relations it swiftly fell victim to the Western craving for definition and became a comparatively well-outlined and restricted buffer.

Between Russia and Tibet there had been, for some time, remote and indirect dealings. The link was through the Mongols, for most of the Mongol tribes which gradually came within the Russian sphere were originally converts to the reformed sect of Tibetan Buddhism during its great diffusion in the sixteenth and seventeenth centuries. There was also a connection through the

Torgot Kalmuks who were pushed out of their native homes in the sixteenth century and gradually migrated to the Volga basin where in the mid-seventeenth century they were eventually accepted as vassals of the Czar. Lhasa continued to be their spiritual home. In 1720 they sent contributions for the repair of the Jo-khang after it had been damaged by the Dzungar invasion; and Kalmuk missions visited Lhasa in 1730 and on several occasions after that. In 1771 the majority of the tribe, dissatisfied with conditions in Russia, set out on a nostalgic migration back to Central Asia. The story of their terrible sufferings at the hands of pursuing Russians, Bashkirs, and Kirghiz, and how the survivors struggled to safety under Chinese protection, has been told by De Quincey in 'The Revolt of the Tartars'. Although there is no trace of organized missions after that, some of the Kalmuk remnant left on the west bank of the Volga probably continued to visit Lhasa from time to time, as did Mongols from other parts of Russia, whose visits are mentioned without any clear identification of their origin by later travellers. Bogle and Turner found in Tibet persons whom they describe rather vaguely as 'Siberians; Kalmuks; and Tartars'; also several evidences of trade goods originating in Russia. They found, too, the Tibetans reasonably well-informed about Russian activities in Asia.

The rulers of Russia do not appear at that time to have attached very great importance to the contact of their subjects with Tibet; but Turner reports that the Russians had made repeated overtures for the extension of their trade with Tibet and that some years before his visit the Empress Catherine had dispatched a special embassy to the Taranatha Lama at Urga, with the same object. The Lama had sent the Empress's presents—including a Bible in Russian which Turner saw—to the Panchen Lama and had also referred the Empress's request to him. The Panchen grudgingly advised that the Russians should be allowed a trading establishment at Kharka (perhaps a place in Mongolia to the south of Lake Baikal).

Traffic with Tibet by Russian subjects of Asiatic origin appears to have been regular and long-established. It was probably a party of 600 such persons that Moorcroft reported as having visited

Gartok about 1812. Asian Russians may have been the carriers
of British goods which Hodgson discovered in 1831 to have been
reaching Tibet by way of Russia. Later, when Tsybikov (himself
a Buriat) visited Lhasa in 1900, he found that while Russians
came under the general ban on foreigners, Buriats and Kalmuks
had been going there annually for the past thirty years. Tibetans
therefore knew something about the Russians and appear to have
had the same suspicions of them as they had of the British.

Curzon's study of Russian expansion in Asia long antedated
his appointment as Viceroy of India. So early as 1889 the possibility had been in his mind that Russia would seek to acquire
influence in Tibet. From about 1894 a few signs of Russian contact with Lhasa began to be known but no great significance was
attached to them until in 1898 reports appeared in Indian newspapers that a Russian mission under a certain Baranov had been
to Lhasa. Coming about the time of Curzon's assumption of the
Viceroyalty and echoing his established fears of Russian ambitions,
that was enough to start a more active concern on the part of the
Government of India and perhaps had some part in inspiring the
attempt to come to terms directly with the Tibetans, which was
mentioned at the end of the last chapter. Nevertheless, it was not
until the activities of Dorjiev came before the public eye that the
Russian scare really blew up in India.

Dorjiev was a Buriat Mongol from Baikal who went to Lhasa
on a religious visit in 1880. He settled there quietly in the great
monastery of Drepung and acquired exceptional learning in
Tibetan religion, philosophy, and history. After gaining a title
of distinction in scholarship he became one of the instructors of
the young Dalai Lama, with whom, it is generally agreed in
Tibet, he acquired considerable personal influence. There is no
evidence that Dorjiev had at first any official backing from, or
indeed any communications with, the Russian Government and
Alistair Lamb has wrongly identified him as a member of Prje-
valski's expedition to Tibet in 1884. In 1898 he went on a journey
to Russia to collect subscriptions for his monastic college. He may
also have had secret instructions from his pupil, the Dalai Lama,
who had recently come of age and asserted his independence of

the authority of a domineering Regent. At all events, on his visit to Russia he came to the notice of officialdom. He was loaded with presents for the Dalai Lama and was instructed to advise him that, as China was weak, he should seek alliance with Russia. The Czar, who was still vaguely regarded in Asian eyes as the White Khan, was described by Dorjiev as having an earnest interest in Buddhism, and an invitation to visit Russia was conveyed to the Dalai Lama on his behalf. The young man was flattered. He sent costly return presents and made preparations for the journey, even sending a suitable throne ahead of him. But the Tibetan Assembly, wedded to the idea of avoiding contact with all outsiders, whether British or Russian, raised strong objection to the proposed journey and it had to be abandoned. Dorjiev was therefore sent once more to Russia, in 1901, and returned soon—through India—with further presents including a gorgeous set of clerical vestments, together with the hint that the Czar (Nicholas II) himself might become a Buddhist. He also brought the suggestion that a Russian imperial prince might be sent as the Czar's resident representative at Lhasa. There was now no concealment of Dorjiev's activities. The Russian press described it exultingly as 'our mission to Tibet' and Dorjiev himself was received by the Czar as 'Envoy Extraordinary from the Dalai Lama'.

In considering these events and what followed from them, it is necessary to see them in the setting and against the conditions of the period; and, above all, to remember the curtain of almost total ignorance about Tibetan thought, policies, political status and very way of life which the aloofness of the Tibetans drew in front of the eyes of their southern neighbours. Nevertheless, it was now evident that, at the same time that the Dalai Lama was rejecting Curzon's overtures, he was busily exchanging amicable messages with the Czar.

THE YOUNGHUSBAND EXPEDITION: 1903–1904

Earlier reports of Russian contact with the Tibetans, including information about Dorjiev's first visit to Russia, had been regarded in India as of no immediate consequence. But after Dorjiev's much-publicized mission in 1901 it began to appear that active Russian interest in Tibet, which had long been considered by Curzon to be a theoretical possibility, was on the way to becoming an established fact.

The British Ambassador at St. Petersburg, who was instructed to inquire formally about Dorjiev's activities, was told by the Russian Foreign Minister, Count Lamsdorf, that the visits had no political significance. That did not allay British doubts; and Count Lamsdorf was informed that the British Government could not see any change in Tibet's status without concern. The Russians repeated their denial and retorted with counter-allegations—quite baseless—that a British railway was being constructed up the Chumbi valley.

In 1902 there were persistent rumours of a secret treaty between Russia and Tibet at which the Chinese Government was reported to be ready to connive. In spite of denials by both the Russian and Chinese governments, circumstantial rumours continued to circulate and it was genuinely accepted, not only by Curzon but also by the British Ambassador in China, that some such agreement existed. Further, there was frequent talk on the Indian border of consignments of Russian arms reaching Lhasa. The Japanese monk Kawaguchi who was in Lhasa in 1901 confirms the truth of such reports. There was, therefore, good ground for the belief, firmly held in responsible British quarters in China, India, and Whitehall, that Russia was on the verge of obtaining a position of influence at Lhasa which could only be inimical to British interests.

Neither Curzon nor anyone else in authority considered that a Russian invasion of India through Tibet was a probable or immediate threat; but a hostile Tibet was capable of upsetting the peace of northern India by causing unease and disturbance along the Himalayan frontier.

Alistair Lamb in a careful and thorough account of the events of the period has written that 'few who then thought about the Tibetan problem would have denied that something had to be done'. Curzon, on whom lay the responsibility, decided that the issue could be settled only by a mission to Lhasa. On 8 January 1903 he set out his arguments in a masterly despatch. In it the overriding consideration of High Policy—the long-term protection of the frontiers of India—is not specifically stated. The despatch concentrates on what was, in a broad sense, the method of achieving that unspoken object by the establishment of friendly relations and regulated commercial dealings with Tibet, including the posting of a British representative at Lhasa. The instrument was to be the dispatch of an official mission. It was, of course, necessary to consider what might have to be done if the mission were opposed. Curzon had earlier discussed such a situation, as a sort of theoretical exercise, and had concluded, as he did now, that if peaceful overtures were rejected, a show of force would be necessary; but the idea of any territorial or political object was firmly disavowed. It is permissible to see some disingenuity in the denial of all political aims, for the displacement of Russian influence and the posting of a British representative, even if his designation was commercial, could not fail to have a political value. Nevertheless, Curzon's despatch was unanswerably convincing as a statement of what India's interests demanded; but as St. John Brodrick said on a later occasion, 'the course of affairs on the Indian frontiers cannot be decided without reference to Imperial exigencies elsewhere'.

When the despatch was received, the British Government was engaged in the search for a general settlement with Russia and in the course of these talks the Russians hinted that, if British pressure was put on Tibet, they would feel free to take action elsewhere. The British Government, therefore, while realizing that the whole problem of our future relations with Tibet must be put on a proper basis without delay, recommended that, for the present, instead of sending a mission, negotiations with China and Tibet— already discredited by half a century of experience—should be continued. It was the beginning of a process in which Curzon kept urging the clear interests of Indian security while the Home Government, although agreeing in principle, kept pleading its other responsibilities and seeking to soften and circumscribe the firm, decisive action which Curzon wanted to take.

In spite of the hesitations of Whitehall, Curzon managed to take a step forward. He secured approval for his proposal that the discussions with the Tibetans and Chinese should take place at Khampa Dzong, across the Tibetan border from North Sikkim; but he could not prevail on the British Government to agree that, in case of difficulties, the Mission might go on to Gyantse, or that the appointment of a British Trade Agent at Gyantse might be considered.

The Mission under Col. Francis Younghusband, who was to conduct the negotiations, reached Khampa Dzong in July 1903. What happened there indicates that the Government of India had fairly summed up Tibetan minds and methods. The instruction that the Mission should not go further than Khampa Dzong seems to have leaked out. At all events, the Tibetans did not trouble to send representatives of any but inferior status who lacked powers to do anything but press for the withdrawal of the Mission. The Chinese were not, it seems, in a position to send suitable representatives even if they had wanted to do so. They later complained that the Dalai Lama had ignored advice from the Amban that he should negotiate with the British and that the Tibetans had refused to provide transport for the Amban himself or his Deputy to go to meet the Younghusband Mission. So low had Chinese prestige fallen in Tibet. One brighter note was the arrival of a high monk official sent by the Panchen Lama. He, too, was commissioned to ask Younghusband to withdraw but in him the British had their first contact with a Tibetan of breeding and status; and although no progress was made, a friendly personal relationship was established with the courteous and dignified abbot.

In this way five months were wasted. Winter was approaching and hostile concentrations were reported between Phari and Shigatse. The choice lay between losing prestige by going back, or taking another step forward. Curzon secured agreement from Whitehall that the Mission should advance to Gyantse; but it was given reluctantly and on the strict condition that the advance should be solely for the purpose of negotiating a trade agreement, that the Mission should return as soon as that was accomplished, and that no permanent representative should be left at Gyantse. The Chinese and Russians, who were informed of this decision, both protested but were suitably answered.

The Mission with its escort of only 200 men now needed military support on a larger scale. Some 3,000 armed men and 7,000 followers under the command of Brigadier-General J. Macdonald were transported over the Himalaya into unknown territory; and the advance force wintered at Tuna, fifty miles inside the Tibetan border, with another detachment at Phari and headquarters in the Chumbi valley. Local Tibetan headmen and petty Chinese officials made repeated requests that the expedition should go back; but no high personages appeared with powers to negotiate. Instead, Tibetan forces began to assemble not far from Tuna. Younghusband frequently tried to discuss the situation with their general—once at considerable personal risk; but he was met only with the polite reiteration of the request to go back.

By January 1904 the expedition was ready to advance. Younghusband warned the Tibetan general of his intention and declared that he would not fire unless attacked. The two forces came face to face, literally at arm's length, at a stone wall which the Tibetans —greatly superior in numbers but mostly armed with primitive weapons—had built not far from Tuna. The Tibetans were advised by Younghusband to put down their arms and go away safely; and the British troops began to dismantle the wall, and to try to take away the weapons from the puzzled Tibetans. Strained nerves suddenly broke. A shot was fired on the Tibetan side followed by a fierce attack, mainly with swords. The British opened fire and in ten minutes the wretched affair was over with hardly a British casualty and at least 300 Tibetan dead and many wounded. Tibetan resistance was broken for the time and the Mission moved on to Gyantse with only one more engagement of any consequence in which a further 180 unfortunate Tibetans were killed.

Once at Gyantse, which was reached early in April 1904, the pattern of Khampa Dzong was repeated. Had its objects been military, the Mission could probably have pressed on to Lhasa

Plate 5

(*a*) King Song-tsen Gampo

(*b*) The Nechung Oracle in a state of possession

Plate 6

(*a*) The Potala, Lhasa, showing procession and great banner

(*b*) An old Tibetan manor house

without difficulty; but Younghusband's orders were to negotiate at Gyantse. As the Tibetans appeared to have abandoned armed opposition, the main body of the expedition was sent back to the Chumbi valley leaving Younghusband and a small escort at Gyantse to await developments. The Mission passed about a month pleasantly enough and made friendly contacts in the neighbourhood; but no one came to negotiate. In the meantime, the Tibetan Government regained confidence and armed forces began to gather between Gyantse and Lhasa. A fierce but not entirely unprovoked surprise attack on the small party at Gyantse made it necessary for the main body to come up again from Chumbi to relieve them and to capture the fort which had been reoccupied by the Tibetans. There was clearly no hope of negotiation there; and at last the British Government sent orders for the Mission to advance to Lhasa.

After one more serious engagement in which the Tibetans lost a further 300 killed, resistance evaporated. The Tibetan Government, at last convinced that the Mission could be delayed no longer, sent several parties offering to negotiate; but experience had shown that delegation of authority was alien to Tibetan practice and that serious discussion was possible only at the capital. When Lhasa was reached—without any great difficulty— the Mission found that the Dalai Lama and Dorjiev, who had been continuing to advise him, had fled. The Chinese Amban was the first to welcome them but he could do little to arrange negotiations and had, visibly, no authority over the Tibetans. The Tibetan ministers had been accustomed to high-handed treatment from the Dalai Lama and his flight had left them in a state of bewildered anxiety to do nothing for which they might have to answer later. Progress became possible only with the appearance of an elderly, strong-minded monk, the Tri Rimpoche of Ganden whom the Dalai Lama had appointed as Regent when he left Lhasa. The Tri Rimpoche obtained the authority of the Tibetan Assembly and, without undue delay, an Anglo-Tibetan Convention was signed. Soon after, the Mission, to the great surprise and relief of the Tibetans, began its withdrawal to India only two months after it had arrived at Lhasa.

The Mission has come in for criticism at various times and on various grounds. It has lately been given much attention by the Chinese Communists as a 'British atrocity'. For that, the Chinese have a transparent motive in their eagerness to conceal what they themselves have done and are doing in Tibet; and the subject is treated with the customary Communist frenzy and exaggeration. The nature and effect of the Convention itself will be discussed in the next chapter; but some of the criticisms of less obviously interested parties, directed at the origin and conduct of the Mission, may be briefly examined.

Certain historians, for example Vincent Smith in his *History of India* and Philip Woodruff in *The Guardians*, have stigmatized the Mission as 'unnecessary and fruitless'. That censure, unsupported by detailed reasoning and made long after the possibility of a Russian threat through Tibet had been dispelled, partly by the expedition itself and partly by other factors, smacks of Olympian omniscience but overlooks the immediate circumstances. It is clear beyond doubt that the Russians were intriguing in the capital of a country bordering on India in which they had no good reason to take an interest. Tibetan, or Chinese, policy, which took advantage of the freedom to enter India enjoyed by the Tibetans but forbade any return traffic, made it impossible for the Government of India to find out what was going on or to represent their own interests—let alone exchange views with the Tibetan authorities. Even if suspicions were magnified by lack of exact information, there was good reason to fear trouble along India's frontiers and perhaps a more serious long-term danger unless Russian influence could be held in check.

As for the fruits, if they were slow to form, the cause should be sought in the climate of Whitehall. Nevertheless, there was a harvest even though it took six years or so to mature.

It has been suggested that force might have been avoided by using Indian Buddhist agents, with lavish presents, to win Tibetan opinion. That underestimates the extent to which fear of British designs had intensified the feeling of the Tibetans that they were the 'inner people' whose religion and whose existence were threatened from outside. Nor was it only the British who were seen as a danger. When the expedition was at Lhasa it came to light that a large body of Tibetan officials had been opposed to the Dalai Lama's flirtation with Russia.

Allegations that the conduct of the expedition was cold-blooded and cruel, Tibetans being 'shot down like partridges' and so on, were made by persons who were not present. Eye-witness reports show that the British commander had the utmost reluctance to begin hostilities and tried to win his object by patient, resolute pressure. There was no instance of firing until his troops were first attacked; and there was no relentless pursuit of beaten men. The heavy casualties of the Tibetans were due largely to their antiquated armament and to inexperienced leadership. There was general sympathy in the expedition for the simple Tibetan peasants who were compelled to enter so unequal a fight; British officers came to admire their courage and appreciate their qualities and character—except, it should be added, those of the monks whose fierce show of hatred did not endear them to the Mission. Tibetan wounded and prisoners were, of course, treated with care and humanity. That and the unexpected withdrawal when it seemed that Tibet was at their mercy inspired in the Tibetans a new opinion of their hitherto unknown neighbours. In particular, a lasting impression was made on Tibetan minds by the frank, honourable, and sensitive character of Young-husband and the gay friendliness and mastery of the Tibetan language shown by his assistant, Frederick O'Connor.

Charges of large-scale looting were also made. They were denied promptly and effectively in Parliament. There can be no doubt that images, paintings, and other such objects were taken from monasteries where opposition had been met and which had to be stormed; but there were strict orders against looting and there is no suggestion of plunder of peaceful monasteries, or private houses—great or small. One rhetorical flourish by the American writer Professor Cammann, suggesting that the British 'looted' Lhasa, is completely unfounded. The city was entered peacefully and personal information from both Tibetan and British eye-witnesses confirms that the behaviour of the troops there was exemplary.

It must remain a source of regret that it should ever have come to the use of force against Tibetans; but, in the conditions and state of knowledge of the day, it is hard to question that the dispatch of the expedition was reasonable. Once it was under way, force was the unfortunate but inevitable development, but the campaign was conducted with restraint, without rancour, and with as much humanity as is possible in war. There is no cause in it for shame.

RESTORATION OF TIBET'S
INDEPENDENCE: 1912

THE ANGLO-TIBETAN CONVENTION OF 1904 AND
THE ANGLO-CHINESE CONVENTION OF 1906

The terms of the treaty to be negotiated at Lhasa had been discussed while the Mission was on its way. The Home Government continued to be unwilling to go as far as Curzon wanted. In particular their anxieties about Russian reactions caused them to shy off the suggestion that a British representative should be established at Lhasa. Avoidance of any appearance of territorial or political aims remained the watchword. Younghusband, who was under pressure to conclude a treaty by a fixed date, was given discretion only to allow up to three years for payment of an indemnity which it was proposed to demand.

The principal clauses of the Convention concluded at Lhasa on 7 September 1904 (Appendix, p. 253) concerned the settlement of the Sikkim–Tibet frontier; the opening of Trade Marts, with resident British agents, at Gyantse and Gartok (in West Tibet) as well as at Yatung; provision for negotiating fresh Trade Regulations; and clauses excluding any other foreign power from political influence in Tibet.

With regard to the indemnity Younghusband arranged that 75 lakhs of rupees (£562,500) should be paid in yearly instalments of one lakh and that the Chumbi valley should be occupied until payment was completed or until the Trade Marts were opened, whichever should be the later. A note was also added to the Convention that the British Trade Agent at Gyantse might visit Lhasa to discuss matters arising out of the treaty. Both these points agreed with Curzon's ideas but exceeded the final instructions of the Home Government.

The Government of India supported Younghusband's actions

strongly; but they recommended the reduction of the indemnity to 25 lakhs of rupees and the period of occupation of the Chumbi valley to a maximum of three years. Younghusband's proposals were greeted with indignation in Whitehall where the obsession with Russian susceptibilities continued and where, perhaps, there was a sense of injured dignity in that a subordinate should venture to exceed his orders. The Convention was, eventually, agreed to with the Government of India's amendment regarding the indemnity and with the removal of the provision for visits to Lhasa by the British Trade Agent. Younghusband was reprimanded for his disobedience. That was palpably unfair. He was a man of honour and initiative; and in the exhilarating atmosphere of a successful expedition in a remote and unknown country he saw the opportunity of securing without difficulty greater advantages for his country than were contained in his instructions. There was no conceivable personal advantage to him and no suggestion of anything underhand.

The importance of the Chumbi valley to India has been demonstrated since the Chinese Communists have adopted an aggressive attitude on the Indian frontier. The Government of India, which has assumed responsibility for the defence of Sikkim and Bhutan, is faced by a salient of Chinese-held Tibetan territory well south of the main axis of the Himalaya, separating Sikkim from Bhutan and cutting the best and most frequented route from India to Bhutan. Although it might have been difficult to find a suitable defensive frontier in the Chumbi valley area, it would have been an advantage to India today if the interruption of the route between Sikkim and Bhutan had been avoided. As for the right of a British representative to visit Lhasa, that was a common-sense proposal which eventually had to be put into effect. There is nowhere in Tibet where matters can be decided except at Lhasa. The hesitations of the British Government thus nullified an opportunity which might have saved both India and Tibet from later troubles.

If Younghusband exceeded his instructions in one direction, there was another important point where he failed to fulfil them. He did not secure the signature of the Chinese Amban to the treaty. Throughout the Mission's stay in Lhasa the Amban was in close touch with them. His help was sought on many points. He was associated by Younghusband in every stage of the proceedings and, although he did not sign it, he was present at the signing of the treaty. Younghusband also was careful to tell the Tibetans that there was no intention of abrogating Chinese suzerainty; nor was there any indication that the Tibetans wanted any change in the existing arrangements so far as that went. On the other hand, it was apparent to everyone that the Amban had no real authority and that the Tibetans did not accept Chinese dictation in their internal affairs. An imperial proclamation deposing the Dalai Lama and instructing the Panchen Lama to act on his behalf was angrily torn down by the people of Lhasa and was completely ignored. In external affairs, too, the events of 1904 had shown that, though the Tibetans might use the Chinese as a stalking horse, they conducted their own policy.

The absence of Chinese participation in the Lhasa Convention brought it about that, whatever may have been the intentions of the negotiators, the treaty as signed was a clear acknowledgement of Tibet's direct power to make treaties and it contained nothing whatsoever to suggest the suzerainty of, or even any special connection with, China. On the contrary, by the terms of Article IX of the Convention, it established Great Britain if not as suzerain at least in a special position as a kind of Protector of Tibet. Perhaps to offset that, Li Tieh-tseng suggests that the Tibetan signature of the treaty on behalf of the Dalai Lama was not valid. That is a point which was never raised by the Tibetans at any time, and the Chinese Government itself recognized the validity of the treaty very soon after. At all events, the British Government had no intention of interfering with the make-believe of the Chinese connection with Tibet. Younghusband was instructed to secure, if he could, before leaving Lhasa the Amban's signature to a separate treaty of adhesion. That was not possible; and some eighteen months of strenuous and tortuous negotiation in Calcutta and Peking were needed before Chinese adherence was secured in the Anglo-Chinese Convention of 1906 (Appendix, p. 256).

What came out of those negotiations was not the simple acceptance of the treaty as it stood, which had been the original aim in the proceedings at Lhasa. The Chinese representatives had pressed for recognition of China's sovereignty over Tibet. That was resisted; but concessions were made with the object of preserving Chinese suzerainty. Neither of these terms was specifically used in the new agreement but its effect was to modify the 1904 Convention very much in favour of China. The peculiarly privileged position which had accrued to Britain from the negotiations at Lhasa was virtually reversed by the recognition that China was not a foreign power for the purposes of that Convention and had the responsibility for preserving the integrity of Tibet. Chinese rights in Tibet were thus recognized to an extent to which the Chinese had recently been wholly unable to exercise them. This diplomatic success for Peking was due partly to British anxiety to allay foreign criticism of the results of the Anglo-Tibetan Convention of 1904.

The Tibetans were neither consulted nor informed about the new Anglo-Chinese Convention. Had they been, they might reasonably have pressed for the specific restriction of Chinese overlordship to what it had been in 1904.

Similar disregard for the Tibetans and a further surrender of the privileged position acquired in 1904 were shown in the Anglo-Russian Convention of 1907 (Appendix, p. 258) in which reference was made to the British recognition of Chinese rights in Tibet. By that convention the British Government also bound itself not to negotiate with Tibet except through the Chinese Government, nor to send a representative to Lhasa.

The barrier to direct relations with the Tibetan Government, which had been demolished in 1904, was thus rebuilt and, as Curzon commented bitterly, the Anglo-Russian Convention of 1907 had thrown away to a large extent the efforts of our diplomacy and trade for more than a century. A British Government has, of course, the right to upset or whittle away the actions of its predecessor; but it seems extraordinarily high-handed or negligent that, after a treaty had been signed directly with the Tibetans, the British Government should have made no attempt to keep them informed of other acts affecting and modifying that treaty. On their part, the Tibetans later professed that they knew nothing of the 1906 or 1907 Conventions by which they did not consider themselves bound.

British policy at that time inclined to regard its dealings with Tibet principally as the search for a buffer between Russia and India and to devote attention chiefly to the effect its actions might have on the Russians. There was little serious thought that a buffer might be needed between India and China. There was every excuse for the miscalculation. The Boxer Rebellion and the Siege of Peking had revealed such chicanery and unrealistic incompetence that imperial prestige had almost vanished; but a revival, at least of the appearance of strength and confidence, was remarkably swift. So far as Tibet was concerned, the revival was a reality.

The British expedition to Lhasa was a serious loss of face to the Imperial Government and was also seen as a threat to its position in Central Asia where, in addition to considerations of prestige, its interest had become centred principally on maintaining a barrier between the Chinese hinterland and the encroaching Western world. The Chinese reacted with unexpected speed and force. At the same time that they were pressing the diplomatic offensive for recognition of their supremacy over Tibet in the negotiations for adherence to the 1904 Convention, the Chinese had begun to take military measures to restore their authority in Tibet. New administrative arrangements were made on the eastern Tibetan border. The immediate effect of pressure there was a violent rising by the Tibetans among whom Chinese prestige had fallen to a very low ebb; but the picture was completely changed towards the end of 1905 with the arrival of the Chinese general Chao Erh-feng. By 1910 through the efficient and utterly ruthless use of a large force, he had brought the whole of the eastern borderland under a degree of control such as had never existed there before. On the Indian frontier, immediately after the Anglo-Chinese Convention of 1906 had been signed, the Chinese announced their intention of paying the Tibetan indemnity in three instalments. They appointed a vigorous High

Commissioner, Chang Yin-tang—(it was significant that he had to travel to Tibet through India)—who let it be seen that he interpreted the 1906 Convention as a recognition of Chinese sovereignty in Tibet. Things were made easier for him by the policy of the Liberal Government which had succeeded that of Lord Balfour in 1905. Fears at Whitehall of appearing to exert any political influence in Tibet meant that the British occupation of the Chumbi valley amounted to little more than allowing things to go on as before, with the temporary elimination of the Tibetan district officials. On top of that, the British expedition had shaken Tibetan confidence and left the Government in a bewildered state. The Dalai Lama was in exile. There was no British official at Lhasa or in contact with the leaders of the Tibetan Government; and Younghusband had been at pains to emphasize the continuation of Chinese suzerainty. The Tibetans therefore had no immediate encouragement to oppose Chang. He set about his work energetically. The Tibetan ministers who had taken part in the 1904 negotiations were dismissed; direct contact between British and Tibetans was prohibited; obstructions were raised to the acquisition of property at the new Trade Marts by British subjects, to trade across the Sikkim border, and to postal communication with Gartok. Approaches were also made to Nepal and Bhutan in an attempt to detach them from the British sphere of influence.

All the official British reaction produced by this activity was a mild telegram to the Ambassador in China protesting against the punishment of the Tibetans who had taken part in the 1904 negotiations, and the request for the recall from Chumbi of a particularly aggressive Chinese official. In 1907 the Government of India reported that the treaty agreements about Tibet were not being carried out; but the British Government declined to take any action, preferring to wait for the negotiation of the new Trade Regulations.

In the 1904 Convention it had been stipulated that the Trade Regulations should be negotiated between the British and the Tibetans. By 1908 the situation had changed and the discussion, on the Tibetan side, was conducted solely by the Chinese representative. A Tibetan minister was present and signed the agreement but took no active part beyond that.

The purpose of the Regulations (Appendix, p. 260) was to provide for Trade Marts and specified trade routes under Chinese supervision, including the provision of adequate police protection. The right of personal intercourse between British officers and Tibetans and the right of British subjects to buy and sell from and to whom they pleased, and to lease land for shops etc., were included. If these provisions had been properly carried out, the Regulations would have been quite advantageous to British subjects; but the same obstructions that had existed before continued unchanged. Sir Charles Bell, who was in the Chumbi valley at the time, has written that the Tibetans greatly resented having Chinese supervision in all such matters thrust on them. All that British officers in Tibet could do was patiently to cultivate the friendship of such Tibetans as they were able to meet, and to hope for a change.

CHINESE INVASION OF TIBET: 1910

The change that soon occurred in the affairs of Tibet was not, at first, of the kind for which the Tibetans or the British had hoped. In 1908 the Imperial Government decided to restore the Dalai Lama; and that was done by a decree which made it plain that he was in future to be considered merely as the 'loyal and submissive Viceregent bound by the laws of the sovereign state'. He returned to Lhasa towards the end of 1909, the wiser for his experience but in no way better disposed to the Chinese whose treatment of him at Peking had been censorious and slighting. He had also reason to be alarmed at the activities of Chao Erh-fêng in eastern Tibet. Having reduced to subjection all the border states which had long maintained a religious connection with the Dalai Lama through the many great monasteries there but which were politically in a condition of near-independence, Chao was now poised for a move into what had long been the unquestioned domains of the Lhasa government; and he had announced his intention of proceeding to Lhasa itself. There seemed to be a clear plan to convert Tibet firmly into an obedient province of China.

For the first time in history the Tibetans appealed to the outside world for help against the Chinese. In his exile the Dalai Lama himself had learned something about other nations, while, in the Tibetan people as a whole, the Younghusband Expedition had sown the seeds of trust and liking for the British. It was therefore to 'Great Britain and the Foreign Powers' that in 1909 the Dalai Lama addressed an appeal for intervention with the Chinese to stop the dispatch of troops to Lhasa. At the same time a British protest was sent to Peking. The Chinese met this situation by explaining formally to the British Ambassador that the troops were only being sent to police the trade routes as provided under the Trade Regulations. At Lhasa, the Amban succeeded in reducing Tibetan anxieties by similar assurances and by understating the number of the troops. The Tibetans, therefore, confused and hesitant to make an open breach with China, hardly opposed Chao's troops, 2,000 of whom under General Chung Ying reached Lhasa in February 1910.

The Dalai Lama only just succeeded in making his escape and fled from his capital once more, this time to refuge in India. An imperial proclamation soon followed, deposing him for the second time and directing that a new incarnation should be chosen in his place. General Chung Ying and the Amban, to all intents, took over the government of Tibet.

The British Government promptly protested against the subversion of existing political conditions without any intimation to them; and asked that an effective Tibetan Government should be kept in being with which they could maintain their treaty relationship. They were answered with vague assurances that the treaty relationship would be fulfilled. The Government of India was gravely perturbed at this alteration of the balance on its borders, but the British Government accepted the bland opinion of Lord Morley, then Secretary of State for India, that the Chinese were simply making their suzerainty effective, which would probably result in a strong internal government in Tibet, and that nothing need be done unless a precise breach of treaty obligations occurred.

The invasion of 1910 is a turning point in the relations between China and Tibet and marks a break with previous Chinese policy. This was the first Chinese army to reach Lhasa against the will of the Tibetans. The expeditions of 1720, 1728, 1750, and 1792 all came to restore order and were not opposed by Tibetans. After each expedition there had been some reorganization of Chinese relations with the Tibetan Government but, except for a brief period in 1720, there had been no question of taking over the administration. In all that had been done before, the Tibetans had acquiesced, and although they never explicitly declared their consent to Chinese overlordship and were unwilling to admit dependence on the Emperor, they did tacitly accept the relationship and never openly questioned the right of the Emperor to have his representative at Lhasa or to send troops into Tibet on occasions. The emperors on their side had been careful for nearly two centuries to do nothing to upset the ostensibly amicable basis of that relationship.

Now, after the Dalai Lama had been restored to his capital and without there being any disturbance in Tibet or any hint of a desire to break with the Empire, a Manchu general had forcibly overturned the existing régime and had in effect taken over the government of Tibet. There was a complete change of atmosphere. Up till then the two peoples had shared the same Asian political ideas and conventions; but the Manchus had come a great distance from their origins, and in addition to being absorbed into their Chinese surroundings, they had lately, through bitter experience at the hands of the Western powers, begun to learn a new political language and method which they proceeded to apply to the still purely Asian Tibetans. Chao's troops had modern arms and modern training. Chinese officials in Tibet were now preaching new ideas and proclaiming that China was being brought up to date and could hold its own with any country in the world. It was not a mood in which much regard would be spared for the leisurely politico-mystical courtesies of the past.

After the deaths of the Emperor and the Empress Dowager in 1908 rivalries between the provinces and the centre developed which were beyond the power of the weak Regency of Prince

Ch'un to control. It is, therefore, not clear whether Chao's actions had specific central authorization. Although he was a very able soldier and had diplomatic skill in a small way, there is no evidence that he had the mind of a statesman. But whether outraged sentiment over the 'shame of 1904' and half-digested schemes of making it impossible for the British ever to come to Lhasa again are to be attributed to him or to the Peking government, the whole episode can be seen as a last feverish symptom of the disintegration of Manchu strength.

Shortly before the collapse of the Empire, Chao worked out a proposal to create a new province called Sikang which was to include parts of Szechwan and great areas of Tibet extending to Giamda, almost sixty miles from Lhasa. The proposal never received imperial assent and, so far as Tibetan territory was concerned, could never be put into effect. Nevertheless, the frontier according to Chao's abortive blueprint may be seen in Chinese maps published in the present century; and many British maps, too, accepting the fictions of Chinese cartography without question, show a similar line.

For all its military success, the invasion of 1910 was an administrative failure. No one would co-operate. Not only was the Dalai Lama in exile, his leading ministers, too, were with him. The Panchen Lama refused to head a temporary administration. The Tibetan National Assembly was sullenly obstructive; and it kept in touch with the Dalai Lama and sent messages to the Government of India through him, denouncing Chinese action. There was still active resistance in parts of south-east Tibet. The Chinese soon realized that the Dalai Lama was the key to the situation and that it had been a mistake to depose him in such a hurry. Several attempts were made to persuade him to return; but his stipulation that the British Government should guarantee any settlement was too much for the Chinese to stomach.

After reaching India, the Dalai Lama repeatedly appealed to the British Government for help. He made it clear that his previous relationship with the Emperor had been ended when it was violated by the invasion of Lhasa and that Tibet no longer accepted the overlordship of China. He claimed the right to recover the status which the Vth Dalai Lama had enjoyed. He pointed also to breaches of the 1904 Convention. The British Government was in an equivocal position, being tied down by the Conventions of 1906 and 1907, with China and Russia respectively, in which the Tibetans had no part. They chose to overlook the disregard by the Chinese of their obligation to see that the Anglo-Tibetan Convention of 1904 and the Trade Regulations of 1908 were properly carried out; and by professing themselves unable to intervene 'between the Dalai Lama and his suzerain' continued to recognize and, indeed, to give a specific name to a hitherto undefined relationship which the Tibetans were now, for the first time in nearly two centuries, driven to disown actively and with good reason. Bell summed it up by saying that 'the *status quo* and the promises of China went by the board. The Tibetans were abandoned to Chinese aggression for which the British Military Expedition to Lhasa and its subsequent withdrawal were primarily responsible.'

Finding no favourable response from the British Government, the Dalai Lama, with that streak of naïvety in the Tibetan character, made a secret approach to the Czar. It was answered, to his embarrassment, through the British Government.

On one issue only was the British Government prepared to protest. Continuous Chinese intrigue in Bhutan and Nepal culminated in the assertion in 1910 that those States also were vassals of China. The Chinese were informed that the claim could not be recognized and that any attempt to put it into effect would be resisted.

During the Dalai Lama's stay at Darjeeling from 1910 to 1912, liaison with his host, the Government of India, was conducted by Charles Bell, Political Officer in Sikkim, who had served there since 1904. Between Bell and the Dalai Lama there developed a warm friendship which was to have a profound effect on the relations between Tibet and India.

THE END OF THE MANCHUS. THE CHINESE REPUBLIC

The Chinese dictatorship at Lhasa would probably have led, in due course, to an uprising when the slow-moving Tibetans considered that the zeal and resolution of the enemy had been sufficiently blunted and undermined. That might have taken a long time, especially as the balance on this occasion was weighted by the modern weapons and military training of the Chinese forces; but the wheel of Cause and Effect produced a speedier deliverance than might have been expected. Revolution broke out in China in 1911 and the shock waves were not long in reaching Tibet. Before the end of the year the Chinese troops at Lhasa mutinied against their officers. Some of them deserted and began to straggle back to China; others took to looting and destruction which roused the Tibetans to furious counter-measures. General Chung Ying, a Chinese, was appointed Amban in place of the Manchu, Lien Yu. He contrived to keep part of his force with him and to get some support by playing on local rivalries. In other parts of Tibet, Chinese garrisons were set upon and in some cases annihilated; but in Lhasa and Shigatse fighting went on for quite a long time. Tentative suggestions by both parties that the British might mediate were turned down by reason of our 'treaty obligations'; but the British Government did tender advice to the Dalai Lama, rather to his surprise, that he should use his influence to stop the fighting, save the Chinese from annihilation, and allow them to be conducted back to China. Eventually, through the good offices of the Nepalese Government, a solution of that sort was agreed and by the end of 1912 the remaining Chinese troops were removed from Tibet by way of India, disarmed, and shipped back to China. In June 1912 the Dalai Lama returned in triumph to Tibet but it was not until January 1913, after the departure of the last Chinese, that he entered Lhasa.

The collapse of Chinese authority in Tibet proper was soon followed by attacks on Chinese garrisons in the many states of East Tibet which had been subordinated by Chao Erh-fêng. Chao himself fell an early victim to Republican vengeance and his removal was, no doubt, an encouragement to the East Tibetans in their fight to free themselves from the domination he had imposed on them. The Republican government of Yuan Shih-kai immediately showed that, although it had expelled the Manchus

Plate 7

(*a*) Tibetan nobles

(*b*) Tibetan ladies

Plate 8

(*a*) Boys chosen to go to school at St. Joseph's,
Darjeeling, 1948

(*b*) A noble's household servants

as hated foreigners, it meant to keep all the territorial advantages which had accrued to China in 200 years of Manchu rule. In April 1912 the President issued a proclamation that Tibet, Mongolia, and Sinkiang were to be treated on the same basis as provinces of China and were to be considered as integral parts of the Republic. At the same time a strong army was raised and dispatched to the Tibetan border where the fierce rising of the Tibetans was driving the Chinese steadily backward.

These events made it necessary for the British Government to reconsider their policy. They could hardly be expected to grasp what a total change the Chinese Revolution had brought about in the basis of the relationship between Tibet and China. The old, unwritten, flexible bond between Patron and Priest had been strained by the deposition of the Dalai Lama in 1904 and by his subsequent treatment at the Peking court. It was ended by Chinese aggression in 1910 which was the first use of force between Patron and Priest and led to the first denunciation of the Emperor by any Dalai Lama. That was the breaking of the ancient bond; and the fall of the Empire removed the whole substance—personal and religious—of the former connection. The President of a modern republic could not take the place of the Son of Heaven—a sort of honorary reincarnation—as Patron of the Dalai Lama.

Considerations of that nature were probably never taken into account at Whitehall. There, the relationship between China and Tibet had been described as 'suzerainty'. A precise definition of 'suzerainty', and of its counterpart 'autonomy', is impossible because the words have to be interpreted in accordance with the circumstances of each specific case; but authorities on International Law hold that suzerainty is by no means the same as sovereignty, and that an autonomous state under the suzerainty of another is not precluded from having an international personality. By using those inexact terms, drawn from the Western political vocabulary, to describe the relationship between Tibet and China, the British Government appear to have been aiming at what, in their view, was a practical settlement of the problem without giving much consideration to what the Tibetan attitude might be. Certainly, the evidence of 1904 and of 1910 might well make it seem improbable that Tibet could maintain active independence in a predatory world. The possibility of establishing a British protectorate over Tibet can never have been seriously contemplated. Even if that had not been excluded by specific undertakings to Russia, the most optimistic imperialist would have shrunk from assuming responsibility for another 2,000 miles or so of frontier enclosing over 500,000 square miles of country, mostly high, severe, and unpopulated and totally lacking in communications. It seemed, therefore, the best solution to patch things up between Tibet and China in a way which would restore a formal connection between them, saving Chinese face but restricting Chinese control.

Declarations of independence by the Dalai Lama and the Tibetan Assembly were accordingly ignored and a message was given to the Dalai Lama on his return to Tibet expressing the desire of the Government of India to see the internal autonomy of Tibet under Chinese suzerainty maintained without Chinese interference so long as treaty obligations were duly performed and cordial relations preserved between Tibet and India. The same object was pursued in China where the British Minister protested against Yuan Shih-kai's statement that Tibet was to be treated as a province of China in contravention of the treaty of 1906 and also at the announcement that troops were being sent to Tibet. Yuan Shih-kai assured the Minister that there was no intention of incorporating Tibet in the Chinese Empire; but he maintained his right to send troops into Tibet to settle frontier troubles. The British Minister then handed over a memorandum in which it was stated that the British Government was prepared to recognize Chinese suzerainty over Tibet but not to admit the right of China to intervene in the internal administration of the country or to maintain an unlimited number of troops there. Acceptance of that position and a written agreement to that effect were to be conditions on which the British Government would recognize the new Chinese Republic. Until then Chinese would not be permitted to travel to Tibet through India.

In spite of the confusion and weakness of the new Republic, the Chinese indignantly declined to make any concessions about Tibet; but, as conciliatory gestures towards the Tibetans, they recalled their Commander from the eastern frontier and issued a decree reinstating the Dalai Lama.

That decree is a good example of what Sir Claude Macdonald, former British Minister in Peking, described as 'the infinite Chinese capacity for misrepresentation'. As early as August 1912, after the Dalai Lama had been in Tibet for some time, Yuan Shih-kai informed the British Minister that it was his intention to restore the titles of the Dalai Lama and allow him to return to Tibet. Not long after, when the Dalai Lama was on his way back to Lhasa and when it was seen that the former Chinese position there was completely lost, Yuan Shih-kai sent a telegram expressing regret for the excesses of the Manchu régime and announcing that he was restoring the Dalai Lama's official rank. The Dalai Lama replied that he wanted no rank from the Chinese and that he had resumed the temporal and spiritual government of his country. That message is regarded in Tibet as a formal Declaration of Independence; nevertheless, the Chinese, blandly ignoring inconvenient facts, issued a decree on 28 October 1912 attributing to the Dalai Lama sentiments about 'affection for the Motherland', which he had never expressed, and purporting to restore him to his former position.

In fact, so far from making any concessions to the Chinese, the Tibetan Government took active measures to establish their own position. They sent strong reinforcements to the eastern front to meet the new threat from Yuan Shih-kai, and, although they did not immediately succeed in recovering Chamdo or in restoring the frontier to its position in 1910, a strong line was established along the Mekong–Salween divide. Within that boundary, and for nearly fifty years thereafter, there was not one Chinese official and no trace of Chinese authority or administration.

Some connection between Japan and Tibet existed at this time. Yajima Yasujiro, a Japanese who had probably found his way to Lhasa on a private adventure, was employed by the Dalai Lama to give military training to the Tibetan troops, which he did for several years. He was not the first Japanese in Tibet. The monk Kawaguchi, who was at Lhasa in 1901, has already been mentioned and there may have been others before him. Later, Japanese visitors were occasionally known to be studying in Tibetan monasteries.

One other event of this period needs to be mentioned. Soon after the Dalai Lama's return to Lhasa, Dorjiev reappeared there. Slight alarm had been caused at the time of the Dalai Lama's departure from India by the delivery to him, in conditions of secrecy, of a message from the Czar. That had proved to be no more than the expression of good wishes; but Dorjiev was a more serious problem. The Russians had taken the opportunity of the troubles in China to establish their influence in Mongolia and rumours soon got about that Dorjiev had negotiated a treaty between Mongolia and Tibet. It transpired eventually that although there had been an expression of common policy on account of the strong religious bond between the two countries, there had been nothing which could be described as a binding treaty. Nevertheless, incidents of that sort made it all the more desirable to find a settlement of the problem of Tibet.

VII

THE SIMLA CONVENTION: 1914

THE SIMLA CONFERENCE: 1913–1914

The Chinese were disturbed by the success of the Russians in Mongolia, by the weakness of their own government, and by the fear that the British might open direct negotiations with Tibet. In January 1913, after an initial display of indignant resistance, they expressed their willingness to negotiate on the basis of the British Note of August 1912. They made strenuous efforts to have the discussions conducted in London or Peking rather than in India and they objected to entering a conference at which the Chinese representative would be on the same footing as the Tibetans. Nevertheless, in June, after some months of argument, the Chinese Government reluctantly agreed to a tripartite conference at Simla. Even then their manœuvring to secure, in advance, recognition of their claims to supremacy over Tibet did not cease until they had received a warning that unless the Chinese plenipotentiary arrived at Simla by 6 October, negotiations would be begun directly between the British and Tibetan Governments. Sir Henry McMahon was the British plenipotentiary and he had the assistance of Sir Charles Bell. China was represented by Ivan Chen and Tibet by Lönchen Shatra, a leading Tibetan minister, each of whom was a properly accredited plenipotentiary whose powers were accepted formally by the other participants in the Conference.

Tibetan aims at the Conference were contained in a statement asking for acknowledgement of the independence they had re-established by the eviction of the Chinese troops and officials. In furtherance of that, they wanted the Anglo-Chinese Convention of 1906 to be declared invalid and the Trade Regulations revised. They also pressed for the acceptance of a frontier with China which would include all Tibetan peoples—i.e. up to Tachienlu and the Koko Nor.

The Chinese, in reply, put forward a claim to sovereignty over Tibet, resting it on the conquest by the Mongol Chingis Khan. They alleged that in the reign of K'ang Hsi the Tibetans had asked for the appointment of Ambans; and they recalled the occasions on which Chinese armies had protected the Tibetans from foreign invaders. They wanted a declaration of what had never been conceded before, that Tibet was 'an integral part of China'; and they claimed the right to station an Amban with 2,600 troops in Tibet and to control the foreign and military affairs of the country. In general, the Chinese Government aimed at a restoration of the political status under the Anglo-Chinese Convention of 1906. As for the frontier, they claimed a line running through Giamda, only some 125 miles east of Lhasa. That would not only have restored the position won by the recent conquests of Chao Erh-fêng but would have improved on it considerably by making a great reduction in the area over which the Tibetan Government had hitherto exercised unquestioned jurisdiction and of which it was, at the time of negotiation, in full control.

The Tibetans surprised both the other parties by the careful and voluminous documentation of their claims. They exhibited revenue records; lists of houses, officials and headmen, charters, agreements, and other material relating to disputed districts. Against that, the Chinese could produce little but verbal statements including the above-mentioned allegation for which there is no historical foundation whatever—that the Tibetans had asked for Ambans in the reign of K'ang Hsi.

The British plenipotentiary, Sir Henry McMahon, was, for much of the negotiations, in the position of mediator trying to find some common ground between two widely divergent extremes. In order to narrow the gap between irreconcilable claims to independence on the one hand and sovereignty on the other, he put forward the concepts of autonomy and suzerainty. A solution in those terms might, it was hoped, restore peace between Tibet and China on a basis similar to that existing before 1904 and allow the development of a stable Tibetan government free from outside influence, but in closer relations than before with the British Government.

The problem was to ensure the reality of Tibetan autonomy but still to leave the Chinese with a position of sufficient dignity. It might have been thought that the Chinese, having lost all authority at Lhasa, would agree without very great hesitation to accept formal suzerainty, at least as a first step. But considerations of face were important and Chinese consent to accept less than sovereign status was conditional on the acknowledgement that Tibet was an integral part of China. On the other side, the Tibetans, who had regained their complete independence, were strongly opposed to accepting Chinese overlordship under any name. Their eventual assent to the concept of suzerainty was due to pressure from the British Government, which for many reasons —disinclination to assume additional responsibilities being possibly the strongest—was not prepared to support Tibet's claim to absolute independence.

But such concessions as the Tibetans agreed to make were strictly conditional. They were one side of a bargain which would guarantee Tibet's freedom to conduct its own internal affairs and would put precise limits to the operation of Chinese suzerainty. The Chinese, on their part, would have to agree not to send any officials into Tibet, except for one high officer with a suitable staff; no Chinese troops were to be sent into Tibet except for a small escort for the high officer; Tibet was not to be converted into a province of China or to be represented in any Chinese parliament. There was not even to be any stipulation that control of Tibetan foreign and military affairs should rest with China.

One concession was resisted by the Tibetans with the utmost determination. They fiercely disliked the proposed description of Tibet as an integral part of China and they finally prevailed, to the extent that this point was not mentioned in the main body of the agreement as eventually drafted but in notes which it was proposed to exchange.

On another point, too, they advanced strong arguments. The Dalai Lama, who remembered how the Chinese had grasped their opportunity when the British withdrew from Lhasa in 1904, pressed for the appointment of a British official at Lhasa as a counterweight to the Chinese officer. That seemingly sensible proposal was rejected by the British Government because of its treaty obligations to Russia. The farthest the British pleni- potentiary could go was an arrangement for a British officer to pay occasional visits to Lhasa to discuss matters arising out of the 1904 Convention. Even that was made contingent on Russian agreement in each instance. Such careful regard for the Anglo- Russian Convention of 1907 seems over-scrupulous in view of Russian advances then taking place in Mongolia. It also tended to endanger the Tibetan position by leaving the field free at Lhasa for a Chinese representative to reassert his country's influence without the restraining presence of a British colleague.

These questions of political status were difficult enough; but further and even more intractable disagreements appeared in the matter of the frontier between Tibet and China. There, both parties had opened their mouths very wide. The Chinese claim to a line running through Giamda, within almost 125 miles of Lhasa, had no basis in history beyond being included in the grandiose projects of Chao Erh-fêng. The Tibetan counter- demand for a frontier which would include the Koko Nor and Tachienlu, although having the justification that the majority of the population there was of Tibetan stock and that there were many monasteries in direct relations with the Dalai Lama and some states recently under the administration of the Lhasa Govern- ment, extended to large areas where it could not be shown that the Tibetan Government had, in the past thousand years, exer- cised actual jurisdiction.

An obvious compromise was the historic boundary, running roughly along the upper waters of the Yangtse, which had existed at least since the time of the Manchu dynasty; but there was a case for saving Tibet's interest in the states and monasteries of Tibetan origin, lying to the east of that line, in country which had never been dominated by the Chinese before the recent campaigns of Chao Erh-fêng and where, since the Revolution, Chinese influence was tenuous and uncertain. To bridge the conflicting claims McMahon devised the idea of Outer and Inner Tibet. Outer Tibet was to be the wide area, to the west of the historic Yangtse frontier, over which the Tibetan Government had for many centuries exercised complete jurisdiction. That was the Tibet where all the restrictions on the proposed suzerainty of China were to apply. Inner Tibet was to be the broad peripheral area, extending in the north to the Altyn Tagh range and in the east to the old provincial borders of Kansu and Szechwan, in which the population was mainly Tibetan by race and religious affinity. There was to be no bar to the appointment of Chinese officials or the sending of troops there but Inner Tibet would be included in the ban against the conversion of Tibet into a Chinese province.

Acceptance of those frontiers, which were shown in a map attached to the proposals, would have meant the surrender by the Chinese of the important town of Chamdo and a strip of territory between the Salween and upper Yangtse which had only recently been seized out of the direct control of Lhasa by Chao Erh-fêng and where the Chinese position was already precarious. It would also have meant that considerable areas outside the historic boundaries of the Eighteen Provinces, which the Chinese had been gradually claiming as new territories, would be described as falling in Tibet—Inner Tibet. In those regions there would be no restrictions on Chinese activities although in theory China would be suzerain rather than sovereign. On the Tibetan side it would have meant the exclusion from direct administration by Lhasa of the valuable districts of Dergé and Nyarong, lying to the east of the upper Yangtse, over which they had extended their authority in 1860.

In effect, there would have emerged two regions with differing status. Outer Tibet would have been something like a self-governing dominion of China, while Inner Tibet would have been the subject of peaceful contention in which the better or more attractive administration could be expected to win.

British concern was primarily with Outer Tibet and, in addition to the political security expected from the clauses regulating the status of Tibet, British interests were to be secured by the cancellation of the virtual monopoly of economic and commercial concessions which the Chinese had obtained through

Article III of the Anglo-Chinese Convention of 1906, by the grant of most-favoured-nation treatment and by suitable arrangements for trade between India and Tibet.

After negotiations lasting six months the various proposals were embodied in a draft tripartite convention. The terms can be seen in full in the Appendix (p. 268) but in view of the importance it later acquired, a summary of its main points may be helpful:

1. The Conventions of 1890, 1904, and 1906 were to stand, except in so far as they might be modified by or repugnant to the present Convention.

2. Britain and China to recognize that Tibet is under Chinese suzerainty, and to recognize also the autonomy of Outer Tibet; to respect its integrity and to abstain from interference in its internal affairs.

3 & 4. China not to send troops or station officials in Outer Tibet except for an Amban and his escort of 300 men. Britain to be similarly bound except for the British Trade Agents and their escorts.

5. China and Tibet not to negotiate about Tibet with one another or any other power except as provided in the 1904 and 1906 treaties.

6. Article III of the 1906 Convention, which virtually gave China a monopoly of all concessions with regard to Tibet, to be cancelled but China's position to be safeguarded by the understanding that the term 'foreign power' in Article IX of the 1904 treaty did not include China. British trade to have most-favoured-nation treatment.

7. New Trade Regulations to be negotiated between Britain and Outer Tibet.

8. The British Trade Agent at Gyantse might visit Lhasa in connection with matters arising out of the 1904 Treaty.

9. Inner and Outer Tibet defined in a map, attached to the Convention.

10. The English text of the Convention to be authoritative.

11. Disputes arising from the Convention, between China and

Tibet, to be referred to the British Government. (This provision was later removed in deference to Russian wishes.)

Notes were also to be exchanged providing, among other things, for the recognition that Tibet forms part of Chinese territory and forbidding the representation of Outer Tibet in any Chinese parliament.

Up to the last moment Ivan Chen continued to press for further concessions but when it appeared that no further modification would be considered he joined the other two plenipotentiaries in initialling the draft. His action was immediately repudiated by the Chinese Government which declined to accept the Convention. The sole reason given then, and to be repeated later, was the inacceptability of the provisions regarding the Sino-Tibetan frontier. It may be doubted whether that was the whole story. The territory in Outer Tibet which would have had to be given up was of no great extent and had been acquired by force only four years earlier. As for Inner Tibet, as a practical issue there was nothing to prevent the Chinese Government—as they were, in time, to prove—from making their influence effective there, by whatever name it was called. But the formal surrender of territory, however acquired, and the prohibition against making Inner Tibet a province may have seemed too great an affront to Chinese pride. There may also have been the fear that once the border area had been given the name of Tibet—Inner Tibet—the British might help the Lhasa Government to occupy it. Even so, the intensity with which the Chinese sustained their dislike of the Simla Convention suggests that indignation about the frontier was the symptom of a deeper resentment against the whole basis of the proposals.

DIRECT AGREEMENT BETWEEN BRITAIN AND TIBET

Strenuous efforts were made by McMahon to save the Conference from failure. The Chinese were warned that, if they would not sign, a direct agreement would have to be concluded with the Tibetans. They reiterated that the frontier was the only obstacle and asked for the continuance of McMahon's mediation; but the Tibetans had gone to the limit of concession. They declared that they would rather go on fighting than concede any more without a corresponding advantage being offered. The British Government, therefore, directed that the Conference should be wound up. On 3 July 1914 McMahon, after taking notice of a Chinese objection to what they understood he proposed to do, proceeded to sign the Convention with the Tibetan minister. Both plenipotentiaries also signed a declaration that the Convention was binding on them and that so long as the Chinese Government withheld its signature it would be barred from the enjoyment of privileges accruing from the agreement.

The advantages of which the Chinese were thus deprived do not appear to have been specifically catalogued but they must be interpreted as follows:

1. The operation in the favour of China of the Anglo-Chinese Convention of 1906. That document had been categorically objected to by the Tibetans, and before the opening of the Conference the British Government had expressed the view that recent acts of war between China and Tibet had rendered the Convention of no effect. Its restoration, by including it in the Schedule to the draft Convention, was one of the concessions the Tibetans had been prepared to make as their part of the settlement.

2. The recognition of Chinese suzerainty over Tibet by the Tibetan and British Governments.

3. The right to appoint an Amban at Lhasa with a military escort of 300 men.

4. The admission that Tibet forms part of China.

5. The admission that China is not a foreign power for the purpose of the 1904 Anglo-Tibetan Convention.

6. Any concern in the appointment of a Dalai Lama.

7. Any limitation of the strength of British escorts in Tibet.

As for the Sino-Tibetan frontier, everything was left in the air. It would be pointless to argue that, in theory, the Chinese were deprived of the right to enter Inner Tibet, seeing that they were there already.

In addition to the Convention and the joint declaration, the British and Tibetan plenipotentiaries signed new Trade Regulations to take the place of those of 1893 and 1908 which were cancelled by Article VII(a) of the new Convention (Appendix, p. 272). They embodied some differences from the former Regulations in detail and also in principle. Restrictions on trade, such as the previously existing duty on Indian tea imported into Tibet and the creation of monopolies, were removed; and British control over the sites of the Trade Agencies was put on a better footing. The change in principle was the absence of any mention of the Chinese who in the earlier Regulations had been mentioned in a sort of supervisory and superior capacity. In the new Regulations trade relations in Tibet were treated as exclusively the concern of the Tibetans and the British; the Chinese were nowhere mentioned. Control over the Trade Marts—except for the British Agency enclaves—the protection of the Trade Routes and the joint trial of cases between British and Tibetan nationals, in which powers had formerly been exercised by the Chinese, were now to rest with the Tibetans. Provisions in the earlier Regulations about the eventual withdrawal of the British escorts and the handing over of British Post and Telegraph installations and Rest Houses to the Chinese were cancelled.[1] The Trade Regulations in effect accepted the new state of affairs established by the eviction of the Chinese from Tibet and recognized the right of the Tibetans to conduct their trade with the British entirely by themselves.

The result of the Simla Conference from the viewpoint of the three parties involved may be summed up as follows:

The Chinese Government gained nothing but the retention—which proved to be for a short time only—of a strip of territory between the Salween and Mekong formerly administered by the Tibetan Government but occupied by Chao Erh-fêng in 1908/9.

---

[1] It is, therefore, irrelevant to refer to them as though they were still valid in 1954 as Mr. P. L. Mehra does in an article on 'India, China and Tibet 1950–1954' in the *Indian Quarterly,* January 1956.

But China reserved, in its own opinion, the right to settle with Tibet in its own time.

The Tibetans, by the failure of the Chinese to sign the Convention, were released from the offer, made under British persuasion, to surrender part of their sovereignty in return for Chinese guarantees of their autonomy and their joint frontier. They were also freed from the implications of the Note acknowledging Tibet to be an integral part of China, which their stubborn dislike and opposition had kept out of the main body of the Convention. They had secured British recognition of their autonomy and the assurance that the British Government would not acknowledge China's suzerainty over Tibet unless the Chinese Government fulfilled their side of the bargain by signing the Convention. The Tibetans could also expect British diplomatic support and, it appears, a modest supply of arms.

The British gained freedom of direct negotiation with the Tibetans, the right to send a representative on occasional visits to Lhasa, and the prospect of better commercial arrangements. The failure of the Chinese to sign the Convention and their exclusion from any part in the Trade Regulations also conferred on the British—almost unawares—exclusive political influence in Tibet and the special position that the only restrictions on Tibetan sovereignty were the obligation not to negotiate with any other power without British consent. There was also the gain of extra-territorial rights accruing under the new Trade Regulations.

One other important advantage came to the British out of the Conference. In March 1914, before the draft of the tripartite Convention was completed, a substantial section of the frontier between Tibet and India was agreed in direct negotiations between the British and Tibetan plenipotentiaries (Appendix, p. 267). The now well-known 'McMahon Line' was fixed roughly along the crest of the Himalaya from the north-east corner of Bhutan to the Isu Razi pass in the north of Burma. It was drawn on a map, in two sheets, attached to the exchange of Notes and sealed by both plenipotentiaties. The Chinese were not invited to take part in the discussions about the Indo-Tibetan frontier and their specific acceptance of it was not sought; but they were provided with information about it, for the McMahon Line was later embodied, on a reduced scale, in the map showing the proposed boundaries of Inner and Outer Tibet under Article IX of the draft tripartite Convention, which was initialled by all three plenipotentiaries. The Chinese objections, on which the Conference eventually broke down, did not relate to that part of the frontier in which, since their eviction from Tibet, they had no practical interest, but were solely concerned with the proposed boundaries between China and Tibet northward from the Burmese border.

The McMahon Line confirmed an obvious geographical frontier to the south of which live a number of tribes most of whom have no close affinity with either Tibetans or Chinese. After British authority was established in Assam, early in the nineteenth century, agreements were gradually made with the individual tribes to check their long-standing propensity to conduct raids into the settled districts of the Assam valley. Against some of them military expeditions had to be sent. Relations were put on a regular basis by the creation of the frontier tracts of Sadiya in 1912 and of Balipara in 1913, under the Governor of Assam. The effect of the McMahon Line was to make an accepted demarcation of the limits of Indian and Tibetan jurisdiction there, following the natural line of the Himalaya. Special considerations applied in certain areas. In the north of the Balipara tract was Tsari, a famous place of Tibetan pilgrimage. Provision was made to ensure access to it for Tibetans. There were also some private estates in the tribal country owned by Tibetan nobles whose rights were specifically safeguarded by the agreement. And there was a large monastery at Tawang whose connection with the parent monastery, Drepung, at Lhasa, was to be respected. Such other Tibetan interest as existed south of the Himalaya, apart from a tradition that the region had been under Tibetan domination in the time of the kings of the sixth to the ninth centuries, was recent and exploratory. As for the Chinese, they had never set foot in the area except during the period of Chao Erh-fêng's invasion of Tibet when a Chinese party made a short expedition to Menilkrai in the upper Lohit valley some ten to fifteen miles south of the Tibetan frontier.

The ultimate legal implications of the agreement with Tibet were probably not examined in detail at the time. The Russian Government was informed of the action taken, but, as the possibility of Chinese adherence remained open, there does not seem to have been any attempt to reconcile the withholding of recognition of Chinese suzerainty under the joint Anglo-Tibetan declaration of 3 July 1914, with the terms of the Anglo-Russian Convention of 1907. At all events, before long, with the outbreak of the First World War, neither the British nor the Russian Government had time to consider Tibet.

The Tibetan Government had to adjust itself to this unsettled state of affairs. It was about 150 years since a Dalai Lama had taken any part in the administration of the country and a further century since the reign of the Vth Dalai Lama—the only active and autocratic ruler out of the preceding twelve incarnations. The XIIIth Dalai Lama intended to assume full power and responsibility, and he concentrated on reorganizing the government to his liking.

Relations between Tibet and China continued on the footing of undeclared and desultory war. In spite of the acceptance of a truce for the period of the Simla negotiations, sporadic fighting had gone on in the border country. After the Conference there were rumours of a forthcoming Chinese offensive. At the same time Chinese frontier officials made overtures to the Tibetan commanders for the conclusion of a treaty between their two countries. The Dalai Lama sent word that the Chinese should be told that it was open to them to sign the Simla Convention. He also urged the British Government to exert diplomatic pressure at Peking; and he asked for a supply of arms and ammunition. The British Government counselled the Chinese to refrain from hostilities and gave similar advice to the Dalai Lama. A small supply of arms was allowed to the Tibetans and some help was given in other ways—by providing rudimentary military training for a few Tibetan troops at Gyantse, and by sending four boys of good family for education in England. But it was all done in a spirit of grudging circumspection, for the British Government, involved in a world war, was preoccupied by its wider obligations.

The Tibetans had never before had to keep an army in being for so long and the strain on their finances and meagre military supplies was severe. It must have been a disappointing time for the Dalai Lama who had pinned considerable hopes on his new friends. His position was made even worse after 1916 when the British Government, on the plea of international restrictions, placed a total embargo on the supply of arms to Tibet from India and also prevented the Tibetan Government from obtaining munitions from Japan.

The diplomatic front, at first, appeared equally bleak. After the fall of Yuan Shih-kai there was for a time no government stable enough to warrant the conclusion of any sort of agreement. The outlying provinces of Szechwan and Yunnan broke away from the centre so that it was with local war-lords that the Tibetans had to contend. The Governor of Szechwan, General P'êng Jih-shêng, was particularly truculent and in 1917 he intensified hostilities with a spate of noisy threats and menacing gestures. The Tibetans, in alarm, appealed for more supplies of arms. They were allowed a small quantity of ammunition and, at the same time, Mr. (later Sir Eric) Teichman of the China Consular Service was sent to the frontier to try to negotiate a truce on the basis of the *status quo*.

General P'êng's threats proved to be bluster. The Tibetans swiftly recaptured Chamdo and drove the Chinese back, with heavy losses, well beyond the upper Yangtse. They even threatened Tachienlu. Teichman therefore directed his intervention towards securing a Tibetan withdrawal. His advice was reinforced by the refusal of the British Government to supply more arms, without which the Tibetans were unable to advance much further. That was, naturally, a blow to the Tibetans who, as can be seen from Teichman's account, had a great opportunity of making good their claims to Inner Tibet. In the hope of a general settlement they accepted an armistice according to which they withdrew to Dergé. The Chinese, on their side, undertook not to advance beyond Kanzé. A line roughly along the upper Yangtse—almost the historic frontier of the Manchu period—was accepted as the provisional frontier. Chinese writers, who inveigh against British designs in Tibet, are inclined to forget the moderating influence exercised at that time.

After the armistice, which was signed at Rongbatsa near Kanzé in August 1918, the Tibetans expected the early resumption of general negotiations; but confusion in the internal affairs of China caused delay and it was not until May 1919 that the Chinese Government made overtures for a settlement. The basis was still the 1914 Convention, to which some modifications were suggested relating principally to the frontier between Inner and Outer Tibet—the Indo-Tibetan frontier, again, did not come into the question. In addition it was proposed that Chinese officers should be stationed at the Trade Marts in Tibet. The Tibetans, elated by their recent military successes, firmly refused to concede any more than they had been prepared to offer in 1914. The Chinese Government then came under criticism in its own country where a recovery of confidence, perhaps connected with a favourable turn of events in Mongolia combined with the resentment caused by the Shantung incident, hardened the attitude of the military leaders and led to a chauvinistic press campaign against any settlement with Tibet in which Britain had a part. The exploratory talks, which had been taking place at Peking, were somewhat curtly terminated by the Chinese.

In spite of another failure to achieve a settlement, neither side seemed anxious to resume hostilities on the eastern frontier. The Truce of Rongbatsa, by tacit agreement, continued in force and it was, in the event, to keep the peace there for a good twelve years. Chinese provincial officials never gave up hope of securing a separate agreement with the Tibetans—as had been attempted immediately after the end of the Simla Conference—and in 1920 a mission from Kansu, with proposals for a treaty, found its way to Lhasa where it was received by the Dalai Lama. Its leader was given the habitual reply—that the Chinese should sign the 1914 Convention.

CLOSER TIES WITH BRITAIN
1920–1933

The British Government, in displeasure at the abrupt way in which the Chinese had broken off the exchanges in 1919, recalled their Minister from Peking for consultation. One more attempt was made to open discussions on the 1914 basis, but without success. Militaristic feeling was on the rise in China while, in Tibet, British prestige was waning because of the failure to bring about a tripartite settlement or to give more material aid to the Tibetan Government. It was, therefore, decided that the time had come for more active encouragement of British relations with Tibet. The chief architects of the new policy were Sir John Jordan, the British Minister in China, who for some twelve years had persistently and firmly tried to bring the Chinese to a settlement, and Sir Charles Bell whose connection with Tibet went back to 1904 and who, to a unique extent, enjoyed the friendship and confidence of the Dalai Lama.

Something had to be done to convince the Tibetans of British goodwill and to let both parties see that the British Government had a live determination to bring about a tripartite agreement. It was decided to send to Lhasa a British officer who should explain to the Dalai Lama how matters stood about negotiations with China and who could make such recommendations as seemed necessary. There was now no need to consider the Anglo-Russian Convention of 1907, which had been declared a dead letter owing to the Russian Revolution; and there was no doubt that the Dalai Lama, who had often asked for such a visit, would welcome the approach. The obvious person for the mission was Bell; and, accordingly, he arrived at Lhasa in November 1920.

It is rather surprising that the lead in advocating a more intimate relationship with Tibet came at that time from Whitehall; and that the Government of India, on the recoil from the Curzonian energy of eighteen years before, should have shown anxious hesitancy lest its commitments in Tibet should expand to an embarrassing extent. After only a few weeks at Lhasa, Bell found himself ordered to return to India. His work had barely got under way, for things move with ceremonious slowness in Tibet. He was able from Lhasa to allay the uneasiness of the Government of India and to convince them that so sudden a recall would have been taken by the Dalai Lama as a suspicious if not an insulting gesture. In the event, Bell stayed nearly a year during which he had many discussions with the Dalai Lama and his principal ministers; and after thoroughly getting the feel of Tibetan opinion he was able to make proposals for a sound basis on which to conduct relations with Tibet.

A good account of all aspects of the visit is contained in Bell's books, *Tibet: Past and Present* and *Portrait of the Dalai Lama*. Its principal result was to demonstrate that the British Government intended to treat Tibetan autonomy as a reality by strengthening to a reasonable extent Tibet's ability to defend itself and by helping, so far as the Tibetans themselves wanted, to develop the country's resources. There was no suggestion of persuading the Tibetans to undertake anything they did not want. Nor was there any thought of trying to influence them by appointing a British representative at Lhasa. It was considered that, so long as there was no Chinese representative, it was not only unnecessary to post a British officer at Lhasa but that such a step would have given a false impression both to the Tibetans and the Chinese.

Underlying the design of strengthening Tibet was the hope that it would make the Chinese Government more ready to join in a tripartite settlement. At the end of Bell's visit to Lhasa, therefore, a formal invitation to resume negotiations was issued to Peking. The Chinese Government was reminded that it had accepted the 1914 draft Convention in principle, with the exception of the boundary clause, both in 1914 and again in 1919, and it was informed that failing a resumption of negotiations in the immediate future His Majesty's Government did not feel justified in withholding any longer its recognition of Tibet as an autonomous state under the suzerainty of China and that they intended to deal with Tibet in future on that basis.

That statement showed a new determination; but in one important respect it failed to give an accurate interpretation of British commitments to the Tibetan Government. In the negotiations at Simla the British Government had been prepared to recognize Chinese suzerainty over Tibet only as part of a bargain involving specific undertakings by the Chinese. Until the Chinese gave those undertakings, by accepting the whole Convention, that recognition remained one of the advantages denied to them unless they actually signed it; and the Tibetans had continuously and resolutely refused to acknowledge China as suzerain. The main object of the British Government was, evidently, to secure what the Tibetans also wanted—Chinese adherence to the Simla Convention; and, in view of Chinese acceptance in principle of the greater part of the Convention, it was probably the intention to avoid a downright ultimatum. At the same time the manner in which Tibetan autonomy would be interpreted was made clear by letting the Chinese understand that, unless negotiations were resumed, the British Government would provide material assistance for the self-development and self-defence of Tibet and would deal with that country without further reference to China.

The Chinese Government fobbed off this approach with a variety of excuses, including the unsettled state of the country and the imminence of the Washington Conference of 1921; but it was stated that negotiations would be resumed after that Conference had ended. The Dalai Lama was informed of these developments in general terms, but without reference to the question of Chinese suzerainty. He was also told that his government would be supplied with reasonable quantities of arms and ammunition on a guarantee that they would be used only for self-defence and that the Tibetans would refrain from provocative or aggressive acts pending the re-opening of negotiations.

The Dalai Lama readily gave the guarantee, whereupon the British Government set about fulfilling their promises to him by giving the specific assistance for which he had asked Sir

Charles Bell. A supply of arms and ammunition was begun; some officers and men of the Tibetan army were given military training —mostly at Gyantse but some also in India; help was given in the construction of a telegraph line from Gyantse to Lhasa for which the Dalai Lama had asked ever since 1912 but which had been refused on account of 'international obligations'; a geological survey of some parts of central Tibet was conducted for the Dalai Lama by Sir Henry Hayden; assistance was given in obtaining machinery for a small hydro-electric plant at Lhasa, but this took several years to complete; a Sikkimese officer of the Darjeeling Police went to Lhasa to organize a small police force; and in 1924 a small English school was opened at Gyantse for the children of noble and middle-class Tibetan families. The cost of all these activities was met by the Tibetan Government.

There was also a lessening of Tibetan isolation by the admission of a small number of European visitors to the country although their travels were intended to be restricted to a few prescribed routes.

These changes, although small in themselves, represented a considerable broadening in outlook; and the possession of a reasonable supply of modern arms strengthened the confidence of the Tibetan Government. But hopes of a resumption of negotiations came to nothing. After the conclusion of the Washington Conference, once again disunity in China, the low prestige of the Central Government, and the prevalence of a chauvinistic spirit made progress impossible. There was great temptation for the Tibetans to claim that their pledge of non-aggression no longer held good. For at least five years after 1920 the Chinese in the border areas were so riven by feuds that the country could have been easily overrun; but the Dalai Lama stood by his word and the Tibetans concentrated on winning a degree of influence over the civil administration of the border states.

It was, nevertheless, thought desirable to maintain personal touch with the Dalai Lama and to explain to him the continuing difficulties in reaching the settlement which he so much desired. Accordingly, Col. F. M. Bailey, who had succeeded Bell as Political Officer in Sikkim, went on a short visit to Lhasa. He, too, had long experience of Tibet and a deep sympathy with the people, and he was able to advise further patience and to discuss in a friendly atmosphere the problems of the Tibetans' limited plan of modernization, the worsening of relations between Tibet and Nepal, and Tibetan reactions to the flight of the Panchen Lama which had taken place in 1923. His visit was evidence of the new era of easier and more natural neighbourly relations between the Government of India and Tibet which had been inaugurated by Bell's mission.

THE VITH PANCHEN LAMA: 1923

The flight of the Panchen Lama, mentioned above, was the beginning of a situation which for fourteen years was to be an unremitting threat and anxiety to the Tibetan Government and which still later was to play a part in the eventual domination of Tibet by the Chinese Communists.

In chapter III, in which the general relationship between Dalai and Panchen Lamas has been described, reference was made to the use of the Panchen Lama by the Emperor K'ang Hsi as a counterweight to the authority of the Dalai Lama. The inevitable and premeditated result of inspiring the Panchen Lama with temporal pretensions was to create lasting rivalry between Lhasa and Tashilhunpo. The emperors were able to take advantage of that according to the circumstances of the day. Early in the eighteenth century when the Dalai Lama was a possible threat to Chinese policy, the Panchen Lama could be played against him. Fifty years later, at the time of the visits of Bogle and Turner, when the period of successive minorities was beginning, the satisfactory relationship between the Regents of Tibet and the Chinese Ambans gave the Emperor adequate security at Lhasa. Thereupon the Panchen Lamas, particularly the IIIrd and the IVth, emerged as champions of greater Tibetan freedom. Although they maintained correct relations with the imperial court, there was no need, at that time, actively to build up their authority against that of Lhasa. The simple fact that the Panchen Lamas were long-lived and had not to compete with the influence of an active Dalai Lama led to a growth in their prestige and authority and to an air of independence in the administration of their fief.

Trouble was clearly on the way when the XIIIth Dalai Lama survived his minority and appeared as a determined autocrat. The VIth Panchen Lama was about seven years younger than the Dalai Lama and, therefore, his spiritual disciple. Bell and others who knew him have described the sweetness and modesty of his nature and contrasted it with the masterful robustness of the XIIIth Dalai Lama. The two Lamas, unfortunately, met so rarely that a close personal relationship never had a chance to develop and the differences between them were therefore more easily magnified by their respective courts. It became a conflict between the determination of Lhasa to reduce Tashilhunpo to the status— on which there was fair reason to insist—of an honoured vassal, and the reluctance of Tashilhunpo to give up any of the privileges which it had acquired in the past century and more.

Signs of an independent attitude on the part of Tashilhunpo were seen when the Panchen Lama, perhaps recalling the old connection of his predecessors with Bogle and Turner, sent a high official to meet Younghusband at Khamba Dzong in 1903. Although his object was the same as that of the Dalai Lama—to persuade the Mission to withdraw—he showed a different attitude from that of the Dalai Lama who would neither reply to communications nor send any reputable delegates to meet Younghusband.

After the Dalai Lama's flight from Lhasa in 1904 the Panchen was wooed by both the Chinese and the British. The Chinese wanted him to become Regent or at least to take the lead in administering Tibet, which would have been quite contrary to Tibetan custom. The British invited him to visit India, where he went in 1905. Bell, who met him at Tashilhunpo in 1906, found him charming and friendly but above all things anxious to avoid being implicated in the policies of either side.

Again after the Dalai Lama's second flight—to India in 1910— the Chinese were in constant touch with the Panchen Lama and, although he himself avoided their insistence and declined to accept any official post, his entourage did not prove so discreet. The atmosphere, therefore, was one of uneasy suspicion when the Dalai Lama returned to power in 1913. A meeting with the Panchen Lama restored their personal friendliness; but the Dalai Lama never overcame his distrust of the Tashilhunpo circle nor did he relax his determination to assert what he reasonably believed to be his rightful supremacy over that administration.

The break came in 1922 when the Panchen Lama appealed to the British Government for mediation between himself and the Dalai Lama, who had insisted on the payment by the Panchen Lama's administration of a contribution to the cost of the Tibetan army. Unfortunately, the request for mediation was refused on the ground that it would have constituted interference in Tibetan internal affairs; and in 1923 the Panchen Lama, in despair, fled from Tashilhunpo leaving a sorrowful letter of protest against the machinations of evil persons who had misled the Dalai Lama. He declared that his absence from Tibet would only be temporary while he sought for someone to mediate between himself and the Dalai Lama.

Having been given no encouragement by the British, the Panchen Lama made his way to China where he was warmly received. The Dalai Lama was considerably disturbed by this development. He rebuked the Panchen Lama for not having brought his troubles personally to his Father and Teacher instead of 'wandering away into uninhabited places, to his great peril, like a moth attracted by the candlelight'. He also warned the Panchen of the dangers of visiting China or Mongolia. All over Tibet the flight of the Panchen Lama caused great sorrow and disquiet. Even the firmest supporters of the Dalai Lama were shaken; and a whole train of portents and oracles, which are wont to appear in Tibet at times of crisis, was reported from all parts of the country. The less well-disposed hinted darkly that this was one of the results of introducing modern ideas.

In China the opportunity was taken, as a matter of course, of blaming 'British intrigue'; but the Chinese Government was not slow to see how valuable a prize they had won. The only figure in Tibet whom they might hope to use as a Pretender had fallen into their hands and for the next fourteen years, until his death in

1937, the mild, unfortunate, and courteous Panchen became the centre of endless scheming. The danger that he would return to Tibet with the backing of Chinese troops was ever-present, to a varying degree, in the minds of the Tibetan Government. Of course, he wanted to return to Tibet, and emissaries from either side were constantly exchanging proposals; but there is no suggestion that the Panchen Lama personally favoured the idea of securing his return by force—at least so long as the Dalai Lama was alive.

So far as relations between Tibet and Britain were concerned, the exile of the Panchen Lama strengthened the hand of the ultra-conservative element which disliked the thought of any change whatsoever; while the danger that the Panchen Lama might be restored by force added to the Dalai Lama's impatience and dissatisfaction at the failure to secure a tripartite settlement. It therefore had a part in the reaction in Tibet against closer relations with the British which led to what was, if not an estrangement, a marked coldness.

A number of factors contributed to the decline in cordiality between Tibet and the British Government which set in about 1925. Disappointment at the failure to bring the Chinese to a settlement has already been mentioned. There may also have been an inclination on the part of the Dalai Lama to think that, once he had obtained a supply of arms, he was at least a match for the disunited Chinese and, therefore, needed to rely less on help from outside. But the principal cause is to be found in the nature of the Tibetan social system and it is against that setting that the episode must be viewed.

The guiding principle of the Tibetan Government, to which both monks and laymen subscribed, was the preservation of the national religion. Since the time of the Vth Dalai Lama in 1642 it was possible to say that State and Religion were interchangeable terms and that the whole administration was subordinated to the demands of the faith. The ascendancy of religion had been won at the expense of the hereditary nobility and there was, even if subconsciously, a constant awareness of that on both sides. The lay nobles were always more open to new ideas and more interested in the world around them than the monks who were, in general, opposed to innovation or change of any kind and simply wanted to preserve the state of affairs exactly as it was. Although that sequestered conservatism was deliberate, it was not cynical and there was no conscious exploitation of the religious devotion of the people for selfish ends; but the concentration of political aims on the preservation of religion, the extent to which monks themselves took part in the administration, and the fact that its head was a Lama, gave their opinions an overpowering weight. There was, therefore, a general reason for latent suspicion and jealousy between Monk and Noble. There were also, as in any country, family feuds and rivalries among the nobles themselves; and similar rivalries existed between the various monasteries—even of the same sect—and often between different colleges of the same monastery. Some noble families had bonds of tradition, kinship, or expediency with other families and similar bonds with different monastic colleges; but none of these alignments or groupings amounted to anything even remotely resembling a political party. Both lay and monk were unquestioningly loyal to the Dalai Lama and their differences were inspired by the pursuit of place and influence in the state.

One may read, sometimes, descriptions of this or that official or section of opinion as 'pro-British', 'pro-Chinese', and so on. That is too facile. The only thing the Tibetans have been 'pro' is the preservation of their Religious State. At different times they have looked for assistance to that end in one foreign quarter or another, but the idea of Tibetans being pro-British, pro-Indian, pro-Chinese or anything of that sort should be interpreted strictly in terms of Tibetan national interest or banished altogether along with the idea of political parties in Tibet.

It was natural for the Dalai Lama, after his bad treatment in China and his stay in India, not only to feel the attraction of some of the ideas of the outside world but also to look to the British for help in putting them into effect. In this he made use of some of the younger lay nobles; but to many of the monks it appeared that he was introducing practices which their tradition declared to be harmful to the country—such as mining and the use of machinery. There was the fear too that possession of a well-trained army would enable the Dalai Lama to dominate the monasteries; and on one occasion he successfully put his new power to the test by subduing a threatened revolt of the huge monastery of Drepung. The three great monasteries of Lhasa, housing between them some 20,000 monks, were the most powerful instrument for dominating the administration. Each of them had a proportion of sturdy, not very highly educated monks, who were maintained more or less as a monastic army, and it was an unwelcome development that a lay army with noble commanders could neutralize their influence. That threat to monastic supremacy was the key to the reaction against innovations and it showed that the Dalai Lama, although the summit and master of the system, was also its creature. No Dalai Lama, however autocratic, could possibly ignore determined pressure from the general body of monks.

The XIIIth Dalai Lama was throughout his life susceptible to the advice of one or more persons whom he chose in succession as his personal companions and assistants. Among these, there was for many years in his household a counterweight to the modernizing lay officials in the very conservative and strong-willed Lord Chamberlain whose work kept him in constant attendance on the Dalai Lama. There was also growing in favour a brilliant, volatile, and unstable lay official, Lungshar, who, although not unattracted by innovations, was temporarily led by family feuds to oppose the nobles who had taken the principal part in their introduction. The Dalai Lama was, moreover, practically out of touch with his friend Bell who had retired into private life.

From that complex of causes came an unmistakable reaction against the programme of modernization. Tibetan officers recently given military training in India were removed from posts in the Tibetan army and given different employment. The drill and general condition of the new Tibetan army was allowed to deteriorate. The police force fell into decay. The English school at Gyantse, after achieving remarkable results in only two years, was closed. A newly introduced motor mail service for the British

Trade Agencies was stopped at the request of the Tibetan Government. Further signs of the Dalai Lama's withdrawal from the British connection were seen in the affairs of the Panchen Lama. The Panchen made several informal requests for British mediation between himself and Lhasa; and eventually the suggestion was put to the Dalai Lama. The approach came at a bad moment, when one of the Panchen Lama's relations, kept under surveillance at Shigatse, had just attempted to escape and had been severely punished. The Dalai Lama coldly declined the offer to discuss the affair.

What had happened was, briefly, that the Dalai Lama had tried to go too fast for Tibetan opinion and was now concerned to draw back and show that he was in no way under outside influence. Thus the British Government which had helped him—even though it had made no attempt to push him further than he wanted to go—was inevitably involved in Tibetan criticism of foreign innovations. Nevertheless, the jubilant description, in the Russian press, of these events as 'the crash of British influence in Tibet' was a wild exaggeration; and, so far as the Russians were concerned, it was disproved in 1927 when a party of Mongolians, spreading Soviet propaganda, appeared at Lhasa. Their arrival was promptly reported to the Government of India by the Tibetan Government. In 1928 a person believed to be a high Soviet military officer from Mongolia also arrived at Lhasa where he stayed for over a year but was unable to make any headway with the Tibetans.

The Chinese, too, were not slow to look for profit from the new situation. Li Tieh-tseng has described the Dalai Lama's attitude as 'turning strongly towards China'. Let us see what happened. From 1925 onwards there were repeated rumours of peace overtures from China; and in Szechwan a noisy propaganda campaign to 'Save Tibet' was heard; but there was no breach of the old armistice on the Tibetan border while, in China, the central government was still too divided and enfeebled to make any decisive step. Eventually, in 1929 and 1930, when some appearance of stability had been established at Nanking, two missions were sent to Lhasa. The first was informal and was led by a Chinese woman born in Tibet, Miss Liu Man-ch'ing. The second and more important was led by the Yungon Dzasa, the Tibetan abbot of the Lama Temple at Peking, who brought from the Chinese Government some specific suggestions and inquiries about a possible direct settlement. The Dalai Lama gave both parties a friendly welcome and, without informing the Government of India, discussed with the Dzasa the Chinese communication and the possibility of reaching an agreement. That is something he would not have done before 1925 when he still had hopes of a tripartite convention. Nevertheless the replies he sent through Yungon Dzasa show an uncompromising stand on the autonomy of Tibet and no acknowledgement in any way of Chinese suzerainty. In effect, he wanted Tibet to be treated as an independent country in close diplomatic relations with China. The Chinese offer of practical assistance was met with a request for the one thing the Chinese were averse from giving—a supply of arms. As for the return of the Panchen Lama, the Dalai Lama was prepared to consider it only on his own terms which categorically excluded the Panchen's Tibetan entourage and a Chinese armed escort.

It was certainly evidence of a thaw in the Dalai Lama's attitude towards China that he should be ready to discuss proposals without reference to the Government of India; but it should not be overlooked that the discussions for the Chinese were conducted by one of the Dalai Lama's own officials, his representative in Nanking. Moreover the tone of his replies suggests that he may have hoped to succeed where the British had failed, and get what he wanted without making any concessions. It is clutching at straws to suggest that the Dalai Lama's reception of such missions showed a willingness to accept Chinese supremacy or that his attitude was turning strongly towards China.

The Dalai Lama himself has left his political testament, written in 1931, in which he declared the basic principles of his policy. Among them is the advice, prudent in the case of a materially weak country, to maintain friendly relations with Britain and China both of which have powerful armies. It was not very long before he found it desirable to restore some of the old warmth to his relationship with the British. The occasion was the severe worsening of relations between Tibet and Nepal which almost led to war.

Since the Nepalese conquest of Tibet in 1856 and the exaction of tribute and extraterritorial privileges, relations between the two countries were far from amicable. Disputes leading to the brink of war had occurred in 1880, 1883, and 1895; and the Nepalese Government had added to its unpopularity by offering active help to the Younghusband Expedition in 1904. The jurisdiction enjoyed over his own people by the Nepalese representative at Lhasa was a constant cause of ill-feeling. A case of that sort in 1922 was aggravated by Lungshar who seized a disputed person by force out of the Nepalese Legation. The Nepalese Government demanded an apology but the Dalai Lama, perhaps misinformed by Lungshar, sought to explain away and justify what had been done. After further sharp exchanges between the two governments the Nepalese prepared to invade Tibet and the Tibetans made counter-preparations. Great concern was felt by the British Government and in India at the threat of war between two countries with which they were in close relations. Advice was tendered to both sides, a special envoy, Sardar Bahadur Laden La, being sent with a letter to the Dalai Lama. Eventually the Dalai Lama, who appears at first not to have grasped the seriousness of the situation, directed his government to make satisfactory amends to the Nepalese Government and the tension died away, to the relief of all concerned. The Chinese Government, too, attempted to profit from the affair by sending envoys to Nepal to offer mediation. The offer was promptly rejected.

As a result of the crisis which had been precipitated largely by his rash arrogance, Lungshar's position with the Dalai Lama was greatly discredited and it was not long before he fell completely from favour. The Dalai Lama came once more to appreciate the advantages of friendship with the British Government. As a sign of his desire for closer relations he invited the Political Officer in Sikkim, Col. Weir, to visit Lhasa, and so provided an opportunity to discuss the problems of the past five years and, above all, to restore mutual understanding and cordiality.

THE LAST YEARS OF THE XIIITH DALAI LAMA
1930–1933

Not long after Weir's return from Lhasa fresh troubles boiled up for the Tibetans. The armed peace on the Tibetan border, which had hardly been interrupted since 1918, was broken at the end of 1930 by a dispute between two monasteries in the debatable area to the east of the Yangtse. The Tibetans sided with one party, the Chinese with the other, and both sent troops to help their friends. The inevitable blaze was touched off by a Chinese attack. The Tibetans retaliated fiercely and forced their way rapidly almost as far as Tachienlu.

The Chinese troops taking part in the fighting were entirely those of the Szechwan war-lord, Liu Wen-hui. About 1928 Chao Erh-fêng's project to make a province of 'Sikang' had been revived. On paper, its limits extended well across the upper Yangtse into territory which had long been, and continued to be, under the direct control of the Dalai Lama's Government. In practice it served as cover for Chinese expansion as far westwards as they were able; but their physical possession was restricted to the 'capital', Tachienlu, and a few outlying garrisons in important places such as Batang. Liu Wen-hui sought to add this new region to his province of Szechwan which he governed in virtual independence of the National Government at Nanking. Nevertheless, Nanking looked on Tibet as its concern. The Nationalist press, although far from the scene of action and from any reliable sources of information, at once launched out into the frantic anti-British propaganda which was almost automatic whenever the Tibetans got the better of the Chinese. British-trained troops with British officers were alleged to have established themselves in Chamdo; and charges of British instigation of the Tibetans were hurled about. In spite of its inability to control Liu Wen-hui, the National Government was untiring in its effort to figure as the arbiter of affairs. A number of telegrams was exchanged between Chiang Kai-shek and the Dalai Lama and in September 1931 a local armistice was arranged in which a National Government delegate took part. By it Tibetan and Chinese troops were left face to face in Nyarong, Kanzé, and other places close to the frontier of Szechwan to which the Tibetans had penetrated.

Such an uneasy situation could not last. In April 1932, after recovering strength, Liu Wen-hui's troops attacked and in five months' fighting drove the Tibetans back to the Yangtse and even threatened to assault Chamdo. The attack by Liu's forces after the conclusion of an armistice by a National Government representative was explained by the statement, not borne out by Tibetan information, that the Dalai Lama refused to sanction the agreement; but in Tibetan eyes it was long considered an act of treachery. It probably caused some embarrassment to the National Government at Nanking by exposing its lack of control over the provincial governors.

In addition to Liu Wen-hui, the Tibetans had to deal with the equally independent Muslim governor of Chinghai (Sining) with whom they imprudently got themselves embroiled by taking sides in another dispute between monasteries in that area, and who concerted his military reprisals with those of Liu Wen-hui. At the same time there was confused fighting at Batang where a half-Tibetan, Kesang Tsering, claiming to act for Chiang Kai-shek, enlisted some support from local tribes and evicted Liu Wen-hui's governor from the town. He soon came into conflict with a powerful freebooter Lama of the neighbourhood who secured support from the Tibetan forces, and eventually occupied Batang but later had to evacuate it.

By August 1932 so much ground had been lost that the Dalai Lama telegraphed to the Government of India asking for help and for diplomatic intervention at Nanking. Weir was sent once more to Lhasa and, at Nanking, the British representative took up the matter with the National Government. The latter, being in no position to control Liu Wen-hui, resorted to bluster and to denunciation of the supply of arms to the Tibetans by the British; but after some pressure, an order to cease fire was issued towards the end of September.

Weir reached Lhasa early in September. He found that, in spite of popular alarm, the position was not so bad as had been feared and the Tibetan Government had taken steps to restore it.

The Dalai Lama, although irate at Liu's treachery and unwilling to admit the provocation on his own part by allowing his troops to advance so far as Tachienlu, was anxious for a final settlement with China; and during Weir's stay, the Tibetan Government drew up proposals for discussion on the basis of the 1914 Convention. These were communicated by the Dalai Lama to the National Government and had their part in bringing about the cease-fire.

Even before the formal instruction from the Nanking Government the military situation had already been greatly eased for the Tibetans by the outbreak of civil war in Szechwan between Liu Wen-hui and his nephew Liu Hsiang. The cease-fire order, which might otherwise have been ignored, was therefore welcome to Liu Wen-hui. It was followed not long after by a local armistice; and early in 1933 a similar armistice was concluded with Governor Ma of Chinghai. The result of those agreements, in which the Nanking Government had no part, was that the Tibetans gave up everything to the east of the Yangtse but kept possession of the Yakalo (Yenchin) district which had hitherto remained a Chinese enclave to the west of the Yangtse.

The breathing space provided by the armistice and by the pre-occupation of Liu Wen-hui with his civil war, restored Tibetan confidence, and the Dalai Lama, while still hoping for an agreement with the Chinese Government, even seems to have contemplated improving his position by an attempt to recover by force some of the territory he had just had to relinquish. Once again he had to be advised against aggression; and once again it was necessary to admit that the state of affairs and of opinion in China made it useless to consider a general settlement. Regardless of its lack of control over Liu Wen-hui and his province of Szechwan, the Nanking Government, now finding its feet, was working out far-reaching plans for restoring its sovereignty over Tibet and was not in a mood to consider British participation in any settlement. From now on the Simla Convention was of no further interest to the Chinese Government as the basis of a settlement with Tibet, even though the British Government continued to refer to it, for some time longer, as if it still remained open to Chinese adherence.

The only prospect of progress was for the British Government to agree that the Dalai Lama might, without prejudice to his obligations to them, do what he could to secure a direct agreement with the Chinese about the eastern frontier—the issue on which the 1914 negotiations had broken down. Perhaps in the hope of facilitating talks with Nanking, the Dalai Lama wrote a friendly letter to the Panchen Lama expressing his desire that the Panchen should return; but when it came to discussing terms no progress was possible because, in the Dalai Lama's view, the Panchen's requests were pitched too high.

In 1933 Mr. F. Williamson, who had succeeded Col. Weir as Political Officer in Sikkim, paid a visit to Lhasa. In December of the same year, after a short illness, the Dalai Lama died at the age of 58.

Before recounting the events which followed the death of the Dalai Lama, it is desirable to look at the explanation of Tibetan policy in the last few years of his life, as given by Li Tieh-tseng. He considers that the rather aggressive attitude of the Tibetan Government at that time was due to the ascendancy of a pro-British 'Young Tibet Party', militaristic lay officials who wanted to substitute some form of civil government for the Lama hierarchy and to introduce widespread reforms including the establishment, with British help, of a Greater Tibet extending, apparently, to the borders of China.

The 'Young Tibet Party' and its activities existed only in the imagination and the published works of Chinese writers. There was not, as has already been said, anything in Tibet approaching a political party or even an organized 'pressure group'—as Li calls it—unless it were the monks of the three great monasteries of Lhasa. The idea of a group of lay officials seeking to subvert the government of the Dalai Lama shows a complete misunderstanding of Tibetan life and the Tibetan mind; while to suggest that the British Government would assist such a group—if it existed—in a revolutionary and expansionist policy is, at the least, inept. It ignores that the constant aim of British policy in Tibet from 1912 onwards was to preserve the peace and to find a solution acceptable to both China and Tibet. To that end the Tibetans were supplied with a much smaller quantity of arms than they would have liked and were repeatedly given the unwelcome advice to use restraint even when aggression had very good prospects of success.

Chinese politicians appeared unwilling to realize that the Dalai Lama and his government after twenty years of independent rule were becoming stronger and more confident. The Tibetans as a whole were always anxious to make good their authority to the east of the Yangtse. That was not a lay militarist aim but was desired also by the monks on account of the numerous great monasteries situated in that area. At all events, the fighting which broke out in 1931 was plainly the chance outcome of a local dispute and its rapid spread to the borders of Tachienlu followed when the commanders in the field found there was no real opposition. The Tibetans were eventually driven back but the experience of twice almost recovering what they considered *irredenta* may well have sharpened the hope of eventually regaining at least part of the debatable territory.

To attribute that aim solely to a young militarist clique is speculation on a flimsy basis. It overlooks the parallel of the events of 1931 with those of 1918—when an elderly monk was commander-in-chief. In 1931, too, one of the commanders was a high monk official. Further, it suggests unawareness that, after the fall of Lungshar, the principal adviser of the Dalai Lama was not Tsarong, whom Li sees as the villain of the piece, but a monk official named Kunphel La.

The 'Young Tibet Party', therefore, seems to have been invented as a whipping boy on which might be blamed every act of Tibetan independence or resistance to Chinese pretensions and every manifestation of that opinion, concisely stated by a distinguished Chinese diplomat, Shen Tsung-lien, who had some years' experience of Tibet, that 'Lhasa believes that to be politically attached to China is more a liability than an asset'.

IX

INTERREGNUM: 1933–1940

THE DEATH OF THE XIIITH DALAI LAMA

The removal of the imperious hand of the XIIIth Dalai Lama left the Tibetan Government dazed and distracted. The air became thick with rumours of poisoning, black magic, and omens of disaster. It was the setting for a medieval drama and into it there burst a flamboyant, daemonic figure such as rarely appears among the Tibetans. This was Lungshar, one time commander-in-chief, the man who had almost brought Tibet to war with Nepal, the adviser of the Dalai Lama during whose ascendancy had taken place the turning away from innovations and the British connection.

In the customary course, a Regent had to be appointed and the choice, perhaps influenced by Lungshar, soon fell on the incarnate Lama of Reting, a young man hardly out of his 'teens and quite inexperienced in affairs of state. He, it was clear, was not likely to dominate the government, at least for some time. Ordinarily the day-to-day administration should have been conducted by the Council (Kashag); but Lungshar, out of favour with that body, sought an instrument for his ambition in the Assembly which he planned to build up into a kind of committee pledged to his support. With dazzling impetuosity he proclaimed that Tibet should be a sort of temporary republic in which the Assembly, under his leadership, should speak for the country. By his energy and forceful persuasiveness he seems even to have swept the monasteries off their feet for a time. A design to subordinate the Council to the Assembly, in which the monasteries had great influence, might well appeal to them and—whether they were taken in by his advocacy or whether from the start they deliberately intended to use him for their own ends—the monasteries gave Lungshar a large measure of support.

In foreign affairs the man who talked of a republic and who

had taken the lead in what Li describes as 'turning strongly towards China' in 1925 might have been expected to look to Nanking for help. But Lungshar's dealings with the Chinese Government were haughty, independent, and almost hostile. On the other hand, he warned the British Government that the Chinese would certainly try to send official representatives to Lhasa and would probably succeed. Perhaps he feared that reconciliation with China would mean the return of the Panchen Lama who would assume first place in the country. At all events, Lunghsar's conduct shows the pitfalls of trying to find Western parallels in Tibetan political thinking.

Li is further misled by his preconceptions about Tibetan politics into believing that it was Tsarong—the idol of the 'Young Tibet Party'—who made this hectic bid for power. In fact Tsarong carefully kept away from Lhasa and if he did not actively oppose his former rival Lungshar, he certainly did not support him.

Lungshar was an unusual phenomenon in Tibet. In him certain qualities inherent in the Tibetan character were overdeveloped and exaggerated. A strain of recklessness made him, in the well-worn phrase, 'drunk with power'. At all events, he does not seem to have seen the warning signs that he was overreaching himself and that his opponents were gathering strength. The Council, cautious and unimpressive, slowly hardened their counter-measures. The monastic mind began to wonder whether any sort of republic would be really compatible with the conservative rule of religion and to have doubts whether the layman Lungshar might not be getting too much power. Conservative sanity was reasserting itself, and suddenly Lungshar, apparently at the peak of success and blind to everything but his ambitions, found the supports drawn from under him. In a last act of theatrical excitement the Council was able to arrest him. After an inquiry into his behaviour he was condemned to lose his sight—a rare penalty, reserved for acts of high treason—and was imprisoned for life.

The erratic and feverish caprice ruling his conduct can be seen in the variety of aims with which, on the evidence of a number of his associates, he was charged: he was alleged to have wanted a republic; a Bolshevist state; the position of co-Regent; the rank of king, like Phola Miwang. It adds up simply to a lust for power—the name meant little or nothing—and to achieve what he wanted, Lungshar was prepared to use bribery, murder, sorcery—anything that lay to hand.

After that exciting interlude, which lasted about four months, the Council settled down to inaugurate the interim government which lasted, without any substantial change in principle, for seventeen years. For guidance they relied chiefly on the testament of the late Dalai Lama, written a year before his death, and they consciously set themselves to change nothing. No doubt the awe which the late Dalai Lama had inspired by his autocratic methods caused them to think ahead to the time of his return when they might be called to account by his successor for straying from his instructions. The régime, therefore, although not uneventful, was mostly cautious and unenterprising with a constant undercurrent of anxiety.

The new government was faced almost immediately with a difficult task. As Lungshar had foretold, a Chinese mission was allowed to come to Lhasa. The pretext was to offer condolence on the death of the Dalai Lama. The object was to discover whether, with the removal of the Dalai Lama who had so resolutely opposed any concessions to China, the interim government could be argued or threatened into compliance. A large party headed by General Huang Mu-sung, a member of the National Military Council, travelled to Tibet bringing with them a wireless transmitting station. To keep an eye on proceedings the Government of India sent a member of the staff of the Political Officer in Sikkim—the very able Rai Bahadur Norbu Dhondup.

The Tibetans gave Huang an elaborate welcome and on his side Huang, a Chinese gentleman of the old school, worked indefatigably at the diplomatic round—visiting monasteries, giving lavish presents, attending receptions, and so on. The lesser officials, with modern republican manners, made a less gracious impression and there were signs of hostility between them and the people of Lhasa, especially the monks. Huang gave out that he had come only for the ceremonies of condolence. A seal, which the late Dalai Lama would never have accepted in his lifetime, was posthumously bestowed; and after suspicious examination of it, it was accepted by the Council when they found it to contain no compromising inscription.

The Tibetans had no doubt that the mission had political designs as well; but Huang, with diplomatic finesse, merely let it be hinted in private that he would discuss such matters if the Tibetans wanted. After a time, they decided to open proceedings by asking for a settlement of the long-standing frontier dispute. From that developed a series of discussions and arguments. At first Huang himself took part; but finding the Tibetan attitude obdurate on the issue of their independence, he turned the negotiations over to one of his staff, Wu Min-yuan, who had been born in Lhasa, ostensibly on an informal footing. Finally Huang returned to the fray with a proposal that the Tibetans should accept all of Wu's proposals with special emphasis on three points, namely: that Tibet should be subordinate to China; that Tibet should cease to have direct relations with foreign countries; and that the Chinese Government should be consulted before the appointment of high-ranking Tibetan officials. In reply the Tibetan Government affirmed that they were willing to acknowledge Chinese suzerainty on the conditions laid down in the 1914 Convention, that they would continue to conduct their own foreign affairs and to maintain their relationship with the British Government and that, as a token of friendship, they would inform the Chinese Government of the appointments of high officers after they had been made. A note was added that the British Government should be a party to any agreement reached between Tibet and China.

Li Tieh-tseng has published an account of the negotiations derived from General Huang's official report. It varies a good deal in detail from the information on the proceedings obtained from Tibetan sources by the present writer, some twelve years before the publication of Li's book. In particular, it is not correct to represent the Tibetans as having made any such concessions as agreeing that Tibet is an integral part of China, that Tibetan officials should, in any circumstances, be under orders from Chinese authorities, or that there should be joint consultation about any treaties. The official Chinese report appears deliberately to ignore the frequent reference by the Tibetan Government to the 1914 Convention as the basis for agreement, or to the need for associating the British Government in any settlement. Certain other discrepancies are due to the translation of Tibetan political language into the irreconcilably different vocabulary of western ideas. For example, the Tibetans repeated their view of the relationship of Patron and Priest but no hint of that appears in the Chinese account.

The affairs of the Panchen Lama were, of course, discussed and a general understanding was reached that he should return as soon as possible provided he did not bring an armed Chinese escort with him.

It is clear that on the issue of their relations with the Chinese Government the Tibetans, while reaffirming their readiness to negotiate along the 1914 lines, made no concessions in principle. Nevertheless, General Huang's mission was successful in making the first breach in the exclusion of Chinese officials from Tibet which had lasted for twenty years. He contrived to leave behind him two liaison officers with a wireless set and that foothold gradually turned into a regular diplomatic mission. From that time too the Chinese Government began to make regular payments to a number of Tibetan officials, from the Regent downwards. These were somewhat disingenuously accepted as private presents. It is clear also that the Chinese considered they had won the support of the young Regent. Li refers to the 'friendly' Regent and thereafter sees him as conducting a struggle with the 'pro-British Young Tibet group'. It was common report in 1934 and on many subsequent occasions that large sums of money found their way to the Regent from the Chinese Government. But, all in all, the Tibetans had stood up quite well to the first serious test of the new régime.

SIR BASIL GOULD'S MISSION TO LHASA

The vague understanding between General Huang and the Tibetan Government proved to be worthless and trouble soon blew up about the return of the Panchen Lama. There were many signs that the Lama was completely dependent on the Chinese Government and that it was they who made the pace.

As a straight issue between Lhasa and the Panchen Lama, the chief differences were his reported wish to control not only the three principal districts of the Tsang province but also the detachments of the Tibetan army stationed there. He also claimed the return to his followers of the estates which had been confiscated when they went into exile with him. Those domestic problems could have been settled between the two parties but the whole dispute was bedevilled and enlarged by the proposal that he should come to Tibet with a Chinese military escort. The Chinese Government were well aware of the steadfast Tibetan opposition to the idea of such an escort but evidence continued to accumulate of preparations to send a considerable armed force to Tibet.

In the hope of finding some peaceful solution, Williamson, the Political Officer in Sikkim, went again to Lhasa in 1935 but his work was cut short by his untimely death.

Li has suggested that the British may have had a hand in opposing the Panchen's return because it would 'solve the issue of the status of Tibet'. That disingenuously begs the question of the relationship between Tibet and China and displays a strange lack of information about British policy. So long as the Panchen Lama was the protégé of Nanking there was a threat to the peace of Tibet and whenever the British Government gave advice on the subject—which was not always welcome—it had been that the Tibetans should do their utmost to come to an agreement. It was to the return of the Lama by force, with a Chinese army, that the Tibetans objected; and British diplomatic intervention at Nanking in 1935 and on subsequent occasions was at the urgent request of the Tibetan Government in support of direct protests from that government to the Chinese. Both British and Tibetan representations were brushed off unceremoniously and there was little doubt that the preparation of a military expedition meant business. The Tibetans, although greatly alarmed and in spite of their realization that diplomatic support was the most they could expect from the British Government, stood firm and the National

Assembly solemnly resolved to resist any Chinese troops that might enter the country.

In these strained circumstances and since the visit of Williamson had been so sadly interrupted before its completion, it was decided that the new Political Officer, Mr. (later Sir Basil) Gould, should accept the invitation of the Tibetan Government and go to Lhasa to continue the search for a peaceful outcome. The presence of Brigadier (later Lieut.-Gen.) P. Neame of Indian Eastern Command in the party indicated that advice on their military problems would be available to the Tibetans if they wanted it. The possibility was envisaged of acting as middleman to the extent of escorting the Panchen Lama from the eastern border if in that way the difficulty could be overcome. In short, the object was to do all that was possible to effect a reconciliation between Lhasa and the Panchen Lama and at the same time to give advice and some material help to the Tibetans to prevent them from being compelled by threats to accept something they had repeatedly stated they did not want to accept. It would also be possible to discover to what extent Huang Mu-sung's mission had increased Chinese influence at Lhasa. Gould was accompanied by a larger staff than any previous British official visitor to Lhasa and he also had a wireless transmitter with him. After a stay of about five months during which he had frequent discussions with the Tibetan Government, Gould returned to Sikkim with the greater part of his staff, leaving H. E. Richardson (myself), with a wireless officer, to maintain contact and report on any further requests the Tibetan Government might make concerning the problem of the Panchen Lama.

The complexities of that problem had become much clearer when it was possible to study them at Lhasa. Gould had frequent and friendly meetings with the Panchen Lama's trusted adviser Ngagchen (Angchin) Rimpoche, who informed the Lama of British anxiety for a peaceful solution. But it became obvious that there were two parties in the Panchen's camp, one in favour of a reconciliation with Lhasa, the other bent on a return by force. In the meantime the Panchen Lama, accompanied by a military escort, moved to Jyekundo, not far from the border, and sent an advance consignment of baggage into Tibet. The Tibetans were not encouraged in their hopes of peace when it was found by chance that the baggage contained a large number of grenades. Nevertheless, negotiations went on feverishly at Lhasa, Nanking, and Chamdo. A further protest was delivered by the British representative at Nanking but it was brusquely rejected and not long after, in August 1937, the Panchen Lama moved to Rashi Gompa, just on the Tibetan frontier. At Lhasa, mobilization was ordered and the intention to resist was reaffirmed. And then, gradually, tension relaxed.

War between China and Japan had broken out in June 1937 but, even after that, the Chinese pressed on with their plan to send the Panchen Lama to Tibet with an armed escort. Perhaps their aim was to test the strength of Tibetan determination. When they found the Tibetans meant business the Chinese could not afford to have another war on their hands and so were compelled to call off the expedition. As soon as this weakening became known to the Tibetan Government they tried a diplomatic counter-stroke by deciding to renew their request to the Panchen Lama to return and were even considering the admission of a small escort which, they believed, they would have no difficulty in handling while the Chinese were involved in war with Japan. But the Lama telegraphed to them that he would not be able to come to Tibet that year. He returned to Jyekundo and there, in December 1937, to the mingled sorrow and relief of the Tibetan people, that gentle, hapless, troubled figure temporarily solved the problem by 'withdrawing to the Heavenly Fields'.

By following the story of the VIth Panchen Lama to its end, this account has slightly outrun the main theme and it is necessary to look back a little.

The prospect that the Tibetan Government might want help in their military problems did not develop to any large extent. Although they were pleased to invite Neame to inspect all their military resources and to ask his advice on possible improvements, their practical interest centred on securing more weapons. The need for constant and expert training in the use of such weapons was something the Tibetans could never bring themselves to face. It was contrary to their nature and traditions and was also a dangerous source of conflict with the monk element. They were in general always more intent on having arms with the idea that in a crisis they would somehow find their men able to use them.

When the main body of Gould's Mission left Lhasa in February 1937, the decision that one of his Assistant Officers should remain was largely due to the existence of a Chinese foothold there. The staff of the Chinese office was of indifferent quality but the possession of a wireless transmitter had created the possibility of swift and regular communication between Nanking and Lhasa. It could be argued that the joint British and Tibetan declaration of 1914 precluded the Chinese from having a representative at Lhasa without first signing the 1914 Convention; but the Tibetans did not consider that the wireless office constituted Chinese representation and they hoped they might be able to secure its withdrawal. In the meantime they were pleased that a British representative should be left at Lhasa and, to Chinese protests on that score, they replied that, if the Chinese would remove their office, the British would certainly do the same.

The wireless transmitter at the British Mission caused great indignation to the Chinese; but the Tibetans, rather enjoying the situation, used the same argument and assured the Chinese that the British wireless would be withdrawn as soon as they took away their own.

In fact, there was no good reason to believe that the Chinese, having once secured a foothold at Lhasa, would voluntarily surrender it. On the contrary, every opportunity of consolidating it was sought. It was desirable, therefore, and was entirely acceptable to the Tibetan Government that, so long as Chinese pressure on Lhasa continued, a British officer should stay there. That arrangement was, and continued to be, of an undefined and temporary nature. There was never, as some writers have suggested, a demand by the British Government for the right to have a permanent Mission at Lhasa to offset the Chinese Mission. There was, in fact, no permanent mission; nor was the presence of British officers at Lhasa based on the right of the British Trade Agent at Gyantse to visit Lhasa to discuss matters arising out of the 1904 Convention.

In his pleasant book of recollections, *The Jewel in the Lotus*, Gould has explained how things worked. His own visit to Lhasa, like those of Bell, Bailey, Weir, and Williamson, was covered by no specific treaty agreement; but there was nothing to prevent the Tibetan Government from inviting the Political Officer in Sikkim to visit Lhasa, and that is what happened. When Gould left Lhasa he arranged, as he has explained in his book, for me to stay on as his representative. But the Mission continued for all its long existence to be, in theory, temporary. Gould himself returned to resume charge for occasional short visits and that practice was followed by his successors, British and Indian. The Lhasa Mission was never exclusively linked with the post of British Trade Agent at Gyantse. Although I myself held both posts jointly for a considerable period, there were several other officers who had charge at Lhasa without any connection with Gyantse. If the exact status of the Mission had ever been questioned by the Tibetan Government there might have been recourse to the provisions of the Simla Convention, but this did not occur and the 'semi-permanent' representation at Lhasa was, therefore, an example of the advantage of falling in with the Central Asian tendency to avoid precise definitions.

The Mission was modest in scale, consisting of one Officer with a clerical staff of two, a Medical Officer with a small staff, and a Wireless Operator. Without any break, it outlasted the transfer of power to the new Government of India in 1947 and was eventually converted into an Indian Consulate-General after the Chinese occupation of Tibet in 1950–52. Its presence created closer and more friendly relations with Tibetans of all ranks and classes and made it possible to acquire a more intimate and thorough understanding of Tibetan policies and aspirations. Gould himself remained as Political Officer in Sikkim for nearly ten years and twice revisited Lhasa, where his reputation for sagacity and dependability was immense. His Mission to Lhasa in 1936 was a landmark in British relations with Tibet comparable with that of Bell in 1920; and, like Bell, he is remembered by Tibetans with deep affection as a friend and a champion of their interests.

THE XIVTH DALAI LAMA

The inclination of the Tibetan Government to avoid making any changes in the absence of a Dalai Lama was seen also on the eastern front. There the principal occurrence was the march of the Chinese Communist Eighth Route Army through the Tibetan borderland. After that threat had receded in July 1936, the Tibetans ventured, once more, to cross the Yangtse into the Dergé area which had been deserted by the outposts of the Nationalist régime. Chinese border officials protested that this was a breach of the agreement reached in 1932. The Tibetans accordingly withdrew and thereafter took no advantage of the numerous difficulties of the Nanking Government, which included the war with Japan and the imprisonment of Chiang Kai-shek by Marshal Chang Hsueh-liang. Later, when the Nationalist Government had to retreat to Chungking, Chinese interest in the Tibetan frontier, which was now so much nearer to their capital, became more active; but the years between the death of the XIIIth and the discovery of the XIVth Dalai Lama were, in general, unusually quiet.

Similarly, in its relations with India, the guiding principle of the Tibetan Government was that nothing should be changed. There was, therefore, some difference of opinion when the Government of India came to realize, in connection with the affair of the Panchen Lama, that Chinese designs on Tibet were hardening and began to look more carefully at the position on their own frontier with Tibet which had been determined in 1914. It was found that there was little exact information about the location of the McMahon Line and that for the past twenty years little had been done to make good the influence of the Government of India among the tribal peoples inhabiting the area between the administered districts of Assam and the Tibetan frontier. As a result, petty officials from the Tibetan border, who had probably been doing the same thing for many years, were making expeditions well south of the accepted frontier in order to collect various taxes from the tribal people. There was also the anomalous position of the large monastery of Tawang which, although in Indian territory, continued its religious connection with the great Lhasa monastery of Drepung. Representatives of Tawang travelled almost to the plains of Assam to collect monastic contributions which it was not easy to distinguish from regular taxes. Measures to rectify the position aroused some resentment from the Tibetan Government. They have a profound respect for treaties and never questioned the validity of the frontier which they had agreed in 1914, but they had no personal knowledge of the country and were given to believe by reports of local officials that something new was being introduced. They reverted to the matter on several occasions, arguing that, although the frontier had been settled by treaty in 1914, there had been an understanding that Tibetan ownership of estates south of the border should not be disturbed, and seeking to extend that principle to the activities of their intrusive border officials. It needed much persistence and tact by Political Officers in the tribal areas of Assam and some patience on the part of British representatives at Lhasa to accustom the Tibetan Government to the idea that the Government of India meant to make good its administration in the sub-Himalayan region right up to the McMahon Line and to stop any trespass or irregularity there.

That was a matter of comparatively small importance to Tibet compared with the discovery of the new incarnation of the Dalai Lama.

By 1938 it was certain that three promising candidates had been found of whom one, born in Amdo, was believed to be exceptional. In addition to uncertainty about the facts there was concern that all the candidates lived so far from Lhasa. It was known that the Panchen Lama had recommended three children and suspicions were felt that this might have been a move to provide another instrument for Chinese designs on Tibet. By common talk the Regent was regularly in receipt of large sums of money from the Chinese which caused anxiety lest he should lend himself to some arrangement that might compromise the Tibetan position.

The account of events from the Chinese angle, as summarized by Li Tieh-tseng, differs substantially from that given by the

Plate 9

(*a*) Nomad headman

(*b*) Nomad headmen

Plate 10

(*a*) Nomads

(*b*) Nomad boy

Tibetans. The principal Chinese source appears to be the official report of Wu Chung-hsin, Chairman of the Commission of Tibetan and Mongolian Affairs of the Nanking Government, who was at Lhasa in 1940. The Tibetan version is related by Sir Charles Bell in *Portrait of the Dalai Lama*, where he attributes his information to Sir Basil Gould. Gould was Political Officer in Sikkim for the whole of the relevant period and visited Lhasa for the enthronement of the Dalai Lama, when Wu Chung-hsin was also present. He has given a short account in *The Jewel in the Lotus* and in the *Geographical Magazine* for 1946. I was myself in Tibet from 1936 to 1940, most of the time at Lhasa. After leaving Tibet early in 1940, I continued in regular personal communication with Gould and on my next visit to Lhasa in 1944, made my own inquiries into the events of 1940 onwards.

To British eyes the discrepancies between the Chinese and the Tibetan versions seem to be due to Chinese eagerness to substantiate their claim to a superior relationship with Tibet; and, with that aim, the Chinese appear to present events as having occurred in the way in which they would like them to have occurred. The Tibetans, who according to habit unfortunately do not publish official accounts, seem to have tried to follow the precepts of the late Dalai Lama and to have extended the greatest cordiality and politeness to the Chinese without in any way compromising the basic principles which they had made clear at the time of Huang Mu-sung's visit. In the account which follows there is, therefore, some disputation. The reader must judge for himself which version is the more probable and convincing.

The picturesque aspects of the discovery—the traditional search following signs and portents, the mission of holy monks and the careful tests—have been well described by Bell and Gould; this outline will concern itself only with the practical issue affecting relations between Tibet and China.

Amdo, where the most promising child was born, is part of the province of Chinghai which was governed by the Muslim General Ma Pu-feng whose administration was practically independent of Nanking. As soon as the Tibetan Government had seen the reports of their search parties that the Amdo child was almost certainly the true incarnation, they tried to keep the matter quiet and to have him brought to Lhasa with the other boys, as one of three candidates. Difficulties were, however, raised by Ma Pu-feng. First, he was not willing to let the child go to Tibet unless he was immediately recognized as Dalai Lama. In that, he had the support of the important monastery of Kum Bum to which the child had been taken and whose monks wanted the prestige of having sheltered a Dalai Lama. That trouble seemed to have been overcome by the payment of 100,000 Chinese dollars to be distributed partly to various authorities in Chinghai, and partly to Kum Bum; but when it came to the point, a fresh series of demands amounting to 300,000 Chinese dollars was made.

Faced with these obstacles the Tibetan Government appealed directly to Nanking to instruct General Ma to let the child go. The Chinese Government had known of the discovery for some time and had, as Li says, 'decided that the Chairman of the Commission for Mongolian and Tibetan Affairs should be jointly responsible with the Regent in supervising the ceremony' of the choice and installation of the Dalai Lama. The Tibetan Government, according to Li, agreed to this. Nevertheless, it soon became obvious that the Chinese Government had no control over Ma Pu-feng. They merely asked him to instruct the Kum Bum monastic officials not to obstruct the departure of the child and advised the Tibetans to negotiate directly with Ma. It was also proposed, early in 1939, that Wu Chung-hsin, Chairman of the Commission for Mongolian and Tibetan Affairs, should go to Lhasa to supervise proceedings. Li states that the Tibetans agreed but asked Wu to travel by sea, thereby leaving the final decision to the British who could block the matter by refusing visas. That is a misunderstanding, if not a misrepresentation, of the course of events. When the Chinese asked for facilities for Wu to travel through India to Tibet, the Tibetan Government, according to established practice, was asked if they wanted to admit the intending travellers. In this case they asked that no facilities should be granted because Wu's presence at Lhasa was unnecessary. About the same time they made a further appeal to Nanking for help in sending the child to Tibet and stated that when he had reached Lhasa the question of admitting a Chinese delegation would be considered. In reply the Chinese Government told them that they should decide which of the boys was the true reincarnation, and if the choice fell on the Amdo candidate the question of payment would be dropped and the boy would be sent to Lhasa with a suitable escort. That proposal, with its ominous echo of the affair of the Panchen Lama, was rejected by the Tibetans who realized that there was nothing for it but to pay the ransom to Ma Pu-feng. Payment of a further 300,000 dollars was arranged against notes to traders which were to be redeemed in India; and in July 1939 the child eventually set out for Tibet as a candidate and with an escort of only twenty soldiers deputed by Ma Pu-feng.

The Government of India helped the Tibetans to raise the ransom money by giving them certain import concessions. The money was well spent. It would have been worth even more to secure the child without Chinese participation in his return. That fortunate conclusion seems to have been due to the virtual independence and the appetite for money of General Ma Pu-feng. He got payment from both sides, for the Chinese Government also made him a grant of some 50,000 dollars for the expenses of the journey.

The above story is questioned by Li who cannot believe that money was demanded by and paid to Ma Pu-feng. His reasons seem to be that there is no mention of the matter in Chinese official records—but why should there be?—and that he himself visited the young Dalai Lama at Kum Bum and heard nothing about it—why should he? Those arguments appear inadequate in face of the consistent and circumstantial story from the Tibetan side of a long series of negotiations and of payments on several occasions. It would be of no advantage to the Tibetans to invent such a story, and that is not their nature. There was also a tail-piece which will be mentioned in due course.

Soon after the child had left Amdo a special Assembly was held at which he was formally declared to be the XIVth Dalai Lama. In September he was met at Nagchuka by a delegation from Lhasa headed by a Minister of the Council who acknowledged him as Dalai Lama, and in that quality he entered Lhasa on the 8th of

October 1939. The child, not yet five, won the immediate devotion of his people by the incomparable self-possession and charm of his behaviour.

The ceremonies of Installation were held in February 1940 and were attended by Sir Basil Gould and by Wu Chung-hsin. The latter travelled through India, having been given facilities at the request of the Tibetan Government. Li's charge that the question of permission for his journey was decided by the British Foreign Office is misinformed and tendentious. There are similar discrepancies in the different accounts of the ceremonies. According to the Chinese, still clinging to the long-discredited mummery of selecting the Dalai Lama by use of a golden urn (see Chapter IV), Wu professed to have satisfied himself at a private interview that the child was the true incarnation and the urn need not be used. After that, in February 1940, the Chinese Government appear to have issued a decree recognizing the child as Dalai Lama. The Tibetans, as has been said, had recognized the child in August 1939 and had been treating him as Dalai Lama ever since. There must have been bad co-ordination in Chinese quarters, for a Chinese press notice had announced in July 1939 that the child had been declared Dalai Lama with the consent of the Tibetan and Chinese authorities.

Wu also claimed that he personally conducted the enthronement and that, in gratitude, the Dalai Lama prostrated himself in the direction of Peking. Those stories, described as false by Bell on the authority of information from Gould, were categorically denied to the writer and dismissed as ludicrous by Tibetans who attended the ceremony. In looking for the truth of the matter, the firm attitude of the Tibetan Government to the demands of Huang Mu-sung may be recalled and, looking much further back, it is permissible to see the origin of such ritual fictions in the fanciful account, in Chinese official histories, of the visit to Peking by the Vth Dalai Lama.

NEUTRALITY PRESERVED: 1940-1946

THE CHINESE MISSION AT LHASA

Wu found the Chinese liaison office at Lhasa in a poor way. From various causes it had been reduced to one man only—a wireless operator—and although additional officials had been nominated, the Tibetans had prevented them from entering Tibet by the overland route. Before leaving Lhasa Wu tried to persuade the Tibetan Government to accept the appointment of a Chinese High Commissioner—the equivalent of the former Amban—but this was immediately refused. He therefore, without securing Tibetan agreement, simply let it be known that the Chinese liaison office would henceforth be a branch of the Commission for Mongolian and Tibetan Affairs; and he put in charge of it an officer of rather better standing than the former incumbents. The change of name brought about no change of nature nor of the Tibetan attitude towards the Chinese officials at Lhasa. They continued to be treated as temporary foreign representatives and had no part whatsoever in the direction of Tibetan affairs.

In 1942 the Tibetan Government sought to emphasize that point by setting up a new Bureau of Foreign Affairs, headed by two officers of very high rank—next in official seniority to the Ministers of the Council. The British Mission readily accepted the new arrangements but the Chinese, for obvious reasons, declined to do so. In practice, the new Tibetan Foreign Bureau was a great advantage. Formerly, routine business and preliminary examination of important questions had been conducted by messages through the official Guide attached to the Mission, and only in matters of great importance did the Mission ask for an interview with the Council. Of course, during visits by a Political Officer in Sikkim, meetings with the Council were frequent and, in his absence, informal meetings between the head of the British

Mission and the individual members of Council took place quite often. But the new Foreign Bureau made it possible for the Mission to remain in constant close contact with the Tibetan Government at a high level and to have friendly personal discussion on every sort of issue arising between the two countries in a less formal atmosphere than was possible in the Council. The Foreign Bureau was in daily touch with the Council where the high rank and the experience of its staff carried great weight, while in matters of exceptional importance it was still open to the British Mission to ask for a special interview with the Council.

By refusing to acknowledge the new office, the Chinese mission, although avoiding the admission of foreign status, put itself in a position of practical isolation. Its business was transacted through a Guide—an official of much lower rank than the heads of the Foreign Bureau—who in effect was no more than a messenger; and meetings with the Council were allowed only on extremely rare occasions.

The Nepalese, who also maintained a diplomatic mission at Lhasa, were in yet another position. By the treaty of 1856 their relations with the Tibetan Government were conducted through a special Office for Gurkha Relations and it was decided to leave that arrangement in force. There were thus three channels of approach to the Council on foreign affairs; but even though neither Chinese nor Nepalese affairs were directly discussed by the Foreign Bureau, the latter was consulted about them by the Council.

In the course of Wu's visit the Chinese Government, perhaps thinking it was necessary to reassure the British Government about their policy towards Tibet, let it be known that their aim was to undo bad traditions established during the Empire and, without interfering with Tibet's self-development, to be ready to help whenever wanted. That statement was brought to the notice of the Tibetan Government by Gould.

Wu also offered to repay the sum of 400,000 dollars which the Tibetan Government had spent on ransoming the Dalai Lama. This was politely evaded but Wu was told that any donation he liked to make towards the religious expenditure of the Tibetan Government would be welcome.

In general, Wu's mission consolidated and improved the Chinese foothold at Lhasa by putting it on a regular basis; but, in spite of the grandiose designation attached to that office, he made no advance on the political front and no breach in Tibetan resistance to Chinese claims to supremacy. Neither Wu nor Dr. Kung, the official whom he left in charge of the mission, could compare in Tibetan eyes with the courtly General Huang. They appeared to retain some of the traditional Chinese attitude of superiority. Nevertheless, since the Sino-Japanese war there had been greater sympathy with China on the part of the Tibetans. It was compounded of the old feeling of esteem for Chinese civilization, the dislike of injustice and oppression inculcated by the Tibetan religion, and the thought that the Chinese were too busy to make much trouble, together with the fear that the Japanese might be an even worse danger. Japanese pressure, driving the Chinese westward, had stimulated the Central Government to try to extend its control over the border provinces and to make roads ever nearer to the Tibetan frontier. That was to cause trouble towards the middle of 1941, but until then, there was an easier relationship and the Tibetans offered prayers for Chinese success.

Nevertheless, in February 1941, before the difference of opinion about road-making, there was an event to which the Chinese attached a sinister significance—the resignation of the Regent, the Reting (Radreng) Rimpoche, on whom they had pinned great hopes. The Regent was highly-strung, somewhat immature, capricious, and with a pronounced liking for money. He was generally believed to favour the Chinese and they certainly looked on him as well-disposed towards their ambitions; but his inclination was probably influenced by the generous payments he received and it is improbable that, in the long run, he would either have wanted or been able to do anything fatally compromising to the Tibetan position.

On the basis of a report by another Chinese writer, whose connection with Tibetan affairs is not clear, Li has invested the incident with an air of fantasy. The imaginary, pro-British 'Young Tibet Party' is called in again to explain a set-back to Chinese hopes—in this instance with peculiar ineptness because two of the Regent's close friends were young officials whom the Chinese generally considered to be 'pro-British'. Li suggests that there was a plot to replace the Regent; but the persons named as conspirators were well known to be out of favour with the Regent and his action against them was simply the outcome of personal dislike and official and family feuds. Talk of a plot is speculative wishful-thinking. It is just as unrealistic to allege that 'the increasing dissatisfaction of the British with the Tibetan situation' had anything to do with the resignation of the Regent. On the contrary, the removal of the threat from the Panchen Lama, the peaceful return of the Dalai Lama, and the difficulties of the Chinese in the war with Japan had almost eliminated causes of uneasiness. A disagreement developed later about a Chinese proposal to make roads through Tibet but that did not arise until after the Regent's departure. The suggestion that there had been increased British help to the 'Young Tibet Party' is equally absurd. There was no such party; and whatever help was given to Tibet and Tibetans was given at the request of the Tibetan Government.

The Regent resigned because of increasing unpopularity which was intensified by his harsh treatment of Khyungram Theji, an elderly conservative official, who had criticized the Regent's rapacity. Even the majority of the monks of Lhasa grew critical and ventured to shout opprobrious remarks about the Regent's excessive devotion to money-making. The appointment as successor of an ultra-conservative Lama—the Taktra Rimpoche —makes nonsense of the story that 'pro-British' or progressive 'Young Tibetan' elements had ousted his predecessor. The whole affair was a Tibetan domestic issue and no international significance can be ascribed to it.

The international aspect of Tibetan affairs actually took a shape that was most disconcerting to the Tibetans—in the new relationship of alliance between Britain and China which followed the entry of Japan into the Second World War. Until then the effects of the war on Tibet had been small. Prices of imports rose considerably but, to offset that, higher prices were obtained for Tibetan exports, especially wool. The Tibetan Government, although sympathetic with the allied cause, did not adopt the openly favourable attitude of the XIIIth Dalai Lama during the First World War. They early decided that it would serve their interests best if they remained studiously neutral; and the prayers which they offered were not for the allied cause but, in general terms, for the restoration of peace.

SUPPLY ROUTE FOR CHINA: 1941–1943

Tibetan neutrality was brought into prominence by a Chinese proposal to make roads through Tibet. In the search for new ways of supplementing the tenuous link of the Burma Road, to which the Japanese invasion had reduced the Chinese Government's land supply routes, Chiang Kai-shek gave orders early in 1941 for the building of a road from south-west Szechwan across a corner of south-east Tibet into Assam via the Lohit valley. It appeared that he intended to override political obstacles; but the British Government, whose co-operation in India was essential to the scheme, had its commitments to Tibet to consider and therefore asked that Tibetan consent should be secured. For that purpose the help of the British Mission was offered and an approach was made at Lhasa. It met with firm refusal. The Chinese then bluntly informed the Tibetan Government that they were going ahead with their proposed road. The Tibetan Government, after deliberations by the National Assembly, determined to resist. Both sides were urged by the British Government to come to an agreement, failing which co-operation in India could not be forthcoming; but the Chinese, without further argument, sent a survey party to the Tibetan border. When it tried to enter the country it was turned back by Tibetan troops and, in spite of a visit by a Chinese official from Chinghai, who mixed persuasion and threats, the Tibetans refused to yield.

In this way, by the end of 1941, when the entry of Japan into the war created a new link between Britain and China, relations between China and Tibet, which had for some years been comparatively amicable, once again became acutely embittered. In February 1942 Chiang Kai-shek visited India and, among other things, he pressed for the opening of new supply routes. In view of the military situation and the need to support Chinese morale it was decided to try a rather different approach to the Tibetans. The idea of a new road through south-east Tibet was shelved while other possibilities were examined. As a result, it was proposed that pack transport of essential supplies along existing routes across Tibet should be organized and greatly expanded.

The plan was put to the Tibetan Government persuasively and with a strong recommendation by Rai Bahadur Norbu Dhondup who was then in charge of the British Mission at Lhasa, but the Tibetans declined to consider it, stating that they could not do anything which might affect their neutrality. Their refusal was not accepted as final. Repeated and increasingly stern arguments were used in a series of discussions lasting several months. There were no threats of force but warnings were given of the possible consequences of the loss of British support.

At the same time the Tibetans were under menacing pressure from the Chinese, and in 1942 an armed incursion was made into Tibetan territory from Chinghai. Whether that raid was actually connected with the negotiations about supply routes is not clear but, however that may be, the Tibetans were in a position in which they had not been before—isolated, and under severe pressure from both British and Chinese. They feared that the Chinese would make use of any concession as a loophole for encroachment and they feared becoming involved in other people's wars.

Some sort of statement by the Chinese Government about its general attitude towards Tibetan autonomy might have eased the situation but, as the Tibetans were now apparently bereft of the British support they had formerly enjoyed, the Chinese felt themselves in a commanding position and the most that could be obtained was a verbal assurance that they would not resort to force.

Eventually, as the tension increased, the Regent and Council took matters into their own hands and, sidetracking the still obdurate Assembly, they agreed to allow goods for China, provided they were not military supplies, to pass through Tibet. That was far from being the end of the matter. Once agreement in principle had been secured, it remained to organize and finance the working of the route. The best hope of success was to keep it on a commercial basis; but the Chinese, unwilling to give up their hopes of some political advantage, insisted on setting up official agencies in Tibet. That revived Tibetan fears and opposition. They refused to allow Chinese officials in the country and declined to have direct dealings with the Chinese Government without British participation.

Had the matter been one of vital urgency to China, supplies could have been moved without difficulty by private agencies. That was proved by Chinese firms on both sides of Tibet, who quickly began to hire Tibetan mule and yak transport and to carry consignments of trade goods from India across Tibet into China where they made fabulous profits; but, for the Chinese Government, face and political considerations were both involved. Demands for official participation in the transport arrangements in Tibet were repeated but, so far from consenting, the Tibetan Government gave orders that no goods for the Chinese Government should be allowed to enter Tibet until full agreement had been reached. That unnecessarily provocative action caused irritation and resentment in Chungking. In April 1943 Chiang Kai-shek directed the Governors of Chinghai, Yunnan, and Sikang to move troops to the Tibetan border. His intention was probably to overawe the Tibetans but there may have been the underlying consideration that, if the provincial governors became involved in fighting with Tibet, the Central Government might find an opportunity of moving its own troops into those provinces where they had still no very satisfactory standing. Governor Liu Wen-hui of Sikang was not anxious for an adventure in Tibet. His troops were in bad shape and his personal advantage lay in maintaining peace and trade on the border. General Lung Yun of Yunnan had some good troops but was not prepared to waste them on profitless exploits of that sort. General Ma Pu-feng of Chinghai took advantage of the situation to ask for supplies of arms and ammunition to enable him to carry out the orders of Chungking. He was sent some fourteen lorry-loads of military supplies and he moved his troops to Jyekundo not far from the Tibetan border. The Tibetan Government, after anxious deliberation, decided to fight if Tibet were invaded and sent troops towards the eastern frontier.

Whether Ma Pu-feng seriously intended an invasion is doubtful; but the threat of military action against Tibet while China was supposed to be straining every nerve against the Japanese aggressor was a situation that could not be overlooked by China's allies. The Chinese Government, when approached on the subject, professed ignorance but gave verbal assurances that there was no intention to resort to force. The Tibetan Government was also very ready to agree not to take any military action unless it was attacked. Gradually the tension relaxed; and the Chinese Government, having failed to make any political capital out of the scheme, lost interest in the passage of goods through Tibet. The traffic was left in the hands of private merchants whose activities in competing for a limited amount of transport forced the rate of hire up to fantastic heights—which still allowed them to make large profits on any consignment which could escape the attentions of Chinese provincial frontier officers. The traditional organization of the Tibetan wool trade was upset and Tibetan traders became drawn into somewhat shady business methods.

Even by honest means it was possible for Tibetans to acquire considerable fortunes at this time and it is interesting to see the change which had come over the trade between India and Tibet. The vision of Tibet simply as a profitable field for commerce, which had attracted Hastings, had long given way to a keener interest in the political importance of the country; and, although the prosperous wool business and the return trade to Tibet were a valuable asset to Indian merchant firms on the border—most of which were in the hands of Marwaris—the trade connection had become of greater economic importance to Tibet than to the Indian Government. So much so that when the Indian Government introduced wartime restrictions on the export of wool, special arrangements had to be made for the consignments from Tibet. Controls on such commodities as cotton cloth, kerosene, sugar, and metals met with an outcry from Tibet and special quotas had to be granted for the Tibetan market. Tibetans of every sort were able to secure a part of the quota and to share in a lucrative trade. The demands of the home market, competing with those of the traders who were dealing with China by the recently re-opened overland route, caused a steep rise in prices which went to enrich many established merchants, small shop-keepers, monks, nobles, farmers, and muleteers.

One result of the trade boom was that many more Tibetans began to travel further afield throughout India looking for trade goods. This led to a new interest in learning the ways and language of the outside world and in 1944, at the request of the Tibetan Government, a small school with an English headmaster was opened at Lhasa. Once again the progressives had moved too fast for conservative monastic opinion and after a short but successful existence the school was closed. A few years later the need for some contact with the rest of the world was recognized by sending a number of Tibetan boys, at government expense, for education in schools in Darjeeling run on Western lines.

One side-effect of the crisis over transport through Tibet was that the Government of the United States of America was moved to take an active interest in relations between China and Tibet. Early in 1942 two United States Army officers, Col. Tolstoy and Capt. Dolan, were sent on a mission to examine routes through Tibet. The United States Government was not able to arrange permission to enter Tibet from the Chinese authorities but had to secure it from the Tibetan Government, through the Government of India. That might have opened their eyes to the practical rela-tionship between Tibet and China; and the actual independence of Tibet was also pointed out to the United States Government in a British memorandum in August 1942. But United States' policy was firmly wedded to Chiang Kai-shek, and American officials appear to have relied on Chinese sources of informa-tion and to have based their views on generalizations which were, perhaps, not very carefully checked: for example, the recent report of the International Commission of Jurists on Tibet quotes United States documents as stating that 'Great Britain and the Soviet Union [*sic*] have by various treaties concluded with China acknowledged Chinese suzerainty . . .' over Tibet.

In 1943, when the threat of Chinese aggression against Tibet was brought to their notice, the United States Embassy in Chungking appeared to consider that the danger was exaggerated; but it seems probable that they exerted some pressure on the Chinese Government to prevent a blatant misuse of military supplies, for most of which the Chinese had to rely on their allies. The incident may have given the United States Government cause to reflect on the nature of a suzerain authority which could not even secure peacefully the right of transit through the territory of its so-called vassal.

Later, when the need arose for United States officials to correspond with the Tibetan authorities, they did so in a way which recognized the *de facto* existence of the Tibetan Government and also its neutrality. For example, a message of thanks was sent by the head of the United States diplomatic mission in India for the help given to the crew of a U.S. aircraft which had crashed in Tibet and an assurance was given that U.S. aircraft had been ordered not to fly over Tibetan territory in future. Messages were similarly sent when the Tibetan Government recovered the remains of U.S. airmen whose aircraft had crashed in an inaccessible border area and also when it was expected that a U.S. consular official from Sinkiang, escaping from the imminent arrival of the Communists, would enter Tibet from the north.

THE TIBETAN GOODWILL MISSION: 1944–1946

The events of 1943 and the successful insistence by the Tibetans on their neutrality had brought Tibet more international attention than for some time past and had shown that, whatever political theorists might say, the Tibetan Government could and did follow a course of action completely independent of the Government of China. Those events also led to a restatement of the

British attitude towards Tibet which ought to leave no doubt that the British Government would not recognize Chinese suzerainty over Tibet unless the prescribed conditions were fulfilled by the Chinese. In reply to a Chinese request for clarification of the British position, a memorandum from Sir Anthony Eden to T. V. Soong, the Chinese Foreign Minister, after describing Tibet as having enjoyed *de facto* independence since 1911, stated that the British Government had 'always been prepared to recognize Chinese suzerainty over Tibet but only on the understanding that Tibet is regarded as autonomous'.

In its effect on the Tibetans, the danger of invasion had renewed their fears of Chinese intentions and increased their anxieties through the shock of finding themselves under pressure from the British Government to make concessions to China. Their thoughts turned more strongly to self-defence and they asked the Indian Government to provide further military training for their troops. The grant of quite small-scale facilities at Gyantse was met by protests from the Chinese to the Tibetan Government coupled with threats of military action; but the Tibetans did not take that very seriously. At about the same time the United States Government made a present to the Tibetan Government of several wireless transmitters which were needed to speed up communication between Lhasa and the eastern frontier. That was, perhaps, seen by the Chinese as an indication that Tibet was winning new friends. At all events, their next move was to send another high-ranking official to Lhasa.

In the summer of 1944, Shen Tsung-lien, an adviser of Chiang Kai-shek, went to Lhasa with the aim of finding a settlement of the Tibetan problem. The Tibetans at first raised strong objections, but eventually gave permission for the Chinese party to enter Tibet. Gould visited Lhasa at the same time and the two representatives were able to have frequent discussions in an atmosphere of friendliness and candour.

Li Tieh-tseng considers that Shen's talks with the Tibetan Government met with no success. That is true to the extent that the Tibetan Government made no sweeping concessions; but Shen, an able, unostentatious, and broadminded man well supported by a capable staff, certainly won a higher degree of Tibetan confidence and regard than any of his predecessors. That was, perhaps, to some extent due to the honesty of mind which led him, in his book *Tibet and the Tibetans*, to admit that since 1911 Lhasa had enjoyed full independence for all practical purposes. Shen was also prudent enough not to mention the latest racial theory of Chiang Kai-shek who in *China's Destiny* had put forward a new claim that Hans, Mongols, Manchus, Tibetans, and Tungans were all tribes of a single Chinese race, thus modifying the old theory of The Five Races of China. But, for all his diplomatic ability, Shen had storms to weather, such as that when he organized a parade on VJ Day at which large numbers of Chinese flags were displayed; the performance ended in hostile scenes and the firing of revolver shots by a member of Shen's guard. Further, he was believed by the Tibetan Government to be supporting the Che College of Sera Monastery, which in 1945 was becoming openly critical of the Regent and which was later to play a leading part in an attempt to upset the Tibetan Government.

In spite of those lesser difficulties, Shen scored a tactical success by persuading the Tibetan Government to send an official delegation to China. He informed them, apparently without explaining that he was referring to a Chinese National Assembly, that there was going to be an important meeting at Nanking in May 1946 to discuss future constitutional arrangements and that the Tibetans should send a high-ranking representative. The Tibetan Government decided not to accept the invitation but with typical naïvety and anxiety to avoid giving offence, resolved to send a goodwill mission to both India and China to offer congratulations on the allied victory. They were warned by the British Mission of the pressure to which such a party would be subjected in China. They were also reminded of the provision of their agreements with Great Britain that Tibet should not be represented in any Chinese parliament, to which they replied that they had no intention that their mission should act as parliamentary delegates. The event was to prove that the Tibetan Government overestimated the ability of their officials—untravelled, inexperienced in foreign

Plate 11

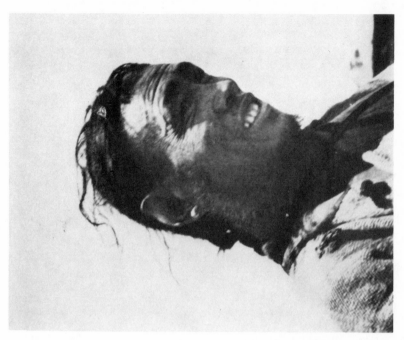

(b) Tibetan farmer

(a) Tibetan yak-herd

Plate 12

(b) Crossing a river

(a) Yak-skin boats

contacts, speaking only Tibetan and lacking qualified interpreters —to hold their own against Chinese wiles.

Early in 1946 the party was welcomed in India with official hospitality and was received by the Viceroy, Lord Wavell, to whom the leaders delivered presents and messages. Even in India they were seen to be under constant surveillance by the Chinese who provided them lavishly with spending money. As soon as they reached China they were announced as delegates to the forthcoming meeting of the National Assembly fixed for 5 May. They delivered their messages of congratulation and were taken on a round of sight-seeing arranged to last until the date of the Assembly. Domestic troubles in China prevented the meeting from being held on the fixed day and it had to be indefinitely postponed. Nevertheless, the Tibetans, in spite of asking for travel facilities, were not allowed to return home. They were kept in China doing nothing, month after month.

In November when it was known that another date had been fixed for the Chinese National Assembly, the Tibetan Government, which had by then become anxious, instructed the mission to deliver a letter to Chiang Kai-shek asking for the return of Tibetan territories still in Chinese hands, and then to return home. But the Chinese, having got the 'innocents abroad' into their web, saw to it that the Tibetans appeared in the Assembly and that one of them was even announced as a member of the Praesidium. The Tibetans tried to get statements published that they were merely observers come to ask for the return of Tibetan territory; but, needless to say, no such statement appeared in any paper.

The Tibetan Government, when asked about reports from China, explained that the mission had been told that the Tibetan Government's letter asking for the return of Tibetan territory could only be answered in the Assembly to which they were invited. The mission had been strictly instructed before they left Lhasa not to sign any sort of document and although they were strongly urged to sign the resolutions of the National Assembly meeting, they declined to do so and made a public demonstration of their refusal.

The incident is an example of Tibetan determination not to

make concessions of substance, but also of their ignorance of foreign conditions and over-confidence in their own ability to handle any situation. The Tibetan Government was not greatly worried by the reports appearing in the Chinese press to the detriment of their position. They argued with bland simplicity that, as what the Chinese said was false, no one was likely to believe it for long. In foreign eyes, the affair might seem to have damaged the Tibetan position but it is apparent from Li Tieh-tseng's account that the Tibetan delegates, in fact, conceded nothing.

There is no doubt that, although the Tibetan Government lacked the skill to put their intentions into practice when it came to competition with the experienced Chinese, they were looking for chances of making the facts of their independence known to the rest of the world. They quickly accepted an invitation to send a delegation to an Asian Relations Conference in India early in 1947. This was organized by the Congress Party of India; it was non-official and by no stretch of the imagination could it be described as 'pro-British'. The Tibetans attended the Conference as an independent delegation, under its own flag, and in no way connected with the Chinese representatives. There was an indignant protest to Pandit Nehru from the Chinese Ministry of Foreign Affairs, after which a map of Asia, showing Tibet outside the boundaries of China, was withdrawn; but the Tibetans by their presence as a separate delegation had scored a clear point.

The visit to India, during which the Tibetan delegates met Mahatma Gandhi and Pandit Nehru, was a step towards the closer relations with Indian leaders which were going to become necessary with the forthcoming transfer of power to the new Government of India and for which the British Mission at Lhasa had been preparing the Tibetans since the end of the war.

XI

WINDS OF CHANGE

THE RETING CONSPIRACY: 1947

About the same time that the Asian Conference was taking place in India, Lhasa was shaken by an attempted *coup d'état* organized by the ex-Regent, the Reting Rimpoche. It is significant that his principal support came from the Che College of Sera Monastery which had for some time been suspected of collusion with the Chinese. In Chinese sources, represented by Li Tieh-tseng, it is stated that the 'Young Tibet Party' had decided to eliminate the ex-Regent and therefore had him arrested on a charge of plotting against his successor. What anyone hoped to gain by 'eliminating' the Reting Rimpoche is nowhere explained.

The course of events, as seen by myself at Lhasa during the crisis, was as follows: on 14 and 15 April the principal representative of the ex-Regent and two other officials suspected of being in collusion with him were arrested at Lhasa and the ex-Regent himself was arrested by a Minister of the Council who had made a speedy journey to his monastery some sixty miles from Lhasa. The reason for the arrests was stated to be that a parcel containing a bomb made from a hand-grenade had been sent to the office of the Regent, the Taktra Rimpoche, with a message that it was to be presented to him as soon as possible. It was opened by a servant who was wounded when the grenade exploded. On 16 April the monks of the Che College of Sera declared their support of the Reting Rimpoche and murdered their abbot when he tried to restrain rebellious talk and warlike preparations. On the same day the Nyung-ne Rimpoche, who was a close associate of the Reting Rimpoche and who by common report had made the bomb, committed suicide. On 18 April the Minister of the Council arrived in Lhasa bringing the ex-Regent with him under escort. As they came near the city the party were fired on from the outskirts of Sera Monastery. On the same day a young

Incarnate Lama connected with Sera Che—the Kartho Rimpoche —was arrested. On the 19th there was desultory firing near Sera and suspicious persons approaching the Dalai Lama's palace of Norbu Lingka were also shot at. On the 20th the Tibetan Government ordered a demonstration against the Che College with a few rounds from their mountain guns. The monks replied with rifles and a home-made cannon. Attempts were then made to negotiate a settlement; and at the same time the trial of the prisoners began before the National Assembly. It had been the intention of the Regent to nominate a small commission to inquire into the conspiracy but under pressure from the great monasteries the trial was transferred to the Assembly where monastic opinion carried great weight. At the hearing, the Reting Rimpoche denied all charges against him; but a detailed and consistent account of the conspiracy was given by the Kartho Rimpoche who broke down under flogging—a customary Tibetan treatment of suspects— and was corroborated by the Reting Rimpoche's principal secretary. It was stated at the trial that the Reting Rimpoche had asked for Chinese help in his attempt and had particularly requested that aeroplanes should be sent to scatter leaflets in his favour coupled with threats of bombing if he were opposed. Official intimation of the events and the trial was sent by the Tibetan Government to the British Mission.

On 27 April, after attempts to negotiate with the Che College had come to nothing, a large-scale attack on it was mounted. By then most of the monks had left the college and only a few remained barricaded inside it. By the 29th resistance had ended in Sera itself, although for some weeks after Tibetan troops pursued fleeing remnants of the hard core of the malcontents from the Che College, many of whom escaped to China where they joined the suite of the late Panchen Lama.

In the end, there were some 200 monks of Che College and 15 Tibetan soldiers killed and 12 badly wounded. During the whole of the crisis, which lasted about three weeks, the ladies of the Tibetan noble families were concentrated under guard in a safe place near the Potala. The officials, both monk and lay, gathered in the Potala itself, all wearing rough, working clothes and carrying arms.

On 8 May the ex-Regent died in prison in the Potala. Although not officially admitted, there can be little doubt that he was murdered; but it is certain that he did not, as stated by Li, have his eyes put out. A few days later, the officials and their families returned to their homes and the Shap-pés invited the Officer in Charge of the British Mission to meet them and hear an official account of the affair.

On 18 May the punishments ordered by the Regent were inflicted. Kartho Rimpoche and the Reting Rimpoche's Chief Secretary were flogged and imprisoned in a specially prepared house. Others of their accomplices—30 monks and one minor lay official—were also flogged, fettered, and entrusted to the custody of members of the nobility. The lay officials who had been arrested at an early stage in the proceedings were found not to have been involved and were released. The monks on whom punishment was inflicted were all from Reting and the Che College of Sera. The attempted coup is therefore seen to have been confined to a comparatively small section of the monastic community. The great monasteries of Drepung and Ganden were not involved; neither were the other two colleges of Sera. The nobility, although a few may have been personally attached to the Reting Rimpoche, were not implicated in any action against the government.

During the trouble the British Mission was entirely unmolested and the wounded from both sides were treated in the Mission hospital. The Mission wireless officer, at the request of the Council, was allowed to set up and maintain the wireless sets belonging to the Tibetan Government which they wished to use at the time of the shelling of the Che College. The statement made by Li Tieh-tseng that the head of the British Mission personally fired guns at Sera monastery is a complete falsehood, and has been withdrawn in later copies of his book.

That the Reting Rimpoche was in communication with the Chinese Government and sought its support is beyond doubt; but it was generally believed in Lhasa that Shen, who had recently returned to China, advised against the sending of aircraft to support him and that Chinese help was limited to financial supplies.

The Reting conspiracy was disturbing to the Tibetan Government not only as a sign of internal dissensions but rather as proof of continuing Chinese machinations just at a time when the transfer of power to a National Government of India was about to sever Tibet's traditional link with the British Government. Although, with the death of the ex-Regent, one potential Chinese danger had been removed, another remained in the supposed reincarnation of the Panchen Lama whom the staff of the late Panchen professed to have discovered and in whom the Chinese were actively interested.

In 1942 there had been ten candidates among whom it was hoped the true incarnation would be found. The Tibetan Government wanted to examine them all and arranged for some of them to be brought to Lhasa; but in 1944 one of the former Panchen Lama's staff who was also a member of the Chinese Central Executive Committee announced that one of the candidates still in China—he was born, like the Dalai Lama, in Chinghai—had been acknowledged and enthroned as Panchen Lama. Such procedure was unprecedented. The selection of a Panchen Lama was the duty of the Dalai Lama (or Regent) and the National Assembly. The Tibetan Government, therefore, declined to recognize the claimant. The Chinese Government, too, did not make any immediate official announcement; but they had, once again, a Pretender in their hands and they hoped to secure Tibetan consent to the choice.

In 1947, just before the Reting conspiracy, it was reported that the child was going to be sent to Lhasa with an escort. The old story of the late Panchen Lama repeated itself in slightly different form. The Tibetan Assembly refused to accept the child until they had seen him, and resolved to fight if any attempt was made by the Chinese to escort him to Tibet. It is probable that the ex-Regent had been kept in touch with the schemes of the Chinese but that his interest in a puppet Panchen Lama was secondary to that of again assuming the Regency. The Chinese Government, at all events, did not press the matter and it was not until 1949 that they decided to give official recognition to the child. Their position *vis-à-vis* the Communists was then desperate and it is not clear why they acted in that way and thereby provided the Communist Government, which almost immediately ousted them, with a ready-made puppet for use against Tibet.

That was for the future. There were other problems to be met first.

THE NEW GOVERNMENT OF INDIA
RISE OF COMMUNIST POWER IN CHINA: 1947–1949

In 1947 the speed with which the British Government was divesting itself of its responsibilities in India caused the Tibetans to wonder whether they were about to be deprived of the diplomatic support they had hitherto enjoyed in their difficulties with China without anything being provided to take its place. They were doubtful about the ability of a future Indian government to give similar help even if it were willing to do so. It was left to the British Mission at Lhasa, with little official guidance, to reassure the Tibetans as far as possible, and it was not until almost the last moment—in July 1947—that formal statements by the British Government and the Government of India were made to the Tibetan Government. They were then informed that after the transfer of power, British obligations and rights under existing treaties with Tibet would devolve upon the successor Government of India and that it was hoped the Tibetan Government would continue with that government the same relations as had formerly existed with the British Government. The British Government assured the Tibetan Government that they would continue to take a friendly interest in the welfare and autonomy of their country and expressed the hope that contact might be maintained by visits to Tibet from British representatives in India. The Tibetan Government acknowledged the message but did not make any immediate reply.

On 15 August 1947 the British Mission at Lhasa formally became the Indian Mission. The transition was almost imperceptible. The existing staff was retained in its entirety and the only obvious change was the change of flag. After about a year the British Civil Surgeon was replaced by an Indian doctor; and an Indian officer joined the British officer in charge of the Mission for training.

In considering their attitude towards the new régime the Tibetan Government contemplated asking the Indian Government to conclude a new treaty with them; but they were dissuaded by the consideration that negotiations of that sort would have given an opportunity for renewed Chinese pressure on Tibet at a time when the Indian Government was not yet securely in the saddle. Nevertheless, the Tibetans did not treat it as a matter of course that they should accept the new situation. They took their time to think over the matter and made it the occasion for airing an idealistic hope that some day all Tibetan-speaking people might be included within the jurisdiction of Lhasa. A message was sent to the new Indian Government asking in general terms for the 'return' of what were described as 'Tibetan territories' from Assam to Ladakh, including mention of such areas as Sikkim and Darjeeling. This was, perhaps, an attempt to test the Indian attitude to border regions where their British predecessors had, by a series of agreements, established the frontiers of India; but it was also an example of the way in which the Tibetans interpreted the political testament of the late Dalai Lama by seeking to balance their actions towards one of their neighbours by similar action towards the other. The request to India was the counterpart of the message conveyed to the Chinese Government by the goodwill mission in 1946, in which they asked, in equally wide terms, for the return of all Tibetan territories still in Chinese hands.

To the message addressed to them, the Indian Government replied that they would be glad to receive an assurance that the Tibetan Government agreed to the continuation of relations on the basis previously existing with the British Government, and suggested that discussion about any new agreements could be taken up later, if necessary. After further deliberation for several months, the Tibetan Government eventually announced their acceptance of the continuation of the former relationship with the new Indian Government.

The effect of the devolution of British obligations and rights upon the new Government of India was that the Indian Government, besides inheriting the British frontier with Tibet, became bound by the Simla Convention of 1914 as between India and Tibet, subject to the modifications introduced by the joint British and Tibetan declarations of the same year. The relationship thus accepted had been most recently defined in the memorandum of 1943, referred to earlier, which had made it clear that there was no unconditional British recognition of Chinese suzerainty over Tibet. The Indian Government also acquired the extra-territorial privileges enjoyed under agreements with Tibet —the right to maintain Trade Agents at Gyantse, Yatung, and Gartok (the last was never a permanent post) with small military escorts; to try cases occurring in the Trade Marts between British subjects; and to hold joint inquiries with the Tibetan authorities into disputes between British subjects and Tibetan or other nationals. A further inheritance was the post and telegraph service and the staging bungalows between the Indian border and Gyantse which had for some time been paid for out of Indian revenues.

Several years later, Pandit Nehru declared that the Indian Government did not want those extra-territorial rights which he implied were a rather disreputable creation of British imperialism. In fact, the rights had never been the subject of Tibetan resentment. The judicial powers had hardly ever been exercised. Tibetan officials and traders made extensive use of the post and telegraph services to their own considerable advantage. Only the military escorts sometimes came under informal criticism from Tibetans who wondered why, in view of the friendly relations between the two countries, any foreign troops need be kept in their country. The answer might have been that, although official opinion in India too often questioned the apparently unnecessary expense of manpower and money which the escorts involved, the right was worth maintaining as a useful bargaining counter in any future negotiations for a settlement with China.

Nehru's protestations should be seen in their proper perspective. The emotional background to his condemnation of acts of the predecessor government can be readily understood but, as this story develops, certain facts will suggest that it was, rather, political expediency which underlay his disapproval of the special rights in Tibet. At all events, in 1947 when an obvious opportunity presented itself for a generous gesture to the Tibetan Government by offering to give up those 'unwanted' rights, nothing of the sort was done. On the contrary, it appeared at that time that the rights were of value to the Indian Government to the same extent as they had been to its predecessor and that the Indian Government was anxious to secure Tibetan consent to the transfer of the whole of the British heritage.

It was not long before the Indian attitude was put to the test. Before the transfer of power the Chinese Government, in an attempt to secure recognition of its claims on Tibet, protested against the activities of officials of the Indian Government in the Assam Tribal Areas south of the McMahon Line. The protests were rejected for the reason that the area was within the accepted frontiers of India. Similar advances were made in 1947 to the new Government of India which treated them in the same way. A different sort of feeler was put out by the Chinese in 1948 with the suggestion that the 1908 Tibetan Trade Regulations were now due for revision. It will be recalled that those Regulations had been cancelled by Article 7 of the Simla Convention of 1914 and replaced by new Regulations signed by the British and Tibetan representatives in the same year. After nearly six months delay the Indian Government replied that it recognized only the validity of the 1914 agreements with Tibet. A protest against that reply was not answered because by then the Chinese Nationalist Government had fallen from power.

In practice, relations between Tibet and India after August 1947 continued on the same footing as before. Whatever misgivings the Tibetans may have had about their dealings with the new Government of India were nothing in comparison with their anxieties about China. Even in 1948 when no one in Lhasa or elsewhere foresaw the speed with which the avalanche was about to descend, the Tibetans were greatly disturbed by a number of baleful portents: one of the gilded dragons which decorate the pagoda roofs of the Jo-khang—the Cathedral of Lhasa—was seen, day after day, to drip water from its mouth although the weather was uniformly dry and no rain fell; a great comet blazed nightly in the sky for several weeks; monstrous births were reported; and the canopy of an ancient stone pillar at the foot of the Potala fell one night, inexplicably, to the ground. Such matters were dealt with in the proper quarter by extraordinary ceremonies to avert evil, in which customary and ancient rites were employed.

In their relations with the world of men the Tibetans became, once again, sensitive about their privacy and were more reluctant than they had been for the past few years to admit foreign visitors. They were also, once more, under pressure from the Chinese Government to send delegates to the first meeting of the new Chinese National Assembly. Again they tried to evade the issue by dispatching a mission, described as a Trade Mission, to India, the United Kingdom, and the United States as well as to China. Although much indignation was aroused in China by the fact that the party travelled with passports issued by the Tibetan Government and accepted as valid documents by the Governments of India, Great Britain, and the United States, the Mission on its arrival in China in April 1949 was at once announced as a delegation to the Assembly; but the evacuation of Nanking before increasing Communist attacks prevented the Nationalist Government from making any convincing use of the presence of Tibetans in their midst. The Mission, in fact, by its reception in Britain and the United States and by the acceptance of Tibetan travel documents, gave some evidence of the practically independent status of Tibet.

Further and very striking evidence of Tibetan independence was given in July 1949 when the Tibetan Government asked the whole of the Chinese official mission at Lhasa, and some Chinese traders also, to leave Tibet. They believed that, with the collapse of the Chinese National Government, the mission at Lhasa had no contact with any official body in China and that some of its members might already be acting as Communist agents. Chinese funds in India, from which the Lhasa mission was financed, were frozen. The Tibetans therefore feared that some if not all of the staff of the Chinese Mission would, if only for the sake of their bread and butter, transfer their allegiance to Mao Tse-tung and the Tibetan Government would thus be faced by an established

Communist foothold in Lhasa. The action was swift and secret. It was a complete surprise to the Indian Mission. It was also embarrassing, in that the Tibetan Government, tardy enough about handling other people's business, expected the Government of India immediately to agree to accept the evicted Chinese mission, some of whom might have Communist sympathies. Even before the agreement of the Indian Government had been received the Chinese were being escorted, courteously and with musical honours, out of Lhasa.

Shortly after taking action against the Chinese Mission the Tibetan Government permitted the American wireless commentator, Lowell Thomas, to visit Lhasa accompanied by his son. It seemed that at last they were becoming alive to the importance of publicity and hoped that through Mr. Thomas they might inform the world of their status and interest it in their difficulties.

Later in the same year the first Indian Political Officer in Sikkim, Harishwar Dayal, visited Lhasa. From 1948 the Tibetan Government had intensified its military preparations. New regiments were raised and the pay and conditions of the soldiers were considerably improved. The need for arms and ammunition was one of the questions put to the Indian Government through Dayal. A favourable reply was received; and, before long, high-ranking military officers visited Sikkim and Gyantse to discuss what could be done. In the upshot, the Tibetans, although anxious to accept arms and ammunition and a limited form of instruction, would not commit themselves to a thorough-going training programme which might have greatly improved their prospects of resisting Communist attacks.

The threat was taking shape; and in their bombastic pronouncements about the 'liberation' of Tibet the Communists were claiming that the new Panchen Lama was supporting their aims. Towards the end of 1949 the Tibetan Government decided for the first time to try its own hand at publicity and, on one or two occasions, statements in English were broadcast from its wireless station at Lhasa denying that the so-called Panchen Lama had been properly recognized and emphasizing the actual independence of Tibet.

With regard to the Indian Government's attitude towards the status of Tibet, the Tibetans had some reason to be anxious. Although the new Government of India continued, as its predecessor had done, to deal with Tibet on the basis of its *de facto* independence, by supplying arms and ammunition and maintaining direct diplomatic contact, the nature of their relations seemed to be misinterpreted in certain pronouncements by Nehru. On more than one occasion he referred publicly to a general recognition of Chinese suzerainty over Tibet. He qualified that statement by describing the suzerainty as 'vague and shadowy'. Nevertheless, the Tibetans were concerned at his disregard for the obligation, which he had inherited under the Simla declaration of 1914, not to accord recognition of Chinese suzerainty over Tibet, of any sort whatsoever, until the Chinese acknowledged Tibetan autonomy in the strict terms of the 1914 Convention. By gratuitously stressing Chinese suzerainty the Indian Prime Minister appeared to serve notice on the Communists that in their designs on Tibet they need not fear any serious opposition from India.

GATHERING CLOUDS

By the beginning of 1950 the momentum of victory had carried the Communists so fast and so far that the only barriers between them and Tibet were the frontier areas of Sikang and Chinghai. It was becoming plain that a move against Tibet was only a question of time, depending on the strength of resistance in the border provinces and on how long the Communists might need to organize an expedition further westwards.

In January 1950 the Indian Government gave formal recognition to the Communist Government of China. That was expedient for more reasons than one. So far as it concerned Tibet, it provided the best hope of preserving Indian interests in that country. The Chinese had never accepted the basis on which the British Government and, consequently, the Indian Government had established its position in Tibet. In such circumstances, if there were no official relations between the Indian Government and the Communists, the prospect was that, in an invasion of

Tibet, Indian representation and rights would simply be pushed out by force or—and this was less probable—the Indian Government would become embroiled with the Chinese by defending its rights there. Once the Communists were recognized, the Government of India could have regular diplomatic exchanges with them. It might even expect some gratitude for being the first non-Communist power to recognize the new régime and it might hope to exercise a moderating influence on Chinese activities in Tibet.

Moderation was certainly not perceptible in Communist pronouncements. A noisy propaganda campaign kept up a flow of charges of Anglo-American intrigue mixed with alternate threats and promises to the Tibetans. At the time, there were three British subjects living in Tibet, myself in the service of the Indian Government as head of their Mission at Lhasa, and two others employed by the Tibetan Government to run their wireless stations. One British subject visited Lhasa to advise on equipment for a small hydro-electric station which the Tibetan Government was planning. The journey of the American citizens, Lowell Thomas and his son, and its objects have been described in a book by Lowell Thomas junior. One other American citizen entered Tibet in 1950, escaping across the northern desert from the Communist occupation of Sinkiang where he had been a language student. On that flimsy foundation, perhaps partly from ignorance but probably as a deliberate policy of self deception and incitement, the Communists built up wild accusations that foreign powers were arming the Tibetans for an attack on China. Perhaps, too, this was a sidelong kick at the Indian Government which had been continuing to supply arms and ammunition to the Tibetans.

By the spring of 1950 the last barriers collapsed when the border governors—particularly Ma Pu-feng of Chinghai, on whom some hope had been pinned—failed to put up any resistance to the Communists. Ma even added to Tibetan embarrassment by asking leave to withdraw with some of his troops through Tibet. At Lhasa there was a great outburst of anxious activity. Military training was carried on to an unheard-of extent. Young officials, both monk and lay, were given arms and some rudimentary instruction from Tibetan army officers in their use and in elementary tactics. The Tibetan Government also decided to send missions to India, Nepal, the United Kingdom, and the United States to explain their case and to ask for help. In addition they chose a party to visit China, in an attempt to come to some sort of understanding with the new régime. Anxiety was increased by a violent earthquake on 15 August which was not only regarded as a very bad omen but also caused great damage and loss of life in East Tibet not far from the threatened border with China.

In the event, only the missions to India and Nepal reached their destination. Neither the United Kingdom nor the United States Government gave any encouragement to the others, while the party for China ran into various difficulties. The Tibetan Government, in its lack of experience and apparently with the vague idea of negotiating on neutral ground, seems to have instructed the mission to go to Hong Kong and meet Communist representatives there. The British Government had not been consulted about the proposal and the Hong Kong authorities were understandably averse from receiving so ambiguous a delegation at such a time. Visas for the journey were not granted but the Tibetans— who displayed no great eagerness to put themselves in Chinese hands by a visit to Peking—were able to meet the recently arrived Chinese Communist Ambassador to India. They had frequent discussions with him and it appears that the Indian Government urged both parties to come to an agreement there; but in Chinese sources it is stated that the Ambassador insisted that the Tibetan delegation should go to China before the end of September.

At the same time, threats of imminent action continued to be uttered by the Chinese propaganda machine. In Peking the Indian Ambassador, Sirdar K. M. Panikkar, made representations to the Chinese Government. It has been claimed by the Chinese that in an *aide mémoire* of 26 August 1950 he referred to Indian acknowledgement of Chinese sovereignty over Tibet. Previously the Indian Government, even though it overstated the position, had been careful to describe China's relationship to Tibet as 'suzerainty'. It seems improbable that they would have authorized their Ambassador to use the word 'sovereignty'. Possibly the Chinese in referring to the *aide mémoire* substituted one word for another, as they appear to have done on a later occasion; but there has been no official explanation of the point.

In reply to his representations Sirdar Panikkar was informed of the Communists' intention to 'liberate' Tibet but was assured—as late as the last week of August—that the use of force was not contemplated. In spite of loudly menacing evidence to the contrary, he appears to have persuaded himself and his Government of the peaceful mood of the Chinese.

The Tibetans in India went on rather ineffectively with their attempts to get visas for Hong Kong but did not, apparently, consider any other way of reaching China. They also continued their talks with the Chinese Communist Ambassador and they were still doing so when, on the 7th of October 1950, Chinese troops launched an attack on East Tibet.

XII

COMMUNIST OCCUPATION OF TIBET

INVASION 1950
TIBETAN APPEAL TO THE UNITED NATIONS

The main attack was in the region of Chamdo, the centre of Tibetan administration on the eastern border. Chinese troops with a large admixture of Khampa irregulars from across the Yangtse were used. The Khampas, as mentioned in the first chapter, are a wild, warlike, feuding sort of people. In spite of their religious loyalty to the Dalai Lama, they had no liking for the Lhasa officials who administered the border areas, and had even devised grand but impractical schemes of themselves taking over control of Tibet. Many of them were deluded by Communist propaganda playing indiscriminately on every sort of local grievance and offering them an independent eastern Tibetan government which had long been one of their vague aims; others were pursuing their own feuds or were simply out for loot. At Chamdo a strong and energetic governor, Lhalu Shap-pé, had just been replaced by a less resolute successor, Ngabo. In spite of individual acts of bravery, the untrained, inexperienced Tibetan troops were quickly overwhelmed and split up. Many were surrounded and had to surrender; and resistance was soon virtually at an end. The story of confusion, divided loyalties and demoralization, and of some fine examples of personal courage and leadership, too, can be read in the books of two British subjects who were captured in the attacks. One of them, Geoffrey Bull, was a missionary on the east side of the upper Yangtse; the other, Robert Ford, was the Tibetan Government's wireless officer at Chamdo.

At the same time as the invasion in the east a small force of Chinese troops from Khotan crossed the Kuen Lun mountains, apparently passing through Indian territory in the barren Aksai Chin region, and entered the uplands of north-west Tibet in a bold drive which took the almost undefended western part of the country completely by surprise. That difficult route had been used only once before by a military force, in 1716 when a Dzungar army from Khotan invaded Tibet. The Communists thus in a few weeks broke well into Tibet on both the east and the west.

With the loss of the Tibetan Government's wireless station in Chamdo, there was for some time no accurate information about events on the important eastern front. As soon as rumours of the attack reached the Government of India a note was dispatched to the Chinese Government expressing concern and suggesting that resort to force would injure the prospects of the admission of the new Government of China to the United Nations. On 26 October, after official reports of the invasion had appeared in the Chinese press, a further note informed the Chinese of the deep regret of the Government of India that their frequent promises to employ peaceful methods towards Tibet should be belied by the use of force. It was also stated that the delay of the Tibetan delegates in reaching China, of which the Chinese Government had previously complained, had not been due to influences inimical to China.

The reply from Peking set the tone for future Chinese communications on the subject of Tibet. It brusquely, almost rudely, declared that Tibet was an integral part of China, the Tibetan problem must be treated as a domestic one and no interference by any foreign country would be tolerated. It was announced that the Communist army would enter Tibet to 'liberate' the people and protect China's frontiers. There was also a suggestion that the Government of India had been infected by foreign influences hostile to China.

That last charge touched the Indian Government on the raw and there is a note of indignation in the reply dated 31 October 1950 repudiating the taint of foreign influence. The Indian Government suggested that a settlement of the Tibetan problem might be possible on the basis of Tibetan autonomy under Chinese suzerainty. It stated that 'Tibetan autonomy is a fact...' and described military operations against Tibet as unprovoked and unjustifiable. It also specified the existing rights of the Government of India in the country which, it claimed, were no detraction from Chinese suzerainty over Tibet, and explained that the Government of India was anxious they should continue. Here may be noted, in parenthesis, the first detailed official reference to those rights which were later to be deprecated as an unwanted relic of imperialism.

The Peking Government was in no mood to argue or to meet the mild reasonableness of the Indian approach in the same vein. Its reply repeated the former position with the addition of the charge that India was trying to prevent the Chinese Government from exercising its sovereignty over Tibet. The Government of India, seemingly taken aback by such aggressive assertion, made no reply.

In Parliament, a statement on 6 November by Mr. Ernest Davies expressed British official support for the attitude adopted by the Indian Government and recalled the assurance given in 1947 about British interest in the maintenance of Tibetan autonomy, which, he said, since 1911 had amounted to *de facto* independence.

While the exchange of notes between India and China was taking place the Tibetan Government, on 7 November, appealed to the United Nations. The case was simply and clearly put, to the following effect: Chinese claims that Tibet is part of China conflict radically with the facts and with Tibetan feelings. Even if the Chinese wanted to press their claim, against Tibetan opposition, there were other methods than the resort to force. The Tibetans described the Chinese attack as clear aggression.

It is difficult to see how the truth of that statement could be questioned, especially by the United Kingdom and Indian Governments which had in succession been treating with Tibet, at least since 1914, as a country enjoying *de facto* independence. Both were well aware that for forty years the Tibetans had resisted all Chinese claims to sovereignty and in that period there had been no trace whatsoever of Chinese authority over Tibet. The United Kingdom had, only three years before, handed over its obligations towards Tibet to the Government of India and could hardly disclaim all responsibility for seeing that they were honoured. Moreover, the Indian Government had, little more than eighteen months earlier, reaffirmed to the former Chinese Government that the agreements of 1914 were the basis of its relations with Tibet. Nevertheless, the Governments of the United Kingdom and India, far from supporting the Tibetan appeal to the United Nations, took a leading part in obstructing it.

Only the Republic of El Salvador had the percipience and the courage to move the condemnation of the unprovoked aggression by the Chinese Communists. It must be recorded with shame that the United Kingdom delegate, pleading ignorance of the exact course of events and uncertainty about the legal position of Tibet, proposed that the matter be deferred. That was supported by the delegate of India, the country most closely affected and, uniquely, bound to Tibet by treaty obligations, who expressed certainty that the differences could be settled by peaceful means which would safeguard Tibetan autonomy. Both the Soviet and the Chinese Nationalist delegates opposed discussion on the ground that Tibet was an integral part of China. The United States delegate agreed to an adjournment solely because of the statement by the Indian representative. The debate was, accordingly, adjourned and the matter not heard of again for nine years. In this way the opportunity was lost of examining the facts when the Chinese were still unsure of world reactions and had not yet proceeded, irrevocably, to extremes. The conduct of the Indian and British Governments amounted to an evasion of their moral duty to make plain what they alone had special reason to know— that there was no legal justification for the Chinese invasion of Tibet. Indeed, subsequent statements by the Indian Prime Minister suggest that he held the surprising view, quite contrary to his Government's arguments to the Chinese in 1950, that the Communist aggression was, somehow, justifiable.

The Tibetans, hardly believing that they could receive such treatment from the civilized world, sent two more agonized telegrams to the United Nations, in the last of which, on 11 December 1950, they asked for a fact-finding commission to be sent to Tibet. They received no answer.

By the end of November 1950 Chinese forces were strongly established in East Tibet and had a footing also in the west of the country. There would have been little, if any, military opposition had they attempted to press on. Perhaps their success had been swifter than they expected and time was needed to reorganize; perhaps the Tibetan reference to the United Nations and the temporizing assurances with which the Chinese had soothed the Government of India made it expedient to delay military measures; but it is more probable that, having demonstrated their overwhelming power, they preferred to complete the conquest of Tibet by the less expensive and less embittering methods of negotiation and political pressure.

After the failure of the appeal to the United Nations, the Dalai Lama, who had been invested with ruling powers although still only sixteen, was advised to leave Lhasa. He and some leading officials travelled to the Chumbi valley from where, if they wanted, they could quickly cross the border into India. The move has been criticized as having added to the demoralization and despair of Tibetan opinion, but by then there was no prospect of successful armed resistance and it was vital to Tibetan morale and powers of negotiation that the Dalai Lama should not fall into Chinese hands as a prisoner. The Communists must have been well aware, as was Chao Erh-fêng in 1910, that the best instrument of any policy of peaceful domination of Tibet was the control of the person of the Dalai Lama. They could, therefore, be expected to use some moderation so long as there was the danger that he might slip over the border into India.

For about four months there was an exchange of messages between the Chinese and the Tibetans in which a leading part was taken by the minister Ngabo, Governor of Chamdo, who had been captured by the Chinese invading forces. From then onwards he has been, after the Panchen Lama, the most important puppet of the Chinese in Tibet. Eventually in April 1951 a Tibetan delegation, headed by the captive Ngabo and containing other high officials from Lhasa, began negotiations in Peking which ended in the signing on 23 May of a Sino-Tibetan Agreement 'for the peaceful Liberation of Tibet'.

An explanation will inevitably be sought for the overpowering desire to possess Tibet which led the Chinese Communists to acts of aggression. There was no hostile move by the Tibetans to account for it. The only answer that appears essentially satisfactory goes deeply into Chinese character and the Chinese past.

The Chinese have, as is well known, a profound regard for history. But history, for them, was not simply a scientific study. It had the features of a cult, akin to ancestor worship, with the ritual object of presenting the past, favourably emended and touched up, as a model for current political action. It had to conform also to the mystical view of China as the Centre of the World, the Universal Empire in which every other country had a natural urge to become a part. The conflict of that concept of history with the violent intrusion of the outside world in the latter part of the nineteenth century led to the obdurate irredentism with which the Republican and Nationalist Governments of China persisted, against all the facts, in claiming that Tibet had always been part of the Chinese fold and was longing to return to it. In the absence of any voice of protest from Tibet, their persistence made some effect even on the minds of other countries.

In spite of the adoption of Western political ideas, the Communists, like their predecessors, continued to be influenced by the traditions of their ancestors. They inherited the same peculiar historical perspective embittered in the more recent past by resentment at the humiliation and exploitation inflicted by the West; and they were the first Chinese to have the power to convert their atavistic theories into fact. They saw their opportunity, calculated that no one was likely to oppose them, and acted.

Many other reasons have been suggested: that the occupation of Tibet appeared to be a strategic or defensive necessity; that there were ideas of economic development or more living room; that Tibet might become a reservoir for reactionary feeling and reactionary organizations; that the zeal of newly converted Communists drove the Chinese to spread their doctrine wherever they could. Those considerations might give colour to the Chinese action and they have varying degrees of force in their own right but, it is submitted, they were no more than secondary to the main object of making good an ancient pretension.

SINO-TIBETAN AGREEMENT OF 1951

The agreement of 23 May 1951, of which the text will be found in the Appendix, pp. 275, was the first treaty concluded between Tibet and China since that of A.D. 821. The Tibetans had no choice but to sign what was put before them. Chinese troops were in occupation of their eastern and western districts, ready to renew operations at any moment.

The long, tendentious manifesto, masquerading as the preamble to the agreement, in which the Chinese took the opportunity of falsifying history and justifying the use of force, cannot conceal that Tibet had lately been a separate entity. The country's future role was defined as part of 'The Motherland', with national regional autonomy under the unified leadership of the Central People's Government.

The provisions of the agreement were artfully drawn up in such a way that they appeared to promise the survival of the characteristic Tibetan form of government. Article 4 pledged the Central Government not to alter the existing political system in Tibet or the status, functions, and powers of the Dalai Lama. Article 7 provided for the protection of established religious customs and institutions. Article 11 declared that there should be no compulsion to reform on the part of the Central authorities.

Those were the principal elements of regional autonomy. The other side of the picture—the establishment of unified central control—prescribed, among other things, the integration of the Tibetan army in the Chinese forces and the appointment of a military and administrative committee at Lhasa to implement the agreement. This transaction, concluded without any reference to the Government of India and including provision for the unrestricted entry of Chinese troops into Tibet and the establishment of a Military and Civil Headquarters at Lhasa, was clearly incompatible with the terms of the 1914 agreements between Tibet and India. But by failing to mention the treaty basis of its interest and its rights in Tibet, either in the exchange of notes with the Chinese Communist Government or at the United Nations, the Indian Government had given plain indications that it no longer regarded the 1914 agreements as viable. Nevertheless, the Sino-Tibetan pact did not necessarily exclude the continuation of a special connection between India and Tibet. It might, also, have meant little more than the establishment of a Chinese protectorate of the kind formerly exercised through the Ambans; and some Tibetans, in particular the monks whose view of China was still coloured by outdated memories of the religious link with the Manchu emperors, believed that the guarantees of their religion and government were substantial and sincere. Everything depended on how the agreement was put into effect by the dominant power; and there was no good cause to expect that the Communists would tolerate the presence of an (Indian) third party or show any measure of liberality and lenience towards Tibetan hopes of self-government.

The British Government's view was expressed on 6 June by their spokesman, Mr. Kenneth Younger, who observed that the agreement purported to guarantee Tibetan autonomy but that there were grave doubts of the value of the guarantees.

The Chinese began carefully but with determination. Their first object was to establish complete physical domination of the country and its government. In July 1951 General Chang Ching-wu, newly appointed Commissioner and Administrator of Civil and Military Affairs in Tibet, travelled through India and met the Dalai Lama in the Chumbi valley. At his request, reinforced by the appeals of the monks, the Dalai Lama soon afterwards returned to Lhasa.

Chinese military occupation was swiftly and smoothly carried out, making use of motor and air transport for the first time in Tibet. At first some 3,000 picked troops were enough for Lhasa and 20,000 more were distributed at key points throughout Tibet. The build-up of forces in Eastern Tibet continued but as the number of troops that could be maintained in Tibet itself depended on adequate communications, the construction of roads for motor traffic was the prime necessity. That work was pressed on with along two main routes from China to Lhasa and on others in the far west of Tibet with impressive efficiency, although without regard for human life. Air-strips were also prepared in several places.

By November 1951 it was clear that, to effect their aim of political domination, the Chinese intended to use the old form of government as their instrument and mouthpiece to control every aspect of Tibetan domestic affairs. The presence of the Dalai Lama at Lhasa was an essential part of that design; but an equally important part was the reduction of his absolute power and divine prestige. Inroads on his authority and on that of the monasteries, from which much of his support was derived, began almost at once.

Early in 1952 the Chinese demanded the dismissal of two Chief Ministers and insisted, in writing, that no new appointments should be made without their consent. Later, in breach of their undertaking to maintain the existing political system and the powers and status of the Dalai Lama, the Chinese sought to appoint him and the puppet Panchen Lama as members of a Consultative Committee and thus put him on a level with other Committee members; they divided Tibet into three administrative regions in an attempt to reduce the extent of the Dalai Lama's authority; they proposed to remove from his personal control the monastic branch of the administration and to combine its officials with those of the lay civil service. As a counterweight to the Dalai Lama the position of the Panchen Lama was built up by conferring on him powers, including the right to maintain an army, which he had never previously enjoyed.

The position of the monasteries in Tibet proper was attacked mainly by derogatory propaganda, by inroads on their position as bankers and general advisers in country districts, and by restricting their special privilege of assuming the administration of Lhasa city at certain festivals. The fate of Tibetan monasteries east of the Yangtse is a matter for later consideration.

In the machinery of administration the Chinese retained in their posts the officials of the old nobility and the monastic service and sought to impose on the government, through them, the pattern which Peking wanted to follow. Apart from a few persons of exceptional spirit, such as the two ministers who were removed for opposing Chinese actions, Tibetan officialdom, both monk and noble, did as they had done at those times when the Manchu emperors sought to assert authority in Tibet—they ostensibly acquiesced in the new arrangements while constantly trying to obstruct and delay changes and to blunt the edge of Chinese zeal. In order to accustom the minds of the Tibetans to change and to new ideas, the Chinese arranged for many parties of visitors to go to China where they were shown all the wonders of modern progress. Lamas, senior officials, and village headmen were included in these groups but particular attention was devoted to young, intelligent monks, young nobles, and commoners of good standing, many of whom were given scholarships for two or three years in schools and colleges of various sorts in China.

When it came to dealing with the peasants, the Chinese found themselves in some difficulty. Before and during their invasion they had made propaganda about oppressive landlords, redistribution of land and so on; but when they took over at Lhasa they found no ready response to their overtures. On the other hand, the Dalai Lama himself, who had been considering his country's need of some progressive measures even before he was invested with ruling power, almost immediately on his return to Lhasa put forward his own proposals for radical reform of the land tenure system. His plan was to resume the estates of the big landholders and of the monasteries on payment of proper compensation and to redistribute them on the basis that the former holders and the peasants—who would receive larger holdings than previously—should all be direct tenants of the state. The Chinese Administrator, perhaps wanting to keep a monopoly of such reforms in Communist hands, objected; and it must, unfortunately, be recorded that it was not difficult for him to find support from the landlords whose property would have been affected. Although his main design was thwarted, the Dalai Lama established his own office for social reform through which he brought to an end some long-standing service demands—such as the provision of unpaid transport—and also decreed the cancellation of agricultural debts and the grant of loans of seed. In this way he took much of the wind out of the Communists' sails. They concentrated therefore on what may be called the benefits of Western science.

Generally speaking, in spite of a barely concealed dislike for the monks, the Chinese in their early contacts with Tibetan officials and people made a genuine effort to be disciplined and to appear friendly and co-operative. Being recent converts to a new ideology and a new way of life, and having shaken off a corrupt and un-popular government, they probably imagined the Tibetans to be in a like case and expected them to welcome the progress and change which they were being offered. Some of those offerings were potentially of real value. Western medicine had been feared by the monks as a danger to their authority; but inroads into that position had been made by the popular acceptance of vaccination since, at least, the beginning of the century. The continuous presence, since 1936, of a small but efficient hospital at the British and Indian Mission at Lhasa had been increasingly welcomed by the lay nobility, large numbers of the common people, and even by many Lamas and ordinary monks. The provision of hospitals and medical training by the Chinese was therefore a beneficial measure for which some preparation had already been made. There was, also, great scope for improvement in agriculture, stock-breeding, irrigation, forestry, and so on. There, too, small beginnings had been made during the British and Indian connection with Tibet and much could be done even without introducing mechanical methods, to which conservative opinion was disposed to object.

The use of motor vehicles, exploration of mineral resources, and introduction of small industries are on rather a different footing. Such innovations portended a new direction of Tibetan life and thought and a breach in that comparative isolation which the Tibetans had hitherto deliberately cultivated. The provision of schools teaching new and foreign ideas is rather similar. Two attempts by the Tibetan Government to start small schools of that sort during the British connection had been brought to nothing by conservative opposition; and although, in Western eyes, the provision of education might be deemed a benefit for the

Tibetans, the big question remained what sort of education would be given.

All the innovating and improving activities of the Chinese had at least two objects—to win popularity and to win minds. The Tibetan people were always curious. They enjoyed seeing or doing something new and were quite prepared to try—at least for a time —such things as Western medicines, seeds, agricultural implements, and motor transport but, to judge from subsequent events, they did so without any feeling of gratitude. A few young nobles, with feelings natural to their years, were temporarily carried away by the attraction of such things as motor-bicycles and by the specious and artfully presented prospect of doing good service to their country by accepting Chinese offers of modernization. But for the most part, neither monks nor laymen took readily to regimentation or attempts to change their way of thinking; and their traditional feeling of separateness caused them to resent deeply all interference in their national domestic affairs and their familiar customs and institutions.

It was not long before the Chinese discovered that, far from being accepted as members of the same family, they were treated with suspicion as intrusive foreigners. Such feelings were made more acute by the trouble which had repeatedly embittered relations between the Tibetans and the Chinese ever since the first Manchu expedition to Lhasa in 1720. The great influx of outsiders brought scarcity of supplies and rocketing prices. Not only did the Chinese empty the Tibetan reserves of grain for the needs of their large armies, they also contrived to borrow—as they put it—some of the country's stored resources of gold and silver. Within less than a year there were signs of growing tension and discontent among the common people. The monks, too, were becoming more openly hostile when they found that, in spite of Chinese promises to respect their religion, a draft constitution was being circulated in which religion was given a very small place. Their discontent led the Chinese to demand the surrender of all weapons held in monasteries and that, in turn, increased the monks' hostility. There were already hints of some sort of organized resistance movement in the widespread distribution of copies of the XIIIth Dalai Lama's political testament, the prevention of most Tibetans from attending social meetings with the Chinese, constant vocal complaints against any interference with existing institutions, and frequent clashes with Chinese workers.

The Chinese gradually lost their initial benevolence and a harder note crept in. The intention to settle 40,000 families of Chinese farmers in Tibet was announced; and, when the roads from China to Lhasa were completed in 1954, there was a great increase in the military forces of occupation.

SINO-INDIAN AGREEMENT OF 1954

Relations between India and China with regard to Tibet remained to be settled. Mention has been made of the acid exchange of notes in 1950 when the Indian Government drew attention, in detail, to its rights in Tibet but failed to secure a response. Later, in December of the same year, the Indian Government made a further direct overture to Peking on the same issue and was coldly informed that no 'unequal treaty' could be allowed to stand.

Faced with that uncompromising denial of the basis of its relations with Tibet, which it had underlined less than two years before by restating its dependence on the Simla Agreements, the Government of India somewhat tamely gave up serious efforts to vindicate the legal origin of its claims. After 1950 its attitude towards its former connection with Tibet became ambiguous and ill-defined.

At first, questions about Indian rights in Tibet were mainly theoretical but when the Chinese took control of the country after the Sino-Tibetan Agreement of 1951 they could not fail to see for themselves the effective existence of those rights. There was an Indian representative at Lhasa and others at Gyantse and Yatung, at each of which places there was an escort of Indian troops. There were also, between Sikkim and Gyantse, a post and telegraph service and a chain of official rest-houses efficiently maintained by Indian staff.

In December 1951 it was rumoured that the Chinese Government 'had asked for the withdrawal of Indian officials from Tibet. That was promptly denied by the Government of India and it is improbable that the Chinese made any such suggestion. They still found it convenient to have communications and a supply route available to them from India and it would have been imprudent to jeopardize Indian goodwill at that stage. It suited their book to preserve official silence and leave it to the Indian Government to make the overtures.

The first move in that direction was the announcement from New Delhi in September 1952 that, as Tibet's foreign relations were now being conducted by the Chinese Government, the designation of the Indian representative at Lhasa would be changed to Consul-General and the Trade Agencies in Tibet would be under his supervision. That decision adroitly transformed the temporary mission at Lhasa into a regular consular post. But it was a practical admission of the fact that Tibet had ceased to be independent and it left unresolved the fate of the special rights acquired when Tibet had been in a position to make its own treaties with foreign powers and enjoyed by the British and Indian Governments for nearly half a century. In December 1953, after a further year in uneasy occupancy of its former position in Tibet, the Indian Government took the initiative in proposing negotiations at Peking to settle outstanding issues between the two countries. About four months later there emerged the Sino-Indian Agreement of 29 April 1954 (Appendix, p. 278).

The central provisions of the Agreement were of comparatively small significance. They dealt with the number, places, and regulation of trade markets, and routes and procedure for trade and pilgrims. The Chinese secured the right to open trade agencies at New Delhi, Calcutta, and Kalimpong in return for the Indian right to similar agencies at Gyantse, Yatung, and Gartok. It is noticeable that, although the subject matter of the provisions was for the most part concerned with routes and markets in Tibet which had existed for a long time, the wording referred to the 'establishment' of such facilities as though they were something completely new. The treaty provisions were supplemented by

Notes dealing with the withdrawal of the Indian military escorts, and the handing over of Indian post and telegraph facilities and the Indian rest-houses to the Chinese. Again, although these were long-standing institutions, there was no hint in the Notes to show how they had originally come into existence or on what treaty they were based.

So far as the status of Tibet was affected, the most important part of the agreement was the acceptance by the Indian Government, in the preamble, and in frequent references to 'The Tibet Region of China', of the position that Tibet forms an integral part of China. That is something which no Indian Government had previously admitted; and in the circumstances of 1954 it amounted to the countersignature by India of the death warrant of Tibetan independence. The result was underlined still further by that part of the agreement which is probably the most widely known and which Nehru was to hold up as a model for the solution of the troubles of the world—the Panch Shila, or Five Principles of peaceful coexistence and friendly co-operation. By those Principles the Indian Government pledged itself *inter alia* to respect the territorial integrity and to refrain from interference in the internal affairs of China—in which it now included Tibet. India thus effectually debarred herself even from making any representations to the Chinese Government about the 'autonomy' of Tibet, in which, by Nehru's own statements, the Indian Government had been especially interested and which in the 1951 Sino-Tibetan Agreement the Chinese had bound themselves to maintain.

What the Indian Government secured, in return for its concessions and withdrawals, was the right to retain representation in Tibet and the belief that the Five Principles guaranteed Chinese good neighbourliness and acceptance of the McMahon Line frontier and the other existing frontiers between India and Tibet. The arrangements about trade and pilgrimage were of secondary importance, depending as they did on Chinese goodwill.

There was some Indian criticism of this settlement both on practical and moral grounds. The former, bewailing the surrender of Indian rights and interests in Tibet, can hardly be considered realistic. The rights in themselves were of small importance. Their value was that they reflected a political influence which could not be expected to survive in the face of external domination of Tibet by an aggressively nationalist China. They served their turn as bargaining counters and even though the Indian Government might have made better use of those counters, it would have found itself treated even worse in its agreement with China if they had not existed. It was in answering criticism of the surrender of those rights—which the Indian Government had enjoyed for nearly seven years and had improved upon by increasing the strength of their military detachments in Tibet—that Nehru first described them as improper and unwanted. None of the critics appears to have pointed out that what the Indian Government was handing over to the Chinese had originally been granted directly by the Tibetans.

There is more substance in the moral criticism which was stated in its sharpest form by Acharya Kripalani in the Indian Parliament on 19 August 1958 when he described the Panch Shila as 'born in sin to put the seal of our approval upon the destruction of an ancient nation which was associated with us spiritually and culturally'. Such attacks could have been even more penetrating if the Indian public had been aware of the fact, which their Government had never revealed, that until the forcible occupation of Tibet by the Communists, India had been associated with that country also by a treaty obligation to withhold recognition even of Chinese suzerainty over Tibet and had been dealing with the Tibetan Government as in practice independent.

That is the point where the conduct of the Indian Government is most open to criticism: that the enunciation of those high-sounding principles should be based on Indian acquiescence in the extinction of Tibetan freedom and territorial integrity and that the long-standing treaty connection between India and a *de facto* independent Tibet—officially acknowledged only five years before—should be allowed to be wiped out without its existence ever being mentioned.

It is a bitter reflection that the main advantage which the Indian Government believed it had secured through that moral surrender—respect for its established frontier with Tibet—soon proved to be an illusion. Probably few people outside New Delhi believed at the time that the lofty generalities of the Five Principles were anything more than pious aspirations or even that the two parties interpreted their undertakings in the same way. There were early portents that might have raised doubts in Nehru's mind. Chou En-lai, when he visited India soon after the conclusion of the Agreement, was noticeably cold and aloof. What Nehru himself learnt from his return visit to China in October of the same year can only be conjectured; but he had at the time cause to complain that the Chinese were sheltering the Nepalese trouble-maker, Dr K. I. Singh. Later in the year Chinese maps were published of a sort against which the Indian Government had previously protested, showing large stretches of Indian territory as part of China. But over four years more were to pass before Nehru, who had stuck nobly, if blindly, to his faith in the Chinese, reached the sad conclusion, forced on him by aggressive Chinese infringements of Indian frontiers, that he had been completely misled by their professions of friendship.

In a tail-piece to the treaty of 29 April 1954, the Indian and Chinese Governments signed, in October, a separate agreement about trade. It covered the 'customary right' of Indian traders to enter the country on business and special arrangements for the transit through Calcutta of Chinese goods for Tibet. In that agreement Tibet was treated, at Indian insistence, not simply as a part of China but as a special territory. It was a gesture, but too late to be of value. The pass had already been sold by the Panch Shila and by India's acknowledgement of Tibet as an integral part of China.

UNEASY CALM: 1954-1956

Between 1954 and 1956 conditions in Tibet were comparatively peaceful—so far as such a word can be applied to any part of Tibetan relations with China after 1950. In spite of occasional alarms there was no serious outbreak of violence at Lhasa. The

Chinese, while trying to refrain from obvious provocation, continued to extend their own influence and ideas and to depreciate the existing system.

In the autumn of 1954 the Dalai Lama and Panchen Lama visited Peking. Mao Tse-tung himself appears to have lavished flattery on the Dalai Lama; and the prospect, beloved by the Tibetans, of uniting all Tibetan peoples under one government was aired in the most deceptively favourable light. There was also much public talk about the excellent relations existing and the progress reputedly being made in Tibet under the new régime. In fact, beyond the rapid extension of strategic communications material progress in Tibet at the time amounted to little more than a few eye-catching exhibitions which might serve as the basis for later developments.

Although the surface was reasonably placid, there was trouble brewing beneath. As early as 1954 occasional reports reached India of the growth of a popular movement inculcating passive resistance and secret sabotage. The Dalai Lama's departure for China in September 1954 and the length of his stay there caused great anxiety and discontent, but fear of unfavourable effects on the absent Dalai Lama kept Tibetan animosity under control. His return to Lhasa in March 1955 was followed by arrangements for the inauguration of a 'Unified Preparatory Committee for the Autonomous Region of Tibet' which had been announced while the Dalai Lama was in Peking. That proposal was resented in Tibet as a further inroad on the Dalai Lama's authority by aiming to subdivide it and impose Chinese influence at the head of each of the subdivisions. The formal inauguration of the Committee was in October of that year and although there was no noticeable increase in the expression of discontent at Lhasa, developments were taking place in Eastern Tibet which were soon to change the whole atmosphere by breaking out into open warfare. The course of events there, which was largely concealed at the time by the Communists' stranglehold on news, was described in detail by Tibetan refugees who reached India in 1959. It will be recalled that when the Chinese invaded Tibet in 1950 they exploited the traditional mistrust of Lhasa officialdom existing

among the Khampa and Amdowa tribes to the east of the upper
Yangtse. For several years, while the construction of the new roads
to Lhasa through Khampa territory was in progress, the Chinese
treated the people generally with restraint. At the start some leading men and others alleged to have been supporters of the Nationalist Government were put to death. But after that initial purge,
Communist activities were mainly devoted to indoctrinating the
young in newly established schools or by taking children for
teaching elsewhere. Propaganda against religion and landlords
was also carried on in a fairly quiet manner. But towards the end
of 1954, once the need for conciliation was past, the Chinese
took active steps to make themselves masters of the country and
to impose their communist ideas.

In a sturdy, independent society where every man carried arms,
the first aim was to get hold of their weapons. Resistance to
that, which showed itself in open discontent and sabotage, led
to a change in Chinese methods. New forms of taxation were
introduced on land, cattle, and houses, also on the value of the
contents of monasteries. Large estates were confiscated and redistribution of land followed, with the customary Communist
accompaniment of humiliating punishments publicly inflicted
on the landowners. Some executions also took place. At the same
time attacks on religion became more violent. Lamas were
assaulted and humiliated; some were put to death. The ordinary
people who refused Chinese orders to give up the practice of
religion were beaten and had their goods confiscated. Attacks on
their religion, property, and social system inflamed the people
to furious resistance, in which their usual fierce loyalty to the
individual clan was absorbed in a wider unity of all Amdo and
Kham. An active guerrilla force quickly came into being in all
parts of the country and by the late spring of 1956 extensive
destruction of roads and bridges and widespread raiding of supply
columns and outposts had compelled the Chinese to undertake a
large-scale military operation with armoured vehicles and aircraft. Monasteries such as Changtreng—which had a traditional
reputation for hostility to the Chinese—Litang, and Batang were
singled out as centres of resistance and were destroyed by shelling

or aerial bombardment. Savage punishment and repression were inflicted on such villagers as remained in their homes and large numbers of Chinese settlers were poured in to take over the land of the dispossessed. The rising spread all over the areas formerly known to the Chinese as Sikang and Chinghai and even had repercussions in Sinkiang. Details of Chinese atrocities in their treatment of the Khampas can be read in the second report of the International Commission of Jurists, published on 8 August 1960. Eye-witnesses have described how monks and laymen were tortured and many killed, often in barbarous ways; women raped and others publicly humiliated; venerated Lamas subjected to brutal and disgusting degradations; other monks and Lamas compelled to break their religious vows; men and boys deported or put to forced labour in harsh conditions; boys and girls taken from their homes, ostensibly for education in China; children incited to abuse and beat their parents; private property seized; monasteries damaged by gunfire; and sacred images, books, and relics carried off or publicly destroyed.

In July 1956 the Dalai Lama sent a delegation including the puppet Minister Ngabo and a highly respected Incarnate Lama of Khampa birth to try to pacify the area. This was probably done at Chinese instigation but it may well have been in the mind of the Dalai Lama that open warfare with China could only lead to harsher measures which might destroy the precarious remnant of Tibetan individuality. The mission failed to shake Khampa and Amdowa determination to resist, and, after a brief lull, fighting went on as fiercely as before.

That was the state of affairs when the Dalai Lama and Panchen Lama visited India in November 1956. An invitation to attend the 2,500th anniversary of the birth of the Lord Buddha had been sent to the Dalai Lama at the end of 1955 but the Chinese did not agree to its being accepted. A further invitation in the summer of 1956 was not answered until a very short time before the beginning of the celebrations, when it was learnt that the Dalai Lama would come to India. The change of mind seems to have been due to the bitter resentment of the people of Lhasa against restrictions being placed on the Dalai Lama's movements, to pressure from the Lama himself and his government at a time when the troubles in the east made the Chinese anxious to have no disturbance in Central Tibet, and perhaps to informal representations by the Indian Government about the effect on Indian opinion if the Dalai Lama should not attend such an important Buddhist occasion. In the event, the serenity and unaffected sanctity of the Dalai Lama, which did not prevent him from being also gay and friendly, won the reverent admiration and sympathy of the Indian people.

A visit of Chou En-lai, the Chinese Prime Minister, was arranged to coincide with that of the Dalai Lama, and the Tibetan Government set great hopes on the prospect of discussions between him and the Dalai Lama on neutral ground. They may have believed that the trouble in East Tibet would incline the Chinese to be conciliatory. The Dalai Lama put forward four requests: the removal of Chinese troops from Tibet; the restoration of the status existing at the death of the XIIIth Dalai Lama; the reinstatement of the Chief Ministers dismissed in 1952 at Chinese instigation; and the abandonment of the Communist programme of reform. It was asking a great deal and the reception was not favourable. Indeed, the Dalai Lama appears to have been so deeply discouraged by the Chinese attitude that he contemplated seeking political asylum in India and not returning to Tibet. He discussed his doubts with Nehru and Nehru informed Chou En-lai, from whom he obtained what he believed to be satisfactory assurance that the Chinese would respect Tibetan autonomy as guaranteed by the 1951 Agreement and that they would not force reforms on the Tibetans. He communicated those undertakings to the Dalai Lama and advised him to return to Tibet. Not long afterwards, in February 1957, Mao Tse-tung announced that Tibet was not yet ready for reforms and that their introduction would be postponed for at least five years.

The Chinese Government carried this show of conciliation further by removing some of their troops from Tibet and by withdrawing the 'political cadres' who were principally charged with the introduction of reforms. Work on such things as new schools, barracks, and a hydro-electric plant was stopped. Those examples of slowing down material progress were astute and prudent and gave the appearance of respect for Tibetan views. Chinese spokesmen admitted that only a small part of the Tibetan masses wanted reforms. There was also considerable self-criticism in the Chinese press, and many mistakes in dealing with Tibet were admitted including 'Great Hanism', bureaucratism, failure to respect local customs and even violence and lawlessness by some Chinese workers. But that did not affect Chinese determination to harden their grip on the all-important political controls. They pressed on with the work of the Preparatory Committee whose aim was to reduce the Dalai Lama's authority.

Perhaps the loss of face in having to admit Indian mediation in what they had unyieldingly claimed as a domestic affair made the Chinese more set on asserting their actual mastery but there were other pressing reasons which made control of the Tibetan Government vitally important. The widespread warfare in the east and schemes for Chinese colonization there had driven many warrior Khampas from their homes. Many young monks, too, had left the monasteries even though the Chinese, as a gesture of conciliation or to conceal what they had done, had begun to rebuild and repair those they had damaged by bombing and shelling. Early in 1958 large numbers of guerrilla bands from the east had made their way into Central Tibet, and hundreds of lay and monk refugees from Kham and Amdo had flocked into Lhasa.

If there had been trust and co-operation between the East Tibetan leaders and the Lhasa Government from the start, the difficulties of the Chinese would have been many times greater. But the two were incompatible. For many centuries the policy of Lhasa had been to yield to force when it appeared irresistible and to look to time and patience to bring their reward. The Khampas' nature was quite the opposite. And so, although there was some ground for their criticism of Lhasa officials as timorous and selfish, it would be unreasonable to expect those officials to give unstinted cordiality and confidence to persons who had recently been plotting their overthrow. But the Khampas and Amdowas were Tibetans; and feelings at Lhasa had been deeply stirred by their terrible sufferings and devoted bravery in the common cause of freedom and religion. The appearance of guerrilla fighters in the near neighbourhood of Lhasa caused greatly increased activity among the local resistance groups and there is little doubt that the Tibetan Government gave clandestine assistance to them. Tension and discontent at Lhasa were further aggravated by overcrowding and by scarcity of supplies following the influx of refugees.

All this seriously disturbed the Chinese and in April 1958 a special body of secret police was sent to Lhasa to root out 're-actionaries'. In an effort to ease the difficulties at Lhasa, they arbitrarily expelled large batches of the male population. That simply added to the strength of the guerrilla forces which by May were alleged to number about 10,000 and were able to annihilate a Chinese military post of 1,000 men within twenty-five miles of Lhasa.

Earlier in the year, when the situation appeared to be deteriorating, the Dalai Lama and his government had sought once more to enlist the help of Nehru. They contrived to put enough pressure on the Chinese Government to invite him to Lhasa. Nehru accepted and it had been expected that he would meet Chou En-lai there in April or May 1958, but the atmosphere was so inflammable that the visit was put off; and in July the Chinese had to ask Nehru to postpone it indefinitely. That was another loss of face. Previously, in the spring of 1957, after initial denials that there had been any trouble in East Tibet, Chinese official circles had admitted that a revolt had taken place in West Szechwan but had been suppressed. Now it could not be concealed that things were going badly at Lhasa itself. In spite of this clear indication and in spite of frequent attempts by Tibetan officials, who succeeded in entering India from Tibet, to explain what was happening, there was a tendency in Indian official circles to play down the whole business. That was inspired, no doubt, by prudent motives, but by the late winter of 1958 it was becoming obvious to disinterested observers that a serious explosion was in the making.

XIII

THE TIBETAN RISING

THE STORM BREAKS

By the autumn of 1958 the guerrillas had grown so strong that they were able to overwhelm and wipe out the garrison of some 3,000 men at Tsetang, the main Chinese stronghold in the valley of the Tsang-po (Upper Brahmaputra), and to secure almost complete control of all districts of Tibet to the south of that river. Fighting also continued in many parts of East Tibet and Chinese communications with Lhasa were restricted by heavy attacks on the roads to Lhasa; but they could now be supplemented, to some extent, by a new route from Sinkiang into N.W. Tibet and by air. The first step taken by the Chinese to meet the trouble was to safeguard their existing positions by bringing in more and better troops to stiffen those already in Tibet, many of whom were indifferent material and of poor morale. At the same time, from early in 1958, they were putting pressure on the Dalai Lama to use his Tibetan troops against the Khampas and Amdowas. It was unthinkable that he could take such action against his own people and his religious followers. With customary Tibetan finesse he played for time, pointing out that the Tibetan troops were not adequate in numbers or equipment for such a task and that, if they were sent against their own countrymen, he could not be sure that they would not take their part.

Feelings on both sides were becoming strained to the limit and there were signs of a stiffening of Tibetan political resistance and of a more defiant public spirit. In order to protect the Dalai Lama from direct dealings with the Chinese, the National Assembly was reconstituted on a broader basis than formerly and declared to be the mouthpiece for decisions of the Tibetan Government. There was also constant anxiety about the safety of the Dalai Lama's person. In the autumn of 1958 he was invited to go to Peking in January 1959 to attend a Chinese National

Conference. The invitation was declined on the valid grounds that the Dalai Lama had to undergo certain tests of religious learning in that month. As soon as that duty had been performed a fresh and urgent invitation to visit Peking was received. The Tibetan Government and people feared, with good reason, that if he were to go to China the Dalai Lama would be subjected to severe pressure, that things might falsely be said or done in his name, and that he would, in effect, be a hostage for the good conduct of the Tibetan people. Anxiety and suspicion reached a new pitch of intensity.

The attitude of the Indian Government at that time was strangely unrealistic. Although reports of the critical situation in Tibet filtered through to India, the Government of India, for reasons which have never been explained but were perhaps dictated by the well-intentioned but misguided hope of avoiding embarrassment to the Chinese, continued to discount all information as greatly exaggerated. It is hardly credible that their Consul-General at Lhasa was unaware of what was going on. Nevertheless, New Delhi went so far as to warn Mr. George Patterson, a British missionary living in Darjeeling, that unless he discontinued sending 'misleading and exaggerated' messages about Tibet to foreign newspapers, the Government of India would be constrained to interdict his residence in the frontier districts. He was told he might send 'normal and objective reports'. Even though the figures in Patterson's reports may have been somewhat inflated—and there is no proof of this—he was particularly well-qualified to grasp the facts of the Tibetan situation, having lived for some time in East Tibet and knowing the Khampa dialect.

On 17 March 1959, when opposition members criticized their government's Tibetan policy in the Indian Parliament, Nehru made the surprising statement that he did not think there was large-scale violence in Tibet and that what was happening was a clash of wills rather than arms. In the same speech Nehru exposed the basic fallacy of his thinking about Tibet by the disingenuous afterthought that 'when the Chinese chose to assert their authority in Tibet in 1950, the legality of that action was not questioned'.

It was his own government that ought to have raised the question. In 1950 the Indian Government certainly held their 1914 Agreements with Tibet to be valid. How could Nehru reconcile that position with even the possibility that the Chinese armed invasion of Tibet in 1950 had a legal justification?

At the moment that Nehru was denying that violence was taking place in Tibet, affairs in Lhasa had reached their crisis. The Dalai Lama was preparing to flee from his country after his summer palace had been shelled by Chinese batteries.

That was the culmination of eighteen days of wild confusion and uncertainty. Tibetan fears for the safety of the Dalai Lama were tried beyond endurance when on 9 March he received an invitation from the Commander at Lhasa to attend a display at the Chinese barracks, specifying that he should come without his Ministers or his usual escort. Possibly that proviso was in good faith, because of the prevailing tension in Lhasa. The truth is unlikely now to be told; but to the Tibetan people there could be only one explanation—that the Chinese intended to seize the Dalai Lama. As soon as the news was known, many of the people of Lhasa crowded to the Norbu Lingka—the Dalai Lama's summer palace—begging him not to entrust himself to the Chinese. At the same time representatives of every class and rank of Tibetan society, monk and lay, went to the residence of the Indian Consul-General asking for his intervention. In the Norbu Lingka the Dalai Lama's Ministers were consulting anxiously whether the danger was so great that the Lama should take refuge in India. They eventually decided to convene the full National Assembly.

On 10 March, accordingly, a great concourse of the people of Lhasa flooded into the grounds of the Norbu Lingka and many more took up positions outside the enclosure, where they began to establish defensive posts at all the approaches. Their temper was made clear by the lynching of a Chinese emissary who tried to enter the palace in disguise. When reports of the events reached the Tibetan troops they, too, were brought by their commanders to join the defenders of the palace. It is estimated that by 12 March 30,000 people were assembled there. At this time, hundreds of

Tibetan women, noble and commoner alike, sought help from the Indian Consul-General.

The Chinese have made much play with three letters sent by the Dalai Lama to the Chinese Commander on 11, 16, and 18 March which, they claim, show that he was under duress and that he was abducted from Lhasa against his will. English translations of the letters, into the Communists' own jargon, indicate that they were written in a time of stress. The Dalai Lama himself has explained that he wrote them when affairs were at a crisis and that he was striving continually to reach a peaceful solution.

In the turmoil and anxiety all round him, he was subjected to much conflicting and excited advice. The one object uniting all those with him—monk and layman, noble and commoner— whatever their personal interests, was the safety of their leader, and it is probable that the majority urged him to leave Lhasa at once. He himself, with his exceptional qualities of mind and character and accustomed from childhood to make his own decisions, would certainly have resisted such advice. For seven years he had worked by calm reasoning, persistence, and moderation to preserve the integrity of his administration; and he must have foreseen the disastrous outcome of open warfare against the Chinese. No one who knows anything of his selfless and determined devotion to his religion and his people can doubt that his mind was concentrated, until the last possible moment, on averting an irrevocable break, as the one hope of saving any part of the traditional Tibetan right to manage their own affairs.

On 17 March, perhaps as a warning or a gesture of strength, the Chinese fired two shells into the grounds of the Norbu Lingka not far from the Dalai Lama's palace. Whatever their reason, the Dalai Lama took it as a sign that his efforts had failed and that he must accept his Ministers' advice to take refuge in India.

He left Norbu Lingka at night, without the Chinese knowing it, even though their troops were encamped not a mile away. Within twenty miles of Lhasa he and his party found themselves under the protection of Tibetan guerrillas and, not long after, they reached the south bank of the Tsang-po where they were safe from the danger of Chinese interference, except from the air. Nevertheless, no time could be wasted on the journey, on horseback and without adequate baggage transport, through sheer valleys and high passes across the Himalaya. The Dalai Lama's escape route, bravely covered by decoys and false trails, was unknown until on 29 March an emissary reached the Assam frontier post at Chutangmo some forty miles from the north-east corner of Bhutan, and asked for permission for the party to enter India. Precautionary instructions had been circulated to all frontier officers. Permission was immediately granted and the Dalai Lama with some eighty persons including his mother and other relations and his leading Ministers, both monk and lay, entered India on 30 March.

After a few days' rest in the great Buddhist monastery of Tawang the Dalai Lama reached Tezpur in Assam on 18 April. There he issued a statement describing the events which led to his departure from Lhasa and making it clear that he had left of his own free will. His radiant serenity and self-possession deeply impressed all who saw him but strict security measures taken by the Government of India made it impossible for him to be asked any questions. Similar precautions, which gave an unfortunate appearance that the Dalai Lama was under some sort of restriction, continued at Mussoorie where the Indian Government had arranged a residence for him and where he arrived on 20 April.

At Lhasa, for two days after the escape, neither the Chinese nor the crowds of Tibetans surrounding the Norbu Lingka knew that the Dalai Lama had left. On 19 March, whether suspecting the truth or tiring of the deadlock, the Chinese began to bombard the Norbu Lingka, dropping shells in a circle progressively nearer to the actual residence of the Dalai Lama. For most of the day the Tibetans outside the enclosure stood their ground and suffered many casualties. It was only late on the evening of 19 March, when the Chinese announced by loudspeaker that the Dalai Lama had been 'abducted', that the Tibetans turned on the Chinese barracks and other buildings in Lhasa itself. Chinese fire from well-protected strong-posts inflicted very heavy losses. Estimates of the Tibetan dead vary from 3,000 to a much higher figure. The Chinese themselves announced the capture of 4,000 prisoners and more than twice that number of weapons. As soon as fighting ceased the execution of so-called 'ringleaders' began; and many thousands of men and boys were arrested and deported to unknown destinations. Several thousands of refugees, monk and lay, succeeded in following the Dalai Lama to safety in India.

The charge that the Norbu Lingka was shelled, on both 17 and 19 March, is denied by the Chinese. It is impossible to disbelieve the evidence of the Dalai Lama himself about the first instance; and it is equally incredible that there is no basis for the numerous and consistent eyewitness reports of Tibetan refugees about the second, large-scale bombardment. To support their story, the Chinese allowed Alan Winnington, the correspondent in China of a Communist newspaper, to revisit Lhasa in August 1959. What he wrote indicates that the Norbu Lingka appeared to be undamaged. Perhaps he was shown only part of the enclosure or perhaps signs of shelling were rapidly patched up. It is known that the Chinese sought very speedily to repair monasteries in East Tibet which they had damaged severely by bombardment; and it is evident from Winnington's account that there was damage in other parts of Lhasa which was being quickly repaired.

After establishing the peace of desolation at Lhasa the Chinese, whose troops had been greatly reinforced, conducted an extensive sweep through areas near Lhasa and south of the Tsang-po which were controlled by bands of Tibetan guerrillas. By May it was claimed that opposition had been suppressed with severe casualties and that many towns and forts had been captured. Many refugees from this fighting swelled the number of those seeking shelter in India. Nevertheless, later reports have shown that resistance is still alive in several places and that fighting continues sporadically.

In the political field the Chinese were quick to make full use of the opportunity that presented itself. The existing Tibetan Government, whose roots went deep into the past, had been the object of an attack by attrition through the Preparatory Committee. Now the Chinese declared its total abolition; and, in its place, they set up a military dictatorship under which they made use of the few Tibetan nobles and monastic officials who were willing to collaborate and, above all, of their puppet Panchen Lama. Tibet was once more promised 'autonomy' and it was announced that the reforms for which the people were alleged to be crying out would be rapidly introduced.

The immediate effect was the fastening of a firm grip on the country and a severe restriction on freedom of movement. Every Tibetan was made to carry an identity card which had to be shown on entering or leaving any town or village. The approaches to Lhasa were heavily guarded and military posts were set up at key points throughout the city. It was hardly possible for two Tibetans to talk in a public place without being asked to show their credentials. Besides controlling the main passes across the Himalaya, Chinese troops were quartered in the more important towns and villages where they were billeted in the houses of the leading men and watched the movements of all travellers. The Dalai Lama has estimated that there are 180,000 Chinese troops distributed through Tibet. Trade and communication with India were almost entirely cut off; and the opportunity was taken of stopping the visits of Indian pilgrims to the holy lake Manasarowar in West Tibet on the plea of disturbed conditions.

Religious institutions came under immediate attack. The great monasteries of Lhasa were suppressed on the accusation that they had supported the rising. The monks were rounded up and examined by the Chinese; some were beaten and some died or committed suicide. Eventually they were told that they would get no food if they stayed in the monasteries. After the monks were evicted in this way it is reported that the sacred images and books were destroyed or removed.What remained of the population of Lhasa was organized for forced labour. Few able-bodied laymen were left; but women, young and old—including ladies of noble family, together with the evicted monks, were made to work day and night on road-building and similar tasks. Obedience was ensured by the grant of a small ration of food; and several hours of propaganda lectures were a daily feature of the régime. According to information received in India, those conditions were unchanged up to the beginning of 1961.

The complete disruption of the political organization, religious institutions, and all the normal life of the country was accompanied also by a social revolution. The landed nobility, a compact and very important stratum of Tibetan society, was almost completely destroyed. The great nobles who had accompanied or followed the Dalai Lama on his flight to India were declared traitors and their property confiscated. It was also made known that the estates of the remaining nobles and of the monasteries would be resumed on the payment of fair compensation, and redistributed to the peasants. In the villages there was at first no violent change. After the flight of the noble landlords there still remained a number of small land-holding yeomen and tenant-labourers. Chinese anxiety to secure the current harvest led them to promise that whoever cultivated the land should enjoy the whole crop for the year; but it was also indicated that agricultural communes would be set up before long. In spite of the inducement offered, it was reported that much land lay uncultivated and that in some places Chinese soldiers were farming it.

To conceal what had been happening from the rest of the world the Chinese propaganda machine poured out stories and accusations of corruption and cruelty in the monasteries and of the brutal oppression of the Tibetan 'serfs' by the former noble landlords and by the monastic officials.

Charges of that sort have become the mainstay of Chinese explanations of their actions in Tibet and have been unquestioningly accepted by others interested to represent Communism in China as a liberal progressive régime. They bear little or no relation to the accounts of conditions in the country and the way of life of its people as reported by experienced and authoritative foreign visitors, from Father Ippolito Desideri in the eighteenth century to Sir Charles Bell in the twentieth. It might also be asked why, if such oppression did in fact exist, it had not been mentioned, let alone removed, in seven years of Communist domination of Tibet. Other attempts to distract attention from the savage use of force by the Chinese were made by reviving stories of the Younghusband Expedition of 1904 and picturing it as a British 'atrocity'. No mention—it need hardly be said—was made of Chou Erh-fêng's capture of Lhasa in 1910.

The question is certain to be asked whether the Chinese themselves may not have engineered the conflict in March which resulted in the social and political revolution which they had desired but had not been able to bring about by gradual methods. It is probable that, although they did not hesitate to increase pressure on the Tibetan Government without any great regard for their opposition, they did not expect so violent a popular reaction at that time. It was undoubtedly a shock that many of the young Tibetans who had received courses of indoctrination in China took a leading part in the rising. Even after seven years in occupation of Tibet, the Chinese do not seem to have come to understand the latent strength of the Tibetans' spirit of nationalism or the extent and intensity of their devotion to the Dalai Lama.

REPERCUSSIONS IN INDIA

News of the flight of the Dalai Lama and the fighting at Lhasa caused an outburst of anxiety and sympathy for Tibet, and of condemnation of the Chinese, in many parts of the world and especially in India. The Indian people and the Indian press gave forceful demonstrations of their commiseration and anger. Even those newspapers which usually supported the Government criticized Nehru for misrepresenting the situation in Tibet as merely 'a clash of wills' and said that unless he spoke up for the incontestable right of the Tibetans to their own way of life, he would not be representing the feelings of his country.

Nehru at first maintained his cool, self-defensive attitude, pleading the delicacy of the problem and his desire not to say anything that might make matters worse. The Chinese, trading on this etiolated caution, made gratuitously arrogant statements, in effect warning the Indian Government to mind its own business. The result was a slightly warmer glow from Nehru who allowed himself a wary expression of sympathy with Tibet, a rejection of 'dictation' from China, and a denial of any intention to interfere.

Even such mildness stirred the Chinese into wild and foolish charges that India had worked with the 'imperialists' by sheltering

Plate 13

Tibetan warrior in ancient ceremonial armour

Plate 14

Tibetan teapot, brass and silver-gilt,
c. eighteenth century

rebels at Kalimpong. That drew a sharp rebuke from Nehru who also, but still guardedly, referred to India's legitimate interest in Tibet and its autonomy. When the arrival of the Dalai Lama in India was welcomed by a tremendous popular demonstration of relief, happiness, and reverence, and when an official spokesman described the Dalai Lama as an 'honoured guest', Chinese comment became even wilder and more unpleasant. By 22 April it was being suggested that the Dalai Lama's statement at Tezpur had been prepared by the Indian Government; and still further provocation · was given in silly remarks made by the Panchen Lama, or put into his mouth, about 'reactionaries in India, walking in the footsteps of the British imperialists, who harbour expansionist activities towards Tibet . . . '.

Although Nehru had been calm and reticent about Chinese treatment of the Tibetans he reacted promptly and with heat to allegations against himself and his Government; and by 28 April he had reached the stage of charging the Chinese with 'using the language of the cold war'. About the same time, he emphasized that he was more deeply distressed by the damage done to the Five Principles than by the tragic happenings in Tibet. The strain on the Five Principles was demonstrated beyond question in a long, inspired article in the *Peking Review* of 12 May entitled 'The Revolution in Tibet and Nehru's Philosophy', criticizing the whole Indian attitude, stigmatizing Indian 'interference' in the matter and questioning the 'truth and propriety' of many of Nehru's statements.

Those exchanges might not have caused such deep concern in India but for the shadow of Chinese actions on India's border. Nehru himself was reluctant publicly to face that shadow. On 22 April, in reply to questions in the Indian Parliament, he discounted the suggestion that China claimed 30,000 square miles of Indian territory and did not accept the McMahon Line as the boundary. It was not long before he had to admit the very opposite; but before examining the contentious frontier question it is desirable to say something about the relations between the Government of India and the Dalai Lama.

The grant of asylum, the provision of a comfortable house,

and above all the generous and friendly welcome by the Indian people were gratefully appreciated by the Dalai Lama. Nevertheless there was a certain magisterial acerbity in Nehru's announcement of the restriction of the Lama to religious affairs and the banning of political activity. In that there was—as *The Times* Correspondent indicated in a dispatch of 21 April—an endeavour to pursue diametrically opposed lines of policy without admitting their incompatibility and to find some sort of compromise between the strength of Indian popular feeling and the need for conciliating the Chinese.

A more material problem for the Indian authorities arose from the unrestricted admission of Tibetan refugees who streamed across the border by widely separated routes in flight from Chinese oppression. Within a few months the number exceeded ten thousand and the influx still went on. There were, inevitably, difficulties in dealing with people from a different climate and with different customs and language. It was not easy to find somewhere for them to live or people able to look after them. Some mistakes and confusion at the start would not be surprising; but whatever may have gone wrong appears to have been magnified by disturbing rumours largely because the Indian Government discouraged visitors from seeing the camps for themselves. More will be said later about the Tibetan refugees in India but it may be stated now that the Indian Government's secretiveness—probably due to concern about Chinese reactions—concealed the generosity and hard work they expended on receiving the refugees and undertaking the considerable cost of supporting them.

On 24 April Nehru had a long meeting with the Dalai Lama and his statements both before and after that suggest that he had in mind the possibility of a reconciliation which might allow the Dalai Lama to return to Lhasa and thus solve some of the Indian Government's perplexities. Without consulting the Dalai Lama, he declared that the Panchen Lama or any Chinese emissary who wanted to meet the Dalai Lama would be welcomed in India. If Nehru was thinking of a repetition of such assurances as Chou En-lai gave in 1956, and which had been promptly and deliberately evaded, he was being unrealistic. At all events, in the Dalai

Lama he was dealing with a young man of unusual perspicacity and determination. The security precautions which made it impossible even for friends to get near the Dalai Lama were gradually relaxed; and, although he could hardly be described as holding open court, that may have been according to his own wish to avoid embarrassing his hosts by appearing to seek the attention of visitors.

On 20 June, after a long silence, he held a Press Conference at which he made his position plain with transparent honesty and with a gracious statesmanship which would have been admirable in the most experienced of rulers. He spoke with unaffected gratitude of his reception by the Indian people, of the asylum given to Tibetan refugees, and of the kindness and consideration shown to him by Nehru. Attempts to extract criticism of the Government of India for their treatment of himself or of the Tibetan refugees were firmly resisted. He would not allow himself to be untrue to his nature as the incarnation of compassion by being drawn into heated condemnation even of the Chinese; but he made it clear that their object was, apparently, to exterminate his people, and that the Panchen Lama and other Tibetans working for the government at Lhasa were mere tools of the Communists. He clearly denounced the Sino-Tibetan Agreement of 1951, declaring it to have been violated by the Chinese. On the question of his return to Lhasa he showed that Nehru's hopes were too sanguine and that he could not go back to Lhasa unless he were guaranteed the practical independence he enjoyed before the Chinese invasion in 1950.

On one other point the failure of Nehru to understand the Tibetan mind emerged. When the Dalai Lama was asked whether Tibetans still recognized him as the Ruler of Tibet he replied, 'Wherever I am, accompanied by my government, the Tibetan people recognize us as the government of Tibet.' That statement was sharply criticized by the Indian Government which announced, yet again, that they did not recognize any Tibetan Government in exile. But there was no other answer that the Dalai Lama could honestly have given. It is fundamental to all Tibetan thinking that a Dalai Lama, once discovered, cannot in any circumstances divest himself of his position as head of the religion and head of the state.

Another statement by the Dalai Lama foreshadowed his intention to appeal to the world at large through the United Nations; and late in August he addressed the Secretary-General on that subject. That step was facilitated by the International Commission of Jurists which, largely through the efforts of Sri Purshottam Trikamdas, a distinguished Indian barrister, had published on 24 July 1959 an interim report on *The Question of Tibet and the Rule of Law*. The Commission found *prima facie* evidence of attempts by the Chinese Communists to destroy the Tibetan nation and religion. After an examination of the international position of Tibet, it also came to the conclusion that Tibet had been, to all intents, an independent country enjoying a large degree of sovereignty and that it was difficult to consider its affairs as within the 'domestic jurisdiction' of the Chinese People's Government.

The Indian Government disapproved of the Dalai Lama's appeal to the United Nations which they found embarrassing in their relations with China. Nehru irritably criticized the Dalai Lama for undertaking political activity and warned him that the plight of his people would only be made worse if the question was taken to the United Nations. But the Dalai Lama himself was convinced that it was the only course left to him. He is understood to have impressed Nehru with his frank sincerity when assuring him that he was deeply concerned at causing embarrassment to the Government of India, to which he was so much indebted, but that he did not think there was anything the Chinese could do to make the life of the Tibetans worse and that he could not escape his duty to his own people. In the event, the Indian Government made it possible for an elder brother of the Dalai Lama to go to New York to canvass support for the Tibetan case.

TIBET AT THE UNITED NATIONS: 1959

By the end of September 1959 the Federation of Malaya and the Republic of Ireland had secured the inclusion of the question of Tibet on the agenda for the forthcoming session of the United Nations; and on 9 October the General Committee of the United Nations debated whether the matter should be recommended for discussion in the General Assembly. The delegates of Malaya, Ireland, and the U.S.A. supported the proposal which was met with heated opposition from Mr. Kuznetsov for the U.S.S.R. He argued that the question had been stirred up, especially by the U.S.A., to revive the diminishing tension of the cold war. He alleged that there was no Tibetan question and that Tibet had been for centuries an inseparable part of China so that its affairs were the domestic concern of the Chinese Government over which the General Assembly had no jurisdiction. As for the allegations of denial of human rights, the Soviet delegate declared that if anything had happened in Tibet it was only the suppression of a reactionary clique of feudal landlords who had made a last bid to prevent their oppressed serfs from winning the rights which had long been denied to them. He and his supporters repeated the allegations of inhuman tortures and exploitation of the 'serfs' which the Chinese propaganda machine had been churning out incessantly since the Tibetan rising. Kuznetsov's unusually intemperate and often abusive manner made it appear that his government was embarrassed at the prospect of a full debate on Chinese actions in Tibet and hoped that by shouting and storming in Committee the question might be prevented from reaching the General Assembly. In spite of that, the proposal was accepted by 11 votes to 5 with 4 abstentions.

On 12 October the General Assembly considered the Committee's recommendation. Similar arguments to those heard before were repeated on either side but it was noticeable that the tone of the U.S.S.R. delegate and his supporters was much milder. The moderation with which the U.S.A. and other countries had met his furious attacks had shown up Kuznetsov and his supporters as the only persons eager to adopt the language of the cold war. Inscription of the question of Tibet was agreed to by 43 votes to 11 with 25 abstentions. The British delegate voted for inscription.

The full discussion took place on 20 and 21 October. The

joint Malayan–Irish resolution was couched in mild terms. There was no mention of the Chinese People's Government; and the status of Tibet was sidetracked by reference to its 'traditional autonomy'. The resolution concentrated on the violation of human rights in Tibet about which it expressed 'grave concern'; and it called for 'respect for the fundamental human rights of the Tibetan people and their distinctive cultural and religious life'. But the mildness of the resolution did not preclude a wide-ranging and outspoken debate. It was ably proposed by Dato Nik Kamil for Malaya and seconded with dignity, warmth, and firmness by Mr. Frank Aiken for Ireland who was the outstanding speaker in this as in the other discussions. The opposition followed the same lines as before but without the heat and fury which had been turned on in the General Committee.

No speaker outside the Soviet bloc gave any credence to charges against the Tibetan ruling class as 'inhuman and reactionary'. Those were the stock arguments of a Communist country against any régime it was able to oppress. They had been refuted in documents circulated by the Dalai Lama's representatives; and they had been questioned, to the wrath of the Chinese press, by Nehru himself in a speech on 27 April 1959. But what the Tibetans had principally hoped for in the debate was a vindication of their claim to be an independent country. Argument on that issue was clouded by a general lack of information about the Tibetan case. The interim report of the International Commission of Jurists had provided useful support to Tibet's claims and the Tibetans had circulated instructive papers to all delegations. The delegate of El Salvador, who had raised the Tibetan question at the United Nations in 1950, and also the delegate of Cuba maintained in notably effective speeches that Tibet had been enjoying *de facto* independence when the Communist invasion took place in 1950; and they made constructive efforts to interpret the effect of the repudiation of the Sino-Tibetan Agreement of 1951 by one side or by both. In that connection it is pertinent that Nehru had said on 5 April 1959 that 'both sides have stated that the agreement has ended or been broken. There is no doubt about that, as both sides say so and events indicate that.' But the delegates of the United Kingdom and India, who were the only countries, apart from Nepal, to have had treaty relations with Tibet and who had special qualifications to give an authoritative clarification of Tibet's status, chose, as they had done in 1950, to dissemble their knowledge.

Sir Pierson Dixon for the United Kingdom, while deploring the tragic events which were reported from Tibet, described Tibet's juridical status as far from clear and he stated that some of the more important facts were in doubt. On the issue whether Article 2(7) of the United Nations Charter—which bars the United Nations from intervention in matters essentially within the domestic jurisdiction of any state—did or did not apply, the British Government was unable to make up its mind. Without putting forward any explanation or examination of the juridical difficulties or of the causes which led to British uncertainty about the applicability of Article 2(7) and without specifying any of the more important facts alleged to be in doubt, the British delegate gave the benefit of the doubt to the Communists and announced that his delegation would abstain from voting on the resolution.

In the absence of any clear indication, it can only be conjectured that one of the British Government's doubts may have been whether the 1951 Agreement between Tibet and China had extinguished Tibet's claim to independence. There should have been no question that at least up to 1950 Tibet had been in enjoyment of *de facto* independence—that had been accepted by a British spokesman in the very same year; nor was there any doubt that Tibet had been invaded by a hostile Chinese army or that after 1951 there had been 'massive repression . . . and ruthless assaults on the historic life of a sturdy and friendly people' as well as destruction of their religious life. The question would arise whether the Agreement of 1951 was signed under duress and how that might affect the international personality of Tibet. About that, the International Commission of Jurists had formed the opinion that 'the matter cannot be dismissed . . . as falling exclusively within the jurisdiction of the People's Republic of China'.

What were described by Dixon as 'our well-known views on Article 2(7)' appear to imply that the British Government preferred to shelter behind doubts of the applicability of the Article and treat the Chinese position in Tibet as possibly comparable with their own position in British colonial territories rather than risk a judgement on the substance of the question of human rights. The immediate effect of such views was to allow a legalistic evasion of long-standing obligations to Tibet. Their benefit, in the long term, could be applied to any successful act of aggression.

To some extent the weakness shown by the British Government may have been due to foreknowledge of the Indian attitude. In a rambling, inconsequent speech, Mr. Krishna Menon, after touching obscurely on many arguments without following them up, announced that his government would abstain, apparently with the idea that that would somehow help towards the possibility of conciliation between Tibet and China. In the course of his speech he threw off, casually and almost inaudibly, the remark that 'India inherited the British position in 1947—that is to say that Tibet was under Chinese suzerainty'. The falsity of that statement must have been obvious to the United Kingdom delegate if to no one else. It can be appreciated by reference to the obligations deriving from the joint Anglo-Tibetan declaration of 1914 (see p. 114) which had devolved on India in 1947 and which in effect bound India *not* to recognize Chinese suzerainty over Tibet except on certain strict conditions—which were never fulfilled.

With such a lead from the two countries which might have been looked to for an exposition of the facts, it was inevitable that powers with colonial responsibilities should abstain from supporting the resolution. Several of them—Spain, Belgium, and France—accepted that there had been violation of human rights in Tibet and sympathized with the Tibetans in their sufferings; but as in the case of the British delegation doubts about the independent status of Tibet prevented them from overcoming their habitual reliance on Article 2(7) of the United Nations Charter, and their fears that a vote for the resolution might expose their flank in some future discussion about their own domestic affairs.

Similarly, the neutralist Afro-Asian countries found nothing in the speeches of the United Kingdom and Indian delegates to move them out of their customary caution.

The resolution was eventually carried by 46 votes to 9 with 26 abstentions. Its terms and details of the voting can be seen in the Appendix (p. 286).

The result of their approach to the United Nations can hardly have given great satisfaction to the Tibetans. They had innocently believed that their case could be considered on its own merits, in isolation from the pre-determined international attitudes of the various Powers. When reports of Soviet charges that the Tibetan question was being used as a weapon in the cold war reached the Dalai Lama he was greatly distressed and sent an appeal to all members of the United Nations expressing his concern at those allegations and repeating that his sole objective was to restore the peace and freedom of his people.

In the end, the discussion not only left the status of Tibet in uncertainty; it also produced no support for the hope which the Tibetans had voiced that a United Nations Commission should be sent to Tibet to inquire into the facts. Several speakers, while appealing to the moral conscience of the world, had regretfully admitted that no resolution of the United Nations could produce an immediate practical alleviation of the plight of the Tibetan people; and it was, unfortunately, obvious that in existing conditions the idea of a U.N. Commission of Inquiry was impracticable.

Nevertheless, for four days Tibetan affairs had received more international attention than ever before. Speakers from countries in every part of the world had expressed sympathy with the Tibetans in their sufferings and in their aspirations for freedom to live their own way of life; and opposition to the resolution had been confined to the nine members of the Soviet bloc. Delegates of many countries may well have found material for further thought about the history and status of Tibet not only in some of the speeches in the debate but also in the report of the International Commission of Jurists and in documents circulated by the Dalai Lama's personal representatives. All that was for the Tibetans a partial success and they might hope that it was the beginning of a process of international enlightenment.

DISPUTE BETWEEN INDIA AND CHINA
ON THE FRONTIER OF TIBET

On the same day that Krishna Menon was talking to the General Assembly of the United Nations about Sino-Tibetan conciliation (see p. 222), Indian feelings were violently outraged by an affray within the frontier between Ladakh and Tibet in which nine Indian border police were killed and ten others—some wounded—were taken prisoner by a Chinese military force.

Something of the sort was not entirely unexpected. After the Tibetan rising of March 1959 growing Chinese ill-will, which had been expressed in increasingly fevered charges against the Indian Government, was also shown in vexatious treatment of Indian nationals in Tibet and a more aggressive attitude along the frontiers. The temperature there had been rising gradually ever since large Chinese forces had occupied Central and Western Tibet in 1951 and had sent patrols along almost every mile of the Indian border.

A detailed study of the about 2,000 miles of frontier between India and Tibet, and the manner in which its various sections came to be established, is beyond the scope of this work; but it may be said, in short, that by far the greatest part of the line from the north—east of Ladakh to Nepal and through Sikkim and Bhutan, running, as it does, through high desert or along the crest of inaccessible mountain ranges, although not demarcated on the ground, was clearly understood and determined by long tradition and practice, embodied here and there in local agreements.

In 1899 the Indian Government conveyed formally to the Chinese Government a description of the frontier between Kashmir and Sinkiang as running up to the Kuen Lun Mountains to a point east of longitude 80°, as had been shown on Indian Survey maps for many years. It is not proposed to examine the Indian frontier, westward of the point, with the Chinese province of Sinkiang but only the Indo-Tibetan frontier of which that point marks the north-west corner. From there the boundary between Ladakh and Tibet runs roughly southward in a traditional line dating back to the seventeenth century and confirmed in the Tibet–Ladakh Treaty of 1842 (Appendix, p. 246). In its northern sector it passes through high, uninhabited country as far as the Lanak La which is a well-established frontier point between Ladakh and Tibet confirmed by travellers from William Moorcroft in 1820 onwards. It is unlikely that anyone on either side ever had a closely detailed knowledge of the frontier in that little-visited desert north of the Lanak La, known as the Aksai Chin, or that the Kashmir authorities ever had cause to exercise active jurisdiction there; but no more had either Tibetan or Chinese authorities exercised jurisdiction there. The line in general had never been subject to dispute with the Tibetan Government, and the frontier now claimed by the Indian Government is shown in maps of the Indian Government's Survey officers from 1865. Southward of the Lanak La the frontier was surveyed in 1846 and the traditional line embodied in Indian Survey maps.

Along the main range of the Himalaya at a few places between the Shipki Pass and the north-west frontier of Nepal, Tibetan claims to grazing rights south of the watershed frontier had been resisted by the Indian Government for many years.

Eastward of Nepal, the frontier of Sikkim had not been in question since 1890; the Bhutan frontier was traditionally accepted by Tibet and from its north-east corner the McMahon Line (see p. 116) determined the remainder of the boundary between India and Tibet.

On the transfer of power in 1947 some adjustment was needed in the juridical basis of the relations of the new India with the border regions. The paramountcy of the British Crown over the Princely States was replaced by a policy of absorbing them into the main body of India by accession. The circumstances in Kashmir were exceptional but the upshot, so far as the Indo-Tibetan frontier was concerned, was that Ladakh, from being a protected state, was converted into an integral part of India although with a form of administration somewhat different from that of the regular Indian States. The former Hill States, between Ladakh and Nepal, acceded to India and were merged in the regular provincial administration. Only Sikkim survived the process of accession. Its previous relationship with India was continued until a new treaty could be concluded. That was hastened by internal trouble in the State which led in 1949 to temporary assumption of control of the administration by the Indian Government which appointed a Dewan to advise the Maharaja. By a treaty signed soon after, Sikkim became a protectorate of the Indian Government to which was entrusted responsibility for the foreign relations and the defence of the State, including the right to station Indian troops in Sikkim. Bhutan had always been on a different footing from the Princely States of India. Its relations with the former government had been established by treaties under which the Bhutanese Government agreed to accept guidance in its foreign relations but was free from any interference in its internal affairs. There was no resident British political representative there nor was there any provision for the stationing of troops in Bhutan. Similar arrangements were continued by the new Indian Government in a treaty concluded in 1949.

The North-East Frontier Area, while constitutionally part of Assam, remained a special Agency of the Central Government of India until such time as it should be sufficiently advanced to be incorporated in the regular provincial administration. Attention to defence arrangements on the Tibetan frontier was intensified and there was also a determined increase in efforts to spread the cultural influence of the Indian Government in these areas. After some initial clashes there appears to have been steady progress in a friendly policy of helping the different tribes to develop their individual way of life along their own traditional lines.

Thus, with the exception of some 800 miles in the independent Kingdom of Nepal, the whole Himalayan frontier from Ladakh to the McMahon Line was the direct responsibility of the Indian Government, although there were slight variations in the manner in which it could discharge its obligations in different sectors.

By geographical necessity Nepal was in specially close relations with India. In 1950 a treaty of friendship was concluded to take the place of that which had existed with the previous government in India; and later in the same year the Indian Government played a considerable part in bringing about the establishment of a new régime in Nepal which it had reason to hope would be sympathetic to Indian policy. Thereafter, India has shouldered the cost of considerable economic development in Nepal and on several occasions Nehru has pointed the importance of Nepal to the security of India by declaring that any aggression against Nepal would be treated as aggression against India.

On the long frontier with Tibet, which the new Indian Government inherited in August 1947, a generation of undisturbed friendship had made for a simple and economical administration. Large-scale defence measures were unnecessary and only a few widely-scattered police posts, at some distance from the border, watched the peaceful traffic. The changed and uncertain outlook resulting from the rise of Communist power in China naturally caused anxiety to the government, the army, and the people of India. That anxiety was reflected early in 1951 by a report that the Chinese had occupied Badrinath, a famous Hindu shrine near the sources of the Ganges, some 25 miles south of the Himalaya. The report was soon denied; but the new situation called for new precautions and it appears that very soon advance posts of border police were established at many points on or as near as possible to the frontier along its whole length, and the strength of the Indian Army Escorts in Yatung and Gyantse was increased.

In the event, in the four years between the Chinese invasion of Tibet and the signature of the Sino-Indian Agreement of 1954 there appears to have been no infringement of the Indian frontier. Indeed, the Chinese appear to have gone out of their way to reassure the Indian Government. According to a statement by Nehru in October 1951, the Chinese Prime Minister referred to Chinese official maps which showed large territorial claims on India, and informed the Indian Government that they should not pay the slightest heed because those were old maps and there had been no time to print new ones.

From the exchange of communications between the Indian and Chinese Governments in September 1959 and February

1960, published in the Government of India's White Papers, it can be seen that when the Sino-Indian Agreement of 1954 was being negotiated, although there was no open discussion about the frontier between India and Tibet, the Indian representative tried to establish the point that no matters relating to Tibet remained in dispute between India and China. That could hardly have been regarded as a substantial gain but after the encouraging remarks of Chou En-lai in 1951 and in view of the continuing calm along the border, the Indian Government appears to have felt that the assurances of mutual respect for territorial integrity contained in the Five Principles were a satisfactory guarantee of its frontiers.

Within three months of the enunciation of the Five Principles, a small cloud appeared on the horizon when the Chinese protested that Indian troops had crossed the Niti Pass—a statement which the Indian Government denied. There was also the report of a Chinese infringement of the McMahon Line—the north-east frontier of India—in which shots were exchanged. Incidents of that sort were treated as minor misunderstandings and would not by themselves have caused any great uneasiness; but the sense of security engendered by Chou En-lai's previous assurances about the maps was shaken by the publication in 1954 of new official maps showing all the former Chinese claims on Indian territory.

For some four years sporadic exchanges continued about further infringements south of the Niti Pass—where, in fact, there had been a long-standing disagreement with Tibet about the exact frontier—and in a few other places between the north-west corner of Nepal and the Shipki Pass near the point where the Sutlej flows out of Tibet. But although by 1956 the Indian Government were issuing warnings that they would resist aggression, there was no serious strain on the relations between the two governments. In December of the same year Chou En-lai, on a visit to India, is on record as having given a sign of friendliness by assuring Nehru that for practical purposes the Chinese Government would recognize the so-called McMahon Line as the frontier in that area. Thereafter there was general calm along the whole frontier until in the autumn of 1958 it was discovered that part of a new Chinese road between Western Sinkiang and Tibet had been built across the Aksai Chin in the north-eastern corner of Ladakh.

It has already been mentioned that the Aksai Chin is a little-frequented and entirely unadministered region. It is a bleak plateau at an elevation of some 16,000 feet which only the rare explorer and an occasional Ladakhi, Tibetan, or Kirghiz traveller ever visited. The Chinese force which invaded Tibet from Khotan in 1950 travelled by that route and it was probably used occasionally after that for supplies before being converted into a regular motor road. The remoteness of the area from effective Indian control is reflected in the fact that the existence of the road does not appear to have been known to the Indian Government until two years after it was actually built.

The Indian Government protested to the Chinese at the violation of their territory; and the Chinese replied by bluntly claiming the territory as their own and objecting to Indian interference there. This repudiation of Indian frontiers in the west probably stimulated Nehru in December 1958 to open a correspondence with Chou En-lai about the new Chinese maps in which old territorial claims had been repeated. He reminded Chou of his assurance in 1956 about the McMahon Line. Chou replied that the frontier between India and Tibet had never been delimited and that there was no treaty of any kind between the Chinese Central Government and the Government of India about their frontiers. He attacked the McMahon Line as a product of British aggression but was willing for practical reasons to take 'a more or less realistic attitude towards it'. He did not claim that the Chinese maps were right in every respect but considered that changes could only be made after a proper survey. He added that Chinese opinion was surprised by the frontier claimed in Indian maps, particularly in the western section. Here may be seen the first hint that a bargain might, perhaps, be arranged of part of Ladakh against the McMahon Line; but the Government of India paid no attention to that veiled suggestion and flatly restated its position, claiming the border as shown in its own maps.

After the events of March 1959 at Lhasa and the flight of the

Dalai Lama to India matters rapidly went from bad to worse. The general state of mind of the Chinese Government can be seen in the intemperate, ultra-sensitive, often contradictory tone of its communications published in the Indian Government's White Paper of 7 September, in which the statement of 16 May 1959 by the Chinese Ambassador in India must mark the nadir of diplomatic discourtesy. Threatening attitudes made it likely that some sort of provocative act would not be long in coming. Early in August there were rumours of large concentrations of Chinese troops at various points on the Indian border and the Chinese general at Lhasa was reported as advocating the 'liberation' of Ladakh, Sikkim, and Bhutan. That moved Nehru to a firm pronouncement of what he had been stating at intervals ever since 1950—and what had also been the policy of the former Government of India—that the Himalaya is India's frontier and that no foreign interference south of that line could be allowed.

It had transpired in June that in furtherance of this policy, arrangements had been made with the Government of Nepal for the manning by Indian troops of fourteen defence posts along the Nepalese frontier with Tibet. Indian intentions were made even more precise in November 1959 when Nehru announced that any aggression against Nepal would be treated as aggression against India. With regard to the McMahon Line he had as long ago as 4 May 1950 declared that 'the McMahon Line is our frontier, maps or no maps'. In March 1959, in a letter to Chou En-lai, he expressly referred to the acceptance of that line by the Tibetans in the 1914 agreements at Simla, and he won applause in the Indian Parliament by announcing that the McMahon Line was 'firm by treaty, by usage and right, and firm by geography'.

On 26 August some 200 or 300 Chinese troops crossed the McMahon Line in the region of the upper valley of the Subansiri and drove out the picket of Indian border police manning a forward post at Longju. Nehru declared it to be a clear case of aggression and ordered the Indian army to take over responsibility for the defence of that part of the frontier. Within a few days Chinese incursions into Ladakh were reported and also hostile concentrations near the Bhutan border.

Plate 15

(*a*) Samyé, the first monastery in Tibet, *c.* 779

(*b*) Samyé

Plate 16

(b) Inside Tashilhunpo, founded 1447

(a) Keu-tsang hermitage, c. fifteenth century

In this time of Sino-Indian tension Tibet and the Tibetans were almost forgotten; but the Dalai Lama brought their existence pointedly to the notice of the Indian Government on 7 September. In an address at Delhi he exposed with lucid brevity the equivocal and imprecise thinking of the Government of India about the status of his country. He remarked that Nehru relied on the McMahon Line as the frontier of India. That was a valid agreement concluded by the British Government and Tibet. If Tibet had been deemed a sovereign treaty-making state at that time, it was still the same when it was invaded by the Chinese in 1950. If the Indian Government did not agree with that, how could they continue to claim that the McMahon Line was valid? That succinct, incontrovertible statement showed up, without ever saying so, that the Indian Government was very ready to claim its rights under the treaties with Tibet which it inherited from the British but was less scrupulous about its obligations.

Nehru found this embarrassing, particularly in view of the forthcoming Tibetan appeal to the United Nations. Without attempting a reasoned analysis of the question, he resorted to censorious bluster and, as he told the upper house of the Indian Parliament on 10 September 1959, he warned the Dalai Lama not to claim any relation between Tibetan sovereign status and the McMahon Line. In the same speech Nehru was careful to avoid mention of the McMahon Line as the basis of Indian frontier policy, and contented himself with the assertion that 'our policy is firm as a rock and will remain so'.

Nevertheless, in a very short time he found it necessary to reaffirm both the validity of the McMahon Line and Tibet's treaty-making competence at that time. He did this in a letter dated 26 September 1959 to Chou En-lai, replying to one from Chou which had not been fully examined at the time of Nehru's statement of 10 September. In his letter, dated 8 September, Chou persisted in his rejection of Indian maps of the Ladakh area and his reassertion of Chinese claims there. He also, in a flood of unconvincing explanations, unmistakably went back on the assurances he had previously given about his acceptance in practice of the McMahon Line.

That letter was a turning point in Sino-Indian relations. Chou's repudiation of his previous statements about the McMahon Line was a severe shock to Nehru who had apparently pinned his faith completely to Chou's promises. Nehru's language became sharp and bitter. He began to wonder—as others had been wondering for some time—whether the two governments meant the same thing when they used similar words. He found that the Chinese attitude had stiffened to the extent of making quite impossible claims on India and saw the explanation in 'the arrogance of might' and 'national paranoia'.

By the end of September passions had begun to abate and the idea of arranging negotiations was in the air. But the storm broke again with even greater fury when on 21 September—the last day of the United Nations debate on Tibet—the serious clash mentioned at the beginning of this chapter took place in Ladakh. The Chinese put out a version of the affair completely contradictory to the Indian account; and irreconcilable national attitudes were hardened still further by the exchange of strong words. The Chinese went so far as to utter barely veiled threats that unless the Indian Government accepted Chinese claims in Ladakh they themselves would not refrain from action south of the 'so-called McMahon Line'.

Indian public opinion was violently excited, Nehru himself used grave and stern language, calling on the people to be prepared to take strong action and to defend Indian territory; but by 6 November, with somewhat contemptuous remarks about public expressions of anger, he began to put on the brake once more and again to speak of conciliation. But conciliation was clearly not to be interpreted as yielding. The Indian army was put in control of the whole frontier and Indian notes, suggesting peaceful means for the solution of minor frontier disputes, contained the suggestion that Chinese methods resembled those of 'the old imperialist powers against whom both India and China struggled in the past'.

There followed a cautious sparring for position in an exchange of proposals aimed at relieving the tension. The Chinese suggested a limited withdrawal which would have meant the evacuation of some Indian-held frontier posts. That was rejected by the Indian Government which made a counter-proposal more favourable to their own interests, drawing a distinction between the uninhabited zone of Ladakh, where a general demilitarization was suggested, and the populated areas of the McMahon Line where the Indian Government could not contemplate themselves withdrawing from established posts and leaving the Chinese in possession of positions recently occupied south of that line. No agreement was reached beyond a tacit understanding to refrain from sending out patrols; but the Chinese, at least temporarily, avoided actions on the frontier which might have precipitated another crisis. Correspondence between the governments continued in which the positions of the two sides became immovably fixed in complete opposition. The Chinese, without making precise territorial claims, insisted that the whole Indo-Tibetan frontier —with the exception of Sikkim and most of Bhutan—was undetermined and needed to be defined by negotiation. The Indian Government insisted that the whole frontier had long been established by treaty and custom, and that only small local adjustments might be open to negotiation. The Indian attitude was so firm that Nehru even declined to meet Chou, arguing that it was useless to discuss an agreement on principles while there was still a complete disagreement on facts. The Chinese Government then produced, on 26 December 1959, a long statement of its case to which the Indian Government replied in a clearly and forcefully argued note dated 12 February 1960. At the same time, Nehru invited Chou to visit India for personal discussions.

Hints of a bargain by which the Chinese might remain in occupation of the road through the Aksai Chin, which was of strategic importance to them, in exchange for their recognition of the McMahon Line and other parts of the frontier continued to be implicit in the Chinese communications. It was also rumoured in India that such a possibility was in the air. But Indian public opinion was so deeply stirred on the subject of the integrity of India's frontiers that even if Nehru had inclined to consider the bargain—which had a good deal to commend it—his government could hardly have taken the risk.

Chou's visit to New Delhi in April 1960 was chilly and, as neither side would make any concessions, no progress was made. The dispute was handed over to the Foreign Ministries of the two countries for examination and a report after six months. It was probably a gain for India that Chou should have seen for himself how deeply moved and determined Indian public opinion was on the issue. After his visit, in spite of rumours of troop concentrations, no overt action against India's frontiers appears to have taken place. The Chinese Government turned their efforts upon frontier settlements with the Governments of Burma and Nepal in which they were anxious to appear reasonable and accommodating in order to suggest that on the issue of the Indian frontier, the Indian Government was being unnecessarily difficult.

The agreement in 1960 with the Burmese Government, while studiously avoiding mention of the McMahon Line, appears for the most part to accept the Burmese section of it as the traditional frontier between the two countries. But it awaits joint demarcation.

The agreement with Nepal which also was supposed to have effected the acceptance of traditional frontiers, subject to possible small adjustments, led to immediate friction and gave an example of Chinese methods. Without waiting for the joint inquiry prescribed under the agreement, the Chinese are reported to have encroached on Nepalese territory and even to have removed boundary marks in order to face the joint commission with a *fait accompli*.

The Himalayan frontier, therefore, continued in a state of uneasy tension through the summer of 1960, with neither India nor China abating any of its demands. Ill-feeling was further increased by charges and counter-charges, of harassment of Indians in Tibet and of Chinese in India. None of this was of advantage to the Tibetans except that, with the possibility of a new approach to the United Nations always in mind, they could remark the reaffirmation by the Indian Government of the validity of the McMahon Line together with the competence of the Tibetans to negotiate it in 1914.

TIBETANS IN EXILE

By the end of 1959 at least 17,000 Tibetans had been received in camps organized by the Government of India and the number was steadily growing. After the first great influx in March to May, which followed the rising and the suppression of armed resistance, a steady trickle of refugees continued to find a way across the border. The initial administrative difficulties were gradually overcome and the refugees were progressively classified and distributed into different camps. At Dalhousie and Buxa Duar about 2,000 learned monks were settled in quiet surroundings where they could resume, so far as possible, their life of prayer, study, and contemplation. Laymen and monk novices were given training in various Tibetan crafts and also instruction in Hindi and English to enable them eventually to learn other skills. In Sikkim and some other places large numbers of the men were found employment on road-making by which they were able to earn a small amount of money. Those who could not readily be fitted into any of the special camps remained in the transit centre into which new arrivals were also received. This centre, at Misamari near Tezpur in Assam, appears to have been chosen hastily as the only place available in an emergency. It has many drawbacks and the damp heat of the rainy season, the mosquitoes, and the bad water make it unsuitable for Tibetans. It therefore acquired a frightening reputation among the refugees and it also came in for wider criticism, based on hearsay. I visited it myself early in 1960 and saw some of the difficulties of handling a shifting population and having repeatedly to adapt newcomers to conditions and habits to which they were not accustomed. The staff of the camp, who had to share the hardships of the refugees, were working with energy and devotion to make the best of admittedly unsuitable conditions and it was understood that the object of the Indian Government was to close the camp as soon as the refugees could be moved elsewhere. The proportion of women and children among the refugees was small and, although some were settled with their menfolk on the road-building sites, many had to remain in the unpleasant climate of Misamari owing to the difficulty of placing them in other camps. Early in 1960 the Government of India were considering plans to solve this unhappy situation by the establishment of village settlements in suitable districts, where the Tibetans could be set up as self-contained communities.

In every camp the Tibetans were well fed and fairly adequately housed—with the exception of the unsuitable site at Misamari. They also had medical help available on a reasonable scale. The expense of all these basic needs falls entirely on the Government of India but much additional relief has been contributed by voluntary organizations. There is a Central Relief Committee set up by non-official Indians through which are distributed extra food, medicines, clothing, and other comforts and necessities. Large contributions have been received from voluntary associations in many foreign countries, with a massively generous proportion from the U.S.A. The share from Britain has been meagre. There have also been offers from European countries of homes and education for selected refugees. Aid from foreign governments, too, has been received, beginning with a gift of £(A)10,000 from the Government of Australia to help in re-settling Tibetans in new villages in India. The British Government, which from its former close and friendly relationship with Tibet should have been the first to give active help, was stated in the House of Lords on 5 May 1960 to be 'watching the situation with the most sympathetic eye'.[1]

In addition to the majority of the refugees, who are cared for by the Government of India, there are several thousands scattered through various parts of northern India. Many are naturally attracted to the neighbourhood of Kalimpong and Darjeeling, with which Tibetans had an ancient connection. But it appears that the Indian Government, perhaps over-sensitive about Chinese reactions in view of the tension on the frontier, wants to dis-

[1] A contribution of £50,000 was made early in 1961.

courage Tibetans from gathering there. As a result the care of these refugees, who include quite a large number of women and children, falls on local voluntary committees which get no help from official sources. Their condition appears much less satisfactory than that of the refugees in the regular camps.

No one who visits the camps and other refugee centres can fail to be struck by the gratitude of the Tibetans for all that has been done for them and by their eagerness to be able to earn their own living and cease to be dependent on charity. On the other side, the warmth of feeling and admiration for their good qualities which the Tibetans have inspired in many of the Indian officials who are responsible for dealing with them is equally remarkable. In general, it may be thought that the Indian Government, which has had to face criticism at home for helping Tibetans while many Indian refugees remain on its hands and has wanted also to avoid additional causes of strain in its relations with China, has tended to hide its light under a bushel and has not received the praise it deserves for its treatment of the Tibetan refugees.

The task is one which will continue for some time, for during 1960 refugees from Tibet were entering India in ever-increasing numbers. I met some of them before they had even been received by the Indian authorities and heard about the conditions from which they were escaping.

These recent arrivals were from villages south of the Tsang-po (Brahmaputra), roughly between Shigatse and Mt. Everest. Owing to the virtual prohibition of travel it appears difficult for Tibetans from north of the Tsang-po to escape southwards and for the same reason the refugees from south of the river knew nothing of conditions at any distance from their own villages. Those reaching India were mostly of the yeoman class whose property ranged from very small holdings to modest estates. All were socially far removed from the nobility but many of them were employers of a few tenant labourers. Since the rising they had been carrying on their farming much as before until about August or September 1959 when teams of Chinese officials with Chinese-trained helpers from distant parts of the country began to arrive in the villages. In each place they appointed a

sort of village council from among those who had no land of
their own. The councils were instigated to arrest, denounce, and
assault the yeoman farmers in the same sort of 'trials' which
appear to have been the practice in China. The landless villagers
had little choice but to take part in the trials because they were
told that unless they accused the landowners they must be in
sympathy with them and would themselves be denounced. The
accusers were reinforced by local beggars and even by gangs of
professional bandits who were brought in from outside by the
Chinese. After the public denunciation and beating, the yeomen
farmers were imprisoned, their land and livestock were confiscated, their hair was cut off and their earrings purloined. The
women and children were left at first in their houses but valuable
property was taken away and some of the children were removed,
ostensibly to go to schools elsewhere. Many of the yeomen were
deported to work on road-making. So long as they were in prison
they received no food and depended on their families to keep
them alive. Starvation was, in fact, the most important weapon
used by the Chinese. Their promises that those who cultivated
the land should have the year's crop were soon dishonoured. The
whole of the harvest of the yeomen was confiscated and an
allowance of about 28 lb. of barley per month was made to each
member of the household who was allowed to remain. The
landless cultivators were not much better off. They were persuaded by arguments which it would not have been prudent to
ignore, to contribute the greater share of the crops they had grown
to 'the people'. In general, they were left with between a quarter
and a third of their harvest, and the organization of agricultural
communes was put in hand to look after future cultivation.

These social 'reforms' were accompanied by religious persecution such as there had been at Lhasa. In each village the Dalai
Lama was publicly vilified. Lamas and senior monks were
denounced, assaulted, and imprisoned. The ordinary monks
were given no food so long as they stayed in the monasteries
and were ordered to marry and settle on the land as the alternative
to starvation. The temples and monastery buildings were stripped
of the sacred images and books, which were taken away or

destroyed on the spot. A few old monks were allowed to stay in the deserted monasteries or to seek shelter in the villages and were given a small allowance of barley.

The refugees from this tyranny included farmers and monks who either fled to avoid the denunciation and assaults they saw being practised on others or who managed to escape from detention either before or after being brought to trial. Many more tried to escape than succeeded. Those who were caught were taken back to punishment and imprisonment or forced labour. Beating and pelting with stones appear to have been frequent and a number of the victims died as a result; there were many suicides; but formal executions seem to have been rare.

So violent an upheaval of a farming society inevitably destroyed the pattern of agriculture and was followed by something approaching famine. In an attempt to restore production the Chinese postponed the idea of collective or communal farming; but, already, many of those on whose work they were counting—the former landless labourers—had joined the flow of refugees into India. Some of them told me, at the end of 1960, that they had been driven to this by broken promises, fear of being moved to another part of Tibet, and—most of all—by the meagre rations which were barely enough to keep them alive.

It is in keeping with the Tibetan nature that almost all the refugees, struggling destitute into India, grieved far more over the attacks on their faith and the sacrilege against their religious teachers and holy places than over the loss of their own small possessions.

In spite of the apparently overpowering military repression, active resistance has not been entirely extinguished and in June 1960 there were reports of fresh outbreaks of fighting in different parts of Tibet, including the border with Nepal. By the end of 1960, Chinese retaliation against the fighters, continued expropriation of small farmers, and the desperate shortage of food combined to swell to about 60,000 the number of refugees for whom—and for those who escape in future—India and Nepal, with the help of the free world, must take responsibility.

From this story the Tibetans emerge as a people deeply conscious of their separateness and resenting foreign intrusion into their way of life; devoted to preserving their peculiar culture, institutions, and above all their religion; united by sharing unquestioningly in the same ideas rather than by being fitted into any close administrative system; not covetously or aggressively inclined towards their neighbours but seeking to maintain their own rights by stubborn persistence rather than by violence; more interested in the reality of independence than in the show of it. For 1,300 years they succeeded in preserving a purely Tibetan form of government, changing and developing to meet different circumstances but always containing elements and ideas which can be traced back to the sixth century.

Attention has been drawn to a regularly recurring pattern in the relations between Tibet and China over those centuries, but it is not intended thereby to suggest that the past can provide a sure pointer to the future. The pattern repeated itself in a wide but clearly defined framework. The rival neighbours, although differing in language and customs, were limited by the same difficulties of communications, and guided by similar political concepts. The possibility of the greater seeking to change the bases of the thought and life of the less never arose.

The shattering of that framework by the irruption of the West into China in the nineteenth century ended the long-existing, latent sympathy and the similarity of thought which had made co-existence possible. Certain considerations of geographical remoteness, climate, altitude, and natural resources delayed the advance of the mechanized and industrially minded age. But from being people of the same Inside world the Chinese became part of the Outside; and having acquired the techniques and taken the measure of that world they have made the Tibetans pay for humiliations inflicted on China by the Outside.

It is, perhaps, significant that the present crisis in the life of Tibet marks the first time that the Chinese proper have ever exercised authority there. The former connection had been with the Mongol and Manchu rulers of China, both people of the steppes and both sharing the same ideas as the Tibetans. In those two periods, but more especially under the Manchu dynasty, the importance of Tibet lay in the need to prevent the religious influence of the Tibetan church from being used against the interests of China. Such considerations had ceased to exist long before the seizure of power by the Communists.

Tibet with its tiny, peaceful population could so easily have been allowed to live on, under remote Chinese control, and to develop on its own lines, preserving those qualities and differences which made its civilization valuable to the rest of the world, without constituting the faintest threat to China. But the mania for imposing conformity, which possessed the Chinese at the same time as they acquired new ideas and overwhelming power, gave little hope that anything so obstinately 'anachronistic' as the Tibetan Government and religion could share in that Brave New World. With the removal of their natural leaders in the cataclysm of 1959 the Tibetan people have been hard put to it to retain their spirit under the pressure of constant haranguing and regimentation. But the conquerors were not content to dominate the spirit. By deporting much of the male population, by dispersing and resettling communities, and by pouring in floods of their excess population the Chinese, who already have been successful in swamping other races, threaten the very existence of the people, the language, the literature, the customs, and even the name of Tibet.

Some politicians and writers, with no personal knowledge of Tibet, have expressed the opinion that what the Chinese have done is only to carry out the long overdue reform of an oppressive social system. Such armchair critics should consider whether they are not in fact giving their approval to the domination of a small people by a ruthless foreign power followed by the abolition of one whole order of society, the destruction of religious institutions, and an attack on the right to private property even on the smallest scale. Two reports by the International Commission of Jurists are available. The second, entitled *Tibet and the People's Republic of China*, published in August 1960, contains detailed statements taken from Tibetan refugees by qualified lawyers. It concludes that the Chinese have committed genocide in a forcible attempt to destroy the Tibetans as a religious group and that they have violated human rights in Tibet in sixteen different ways including murder, rape, torture, destruction of family life, and deportation. The Dalai Lama, who himself gave evidence to the Commission, has stated that between 1955 and 1959, 65,000 Tibetans were killed and at least 10,000 children deported to China. On the other hand, the Commission finds that there is no support for Chinese allegations that no human rights were enjoyed by the people of Tibet before the entry of the Chinese.

With regard to the international position of Tibet the jurists consider that the Agreement of 1951 between Tibet and China, whether or not it can be held to have been concluded under duress, came to an end when it was formally repudiated by the Tibetans in 1959. Tibet then resumed the status of independence and, in the view of the Commission, there is no obstacle in the Charter of the United Nations to the question of Tibet being raised before and decided by organs of that body.

But the Communist occupation of Tibet, however illegal, is, for the present, a hard fact and what can be the future of the Tibetans in their terrible plight is hard to see. Those now in India as refugees will have a focus for their devotion and their hopes in the person of the Dalai Lama, whose presence and religious authority will continue to inspire a feeling of unity and individuality. It is, of course, necessary and it is desired by the Tibetans themselves, that they should adapt themselves to the world in which they have to live; but they will need to be given both help and encouragement to preserve the essence of their way of life. The key, as always, is religion and so that it may be given full opportunity to continue as a living force, it is desirable to keep the Tibetans together, as far as possible, in self-contained communities, as the Indian Government is planning to do. It is of vital importance that in each community provision be made for the practice and teaching of religion. The introduction of Tibetans to Western knowledge and ideas should be done with great care. It will not be enough simply to bring them, at the hands of foreign teachers, some ready-made methods of education. The Dalai Lama has himself made a beginning by setting up a school under his own supervision where the refugees will be taught by his own people. If the Tibetans themselves and especially the religious teachers can make a synthesis of their own beliefs and ideas with the learning of the outside world, a distinctive and valuable Tibetan community may survive in the foothills of the Himalaya.

As for the Tibetans remaining in their own country, the odds seem all against them. A few million Tibetans are faced by overwhelming and brutal power and by a vast number of aggressive, doctrine-infatuated, rapidly increasing Chinese. It is not easy to get a great deal of accurate information. The two neutral observers at Lhasa—the Indian Consul-General and the Nepalese Officer—are restricted in their contacts and movements; the Dalai Lama himself can receive occasional reports although the danger to informants and agents is obvious; the refugees know only about their own limited areas. But none of the obstacles can prevent news finding its way out and the Chinese themselves have had to admit that resistance is continuing. The spirit of the Tibetans has not been crushed and those who know them will continue to believe that even in the darkest adversity the embers of the faith will be kept alive, as they were before, and that something of the Tibetan character with its patience, courage, devout simplicity, honesty, and kindliness, will survive to add its rare value to the rich diversity of the world.

EPILOGUE

Since 1960 the Tibetan scene has undergone various changes. The iron grip fastened on the personal freedom, religion, agriculture, economy and whole way of life of the Tibetan people after the bloody suppression of the 1959 rising was methodically strengthened. A large number of men, women and children of the nobility and middle class, described as oppressors of the people, together with leading monks and lamas, were kept in prison or hard labour camps where many died under brutal treatment and others were to remain for long periods of up to twenty years. Both in towns and villages family life was deliberately broken up, husbands being separated from wives and children from their parents.

The monasteries had been emptied of all but a handful of elderly monks and robbed of much of their wealth; the public practice of religion was proscribed and those who remained openly steadfast in their faith were derided and sometimes assaulted.

Local supplies of food for their forces and civilian officials were a necessity for the Chinese; and to carry out their policy they set up a network of committees down to village level, dominated by their own party workers and responsible, under overriding military supervision, to the Tibet Working Committee of the Chinese Communist Party. Their duties included the organization of agricultural communes or mutual aid groups, the collection of the harvest, allocation of work, distribution of rations, control of the movement of the people—who were strictly confined to their own villages—and the rooting out of "reactionaries" by means of so-called public trials in which children were forced to accuse their parents, and neighbour to give evidence against neighbour. Those who were not being hard driven in agricultural labour were organized into gangs for work on building roads, bridges and military installations, with nominal pay, frequent penalties and punishments, constant indoctrination, and always inadequate food.

Chinese propaganda spoke of increased agricultural production; but the benefits went to support the occupying forces and did not find their way to the Tibetans. A ruthless system of rationing not only of food but of cloth and every other commodity was an important element in the Chinese machinery of government. It was used also to discriminate against former landlords, monks, and the middle classes who were kept in near starvation while those who were regarded as inoffensive and who were able to work were given slightly better treatment; but all except a few favoured puppets were perpetually hungry and apprehensive.

Despite such extensive surveillance, resistance movements continued to trouble the new regime and many young men suspected of sabotage or other rebellious activities were tortured and executed.

Meanwhile the world outside was being told of great progress in modernizing the country on democratic lines with improvements in education, medical facilities, communications, agriculture, animal husbandry, and small industries; and in 1962 a few reliable Communist sympathisers from foreign countries were allowed to visit Lhasa and Shigatse for a carefully window-dressed inspection.

By 1965 the Chinese were ready for a formal change in administrative arrangements. The Preparatory Committee for the Autonomous Region of Tibet had continued in name after 1959 though completely subordinate to the military dictatorship. Now, after dividing the country into eight military zones, the Chinese announced the creation of the Tibetan Autonomous Region, a change more in name than in substance, for the same Chinese masters controlled the shadowy existence of the same Tibetan puppets—and yet, not quite the same, for in 1964 the Panchen Lama, who had been groomed as a substitute for the Dalai Lama, declined to co-operate any further and was denounced as subversive, dismissed, and kept in harsh custody.

And in an empty gesture the Dalai Lama, who had been retained as a make-believe member of the Preparatory Committee, was now formally discarded.

The nominal change in status did little to convince outside observers that the Chinese had won Tibetan support. It was impossible to prevent information finding its way across the borders; Tibetans still managed to escape to India while repeated tirades in the Chinese press against reactionaries made it clear that violent resistance and sabotage continued. An embarrassing and dangerous threat to Chinese troops was posed by the successful guerrilla operations by refugee Khampa warriors based in mountainous regions on the Nepalese side of the Tibetan frontier.

Tibetan discontent and the presence in India of the Dalai Lama with many active followers who were able to publish unpalatable news about events in Tibet led to unsuccessful efforts as early as 1965 to persuade him and other refugees to return home.

In 1966 another violent convulsion alarmed and bewildered the long-suffering Tibetan people and disrupted all Chinese administrative arrangements and plans for the future with the arrival at Lhasa of the Red Guards and the Cultural Revolution. That evil, spawned in China, led in Tibet to thorough-going barbaric vandalism in which an attempt was made to obliterate all outward signs of Tibetan individuality and culture. Although religion had for some time been persecuted and deprived of most of its priestly practitioners, about three thousand temples and holy places were now systematically looted and desecrated; religious books, images and ritual vessels were destroyed or stolen and many of the buildings were razed to the ground. In these outrages Tibetans were compelled by threats or induced by bribery to take part.

The leading Tibetan collaborators in the Chinese administration were maltreated and dismissed; and when General Chang Kuo-hua, who had been virtual dictator of Tibet since 1959, tried to curb their excesses the Red Guard turned on him and, having insolently disgraced and arrested him together with his lieutenant Wang Chung-mei, they set up their own temporary government. The situation was reversed by the Peoples' Liberation

Army (PLA) which, after some equivocal behavior, restored Chang Kuo-hua to much of his former authority; but in 1967 he was transferred to Sichuan. Thereupon disorder broke out again; but the position of Chinese Communist Party officials was eased by the development of rivalry and fierce internecine fighting between factions of the Red Guards. The Tibetans took the opportunity of siding with one or other of the parties to attack its rivals.

It was not until 1970 that the chaos was gradually brought to an end after the collapse of the Cultural Revolution in China and the reinforcement of the PLA troops at Lhasa. The immediate sequel was the arrest, torture and execution of Tibetans who had taken part in widespread guerrilla actions against the Chinese all over the country during the turmoil of the past four years. Eventually, in 1971, the Chinese under the influence of Chou En-lai found it prudent to try to conciliate and reassure minority peoples after the infamous savagery of the Red Guards; and a new Governing Committee with Tibetan puppet members was set up at Lhasa. In 1974 a special delegation of the Chinese Communist Party came to Tibet to try to improve relations. Blame for what had happened was laid on Lin Piao; an amnesty was declared; Tibetans were appointed as nominal heads of village communes; and former noblemen and landlords were rehabilitated and put on the same level as the rest of the population. In order to expiate in the eyes of the world the vandalism of the Cultural Revolution the Chinese, though continuing to prohibit the public practice of religion, set about restoring some of the famous holy places of Lhasa whose main fabric had survived. Images and sacred vessels had to be made to replace those destroyed; frescoes had to be repainted and silk hangings renewed.

A new call went out to the refugees to return; and in an attempt to persuade the outside world of the past success and future good intentions of the regime there was a gradual opening of Tibet's doors to foreigners. After an interval of ten years, the first visitors to be invited were trusty Communist sympathizers. Then in 1976 the king of Nepal came on a stage-managed tour and a gradually increasing trickle of privileged travellers

included Mr Arthur Schlesinger, the Defence Secretary of the
U.S.A., and leading international journalists and Western scholars. By 1979 regular tourist parties were being organized. The
resulting publicity must have been a disappointment to the Chinese. Discerning foreign visitors saw the hollowness of many of
their claims. Lhasa was found to consist of two cities with some
fifty thousand Tibetans, many in rags, segregated in the old city
while a new town had been built by their labour for seventy
thousand Chinese civilians and an unknown number of troops in
their separate barracks. Chinese treatment of Tibetans was
openly contemptuous and often rough. In the few instances
where direct communication was possible Tibetans would refer
to some Chinese mentor before giving an answer. The new religious toleration had converted the restored holy places into mere
museums and it was seen that public worship was allowed in the
Cathedral of Lhasa—the Jokhang—at first only between a few
fixed hours and on payment for entry. Even the vaunted economic developments were less impressive than had been claimed.
The Tibetans clearly had a deep dislike of the Chinese and the
general impression of Chinese rule was of an unsympathetic and
oppressive colonial dictatorship.

Together with their gesture to foreign opinion the Chinese
increased their efforts to encourage Tibetan exiles to return.
They released many of the nobles and lamas, some of whom had
been in prison since 1959, and they allowed Tibetans, including a
few of the released prisoners, to visit their relations in India
provided they left family hostages in Tibet. These visitors
brought first-hand reports of conditions there and of their harsh
and anxious existence since 1959. In the reverse direction refugees in India and elsewhere were allowed to visit Tibet where
they could compare what they saw with life as they had known it
before the Chinese occupation.

The first significant breakthrough in authoritative information
came in 1979 when Tsultrim Tersey, a well-educated and intelligent Tibetan refugee living in Switzerland, succeeded on his own
initiative in reaching Shigatse and Lhasa where he met his family
and many friends. His report confirmed the stories which had

been reaching India for many years about the inhuman treatment of the Tibetan people, their general wretchedness and depressed economic condition. He found that food, cloth, and other commodities were strictly and sparingly rationed. All shops were owned by Chinese-controlled co-operatives and nothing could be bought without a ration coupon. Tibetans were excluded from the world of trade in which they used to excel. Although there had been a move to break up some communes and permit the private holding of small plots of land and a few cattle, the whole crop on land held by a commune was taken over by the Chinese and it was they who distributed the meagre ration to each person. Tsultrim Tersey found the roads in bad repair; and charges for those Tibetans who secured permission to use the buses were very high. In the villages he found children, who should have been at school, working long hours in the fields. At the time of his visit the Jokhang was open only twice a month but that restriction was eased by 1980.

Several other Tibetan men and women from India and America added details from their personal experience. But the most important further development was the invitation of official delegations from the Dalai Lama's headquarters in India who were able to cover much more of the country than the restricted organized tours by foreign visitors. The first mission went by way of Peking in 1979. Little news about its findings was released. The second, in 1980, produced an informative and revealing report. It was greeted with scenes of wild emotion and enthusiasm. Its members, having come from the presence of the Dalai Lama, were treated almost as holy beings. The clippings of their hair were seized on as relics and people struggled to touch even their clothes. This demonstration of devotion was all the more embarrassing to the Chinese because visiting journalists were in Lhasa at the time. The party, which travelled more extensively than Tsultrim Tersey, was able to confirm and expand his information. Wherever they went they were told of the misery of the people and were besought with tears not to be deceived by the Chinese but to go on striving for freedom. They found education in Tibetan lamentably inadequate and subordinated to Chinese, a knowledge of which is essential if a Tibetan wants employment—for example in the small industries which were found to be largely manned and wholly managed by Chinese. Even with a knowledge of Chinese, Tibetans could expect only secondary positions. Medical facilities apart from the towns, where there are good hospitals, are rudimentary. Agriculture, except for some misguided cultural experiments, was generally good thanks to new irrigation and the large labour force conscripted by the Chinese. Industrial and agricultural developments would be of value to the Tibetans if they were allowed to enjoy the fruits. The same was seen to be true of the extensive extraction of trees from the forests of south Tibet which was being carried out by poorly paid Tibetan labour while the timber went to China. Like other travellers the delegation could not see the extent of the military occupation which Indian sources put at around 200,000 men and the Tibetans at many times more. Needless to say they were not informed about missile bases or nuclear tests in Tibet. A sad observation was that the once abundant wildlife had almost vanished.

The most moving aspect of Tibetan life today is the longing of the whole people for the return of the Dalai Lama and their unshakeable devotion to their faith. Every visitor to Lhasa tells of Tibetans, young as well as old, crowding into the Jokhang to pray and make offerings while worshippers prostrate themselves ceaselessly outside the holy place. This evidence of the deep-rooted power of Buddhism in Tibet gives the lie to Chinese propaganda that the people were browbeaten into conformity and exploited by the domination of the large body of monks. Today, as eleven centuries earlier when religion was persecuted and monks almost exterminated, the embers of the faith have been kept alive in the hearts of the common people.

Partly, perhaps, because that lesson had some effect and partly as a result of the reports by the Tibetan official delegations and the critical view of their regime by foreign observers, the Chinese made a remarkable *volte face* which must have disconcerted the fellow-travellers who had so sedulously followed the earlier propaganda line. In 1980 a high-level delegation headed by Hu

Yao-bang, the General Secretary of the Chinese Communist Party, came to Lhasa and almost immediately announced extensive new measures to create better relations with the Tibetans and to improve their standard of living. In a surprising denunciation of almost everything that had been done since 1959 as mistaken, ill-judged or corrupt, it was alleged that vast sums which should have been used for the good of the Tibetans had been misappropriated, officials had abused their power and the Chinese had consumed a disproportionate amount of Tibetan production. The blame for all this was laid on the Gang of Four. It was proposed that a number of Chinese officials should be withdrawn and replaced by Tibetans; but nothing was said about limiting Chinese immigrant settlement in Tibet and it was reasserted that Tibet is an inalienable part of China. The Panchen Lama was dug out of his long-enforced retirement and allowed to visit Lhasa and Shigatse. Although temples and monasteries were still regarded as cultural museums, stress was laid on research by Chinese scholars into Tibetan history, society and archaeology. A few Chinese Tibetologists were allowed to travel abroad and to meet Western scholars and Tibetan students in exile. There is a considerable tradition of Chinese scholarship in such matters but the interpretations of the present breed are inevitably coloured by Marxist theory.

The reaction of the Tibetan people to the changes was cautious. Many were still held in prison and reports of risings and sabotage continued to be heard well into 1981. So, although there was welcome for an improvement in the food ration, the right to hold a little private property and to take some part in trade, the reforms were not seen as ushering in a golden age. Above all, the longing for the return of the Dalai Lama is unabated.

Meanwhile the refugees in free countries pursue many different activities. The majority are in India where the government very generously made them welcome and provided land, cattle, agricultural implements and all that was necessary to settle them gradually in villages in several parts of the country. The governments of many foreign countries also gave large sums of money and other assistance; and financial, material and technical help was rapidly given and continues to be given by charitable organizations and private persons throughout the world where the plight of the Tibetans, their courage in adversity and eagerness to work met a sympathetic response.

About fifty thousand of the refugees are now living in agricultural settlements in India and some fifteen thousand in Nepal where also they have had help from international institutions and private sources in addition to finance from the Nepalese government. The fortunes of the villages have varied according to the climate, the nature of the soil, the quality of leadership and the amount of financial support they receive. The most prosperous are the earliest settlements in Karnataka which now have a population of about twelve thousand who have achieved self-sufficiency and are able to employ Indian labour and to send contributions to the Dalai Lama's office at Dharamsala. Their organization is impressive—they have tractors, vehicle repair workshops, efficient co-operative societies, schools, a hospital and dispensaries, a dairy farm and carpet factory. Other villages in Maharastra, Orissa and Bengal still need to be subsidized, mainly from the Dalai Lama's resources, on a gradually decreasing scale. The Tibetans have been tolerantly accepted by their Indian neighbours with whom they are on easy and amicable terms; and overall, the villages are evidence of Tibetan adaptability and determination to earn their own living in new and unfamiliar surroundings. For their success the humane and generous hospitality of the Indian government deserves great credit.

Not all the refugees are in the villages. A number of craft centres were set up by the Dalai Lama with foreign help; they now give employment to over three thousand men and women; but there are several thousand still in makeshift accommodations waiting for resettlement and mainly working on road construction. Others with some private means prefer to be independent and have set up small businesses, shops, restaurants and hotels. The Tibetan flair for trade has created a new and thriving small industry with refugees making or buying up woollen sweaters during the summer and travelling round north India to sell them in the cold weather. The Indian army has provided another opportunity for young Tibetans in a special formation where they are proving their worth.

The focus of Tibetan life in India is the religious and secular headquarters of the Dalai Lama's shadow government at Dharamsala to which all his people look and which keeps in touch with them through frequent visits by his representatives and sometimes by the Dalai Lama himself. It is his aim to keep alive as much as possible of Tibetan culture and tradition; so as well as administrative offices there are at Dharamsala a library of Tibetan works and archives, a museum of art, a school of drama and music, a college of Tibetan medicine, and a centre for higher religious studies, principally traditional and doctrinal but covering modern subjects also.

Dharamsala, now almost a Tibetan town, is not the only religious centre in India. Important lamas of other sects have successful establishments elsewhere—the Sakyapa near Dehra Dun, the Karmapa near Gangtok, the Nyingmapa at Kalimpong and a Bonpo community near Simla; and wherever groups of Tibetans are found, however small, there is some sort of chapel with its monk or monks. The three or four thousand practising monks and lamas scattered throughout India, Nepal and the Western world are the remnant of the devout and learned men of religion in the many and frequently overgrown monastic institutions in Tibet which used to house probably a hundred times that number, among whom it is fair to say there were many less serious and worthy members. The first object of most of the dedicated monks who managed to reach India was to acquire some means of printing doctrinal works; and the output of religious texts and commentaries is now astonishing. Although most of them retain their orthodox traditionalism, contact with Indian and Western thought has led to some broadening of their outlook and there are new works also on customs, history and language.

In the villages Tibetan identity is kept alive through religion and language. There is always a religious teacher and small temple and the principal festivals of the Buddhist year are duly observed. It is perhaps true that the more sincere piety is to be found among the older people; the young, while honouring their Buddhist faith as part of the Tibetan tradition, have not the crude stimulus of persecution which has produced the emotional fervour of faith in Tibet itself. The recruitment of novice monks is now restricted to a few with a sense of vocation; but Tibetans from all over India, with their characteristic love of travel and pilgrimage, make a great effort to visit Dharamsala and receive the blessing of the Dalai Lama.

One of the first concerns of the Dalai Lama after his escape to India was the care of several hundreds of children in the refugee camps. Some had lost their parents in the exodus; others came from families too poor to support them. Within a year a rudimentary nursery was set up at Dharamsala into which nearly five hundred children were crowded. It has since been developed with substantial foreign aid into a well-housed, well-managed Children's Village of a thousand boys and girls under the supervision of the Dalai Lama's younger sister. Another very successful home for Tibetan children was founded at Mussoorie where there are twenty-eight houses with some seven hundred children; and there are smaller homes elsewhere.

The Dalai Lama's other principal anxiety was that young Tibetans should receive a sound Western education and he very quickly began two schools from his own resources. In 1961 he persuaded the Government of India to form a Tibetan Schools Society in which Indian officials and Tibetan members supervise the management of some fifty schools under the general responsibility of the Indian Ministry of Education which, in another example of Indian generosity, makes a grant for each child. There are four flourishing residential schools, mainly in the Himalayan foothills, day schools in all the village settlements and smaller schools in other places. The state-supported schools are staffed by Indian teachers and by Tibetans trained in a special college at Dharamsala. There are also several small independent schools which rely on local and foreign support. Originally education was free but with increasing prosperity in the villages fees are paid by those who can afford them. In addition, the education of many needy children is sponsored by private persons and charitable societies in many countries.

Inevitably there is considerable variety in the standards of different schools but in general the intelligence and keenness of children whose education in their own country would, if any, have been restricted to religious studies have blossomed in the air of Western thought and they learn quickly to speak and write English and Hindi.

The Dalai Lama's intention was that education should be directed mainly towards vocational training rather than academic learning but within eight years from the founding of the first schools a number of boys and girls qualified for higher studies in Indian colleges. Most of them are absorbed into the Dalai Lama's administrative service and a few others have obtained medical and nursing qualifications which are of value to their community. The young intelligentsia show a remarkable facility for the clear and effective use of idiomatic English in acute political and philosophical argument. In the freedom of new ideas they do not hesitate—while retaining their reverence for the Dalai Lama and admiration for his personal leadership—to criticize the more traditionally minded Dharamsala bureaucracy.

The horizon of several hundred Tibetans has also been widened by education and travel in Europe and America. In the very earliest days of the flight to India leading officers of the Rockefeller Foundation appreciated the opportunity of finding learned Tibetans to act as informants for Western scholars, and themselves to learn something of Western ideas, in a way which had never before been possible. They arranged to finance for five years several monks and lamas, and a few laymen with special qualifications, to be attached to universities in France, Germany, Italy, Japan, the Netherlands, the United Kingdom and the U.S.A., where Tibetologists were available to make use of this project.

Further, voluntary organizations, private persons and some governments in several countries arranged to receive a number of young Tibetans individually or in groups. Parties of children were sent to the Pestalozzi schools in Switzerland and England;

young men and women were chosen for vocational training in Switzerland, Norway, Denmark and Canada; some families were given employment in factories, especially in Switzerland. More recently some young men and women who have passed through the Tibetan educational system in India have won scholarships or sponsors at universities and other institutions in Europe and the U.S.A.

With their natural ability and initiative they have made good use of these opportunities and there are now young Tibetans fluent in English and some in French, German and Italian, fitting easily into the society of the host country in a wide range of employment and at different levels of prosperity but seeming always to enjoy what they are doing whether they work in banks, offices or hospitals, as university technicians, waiters in restaurants, in bakeries or public parks; some run their own trading businesses and own comfortable houses. Their friendly and open nature makes them welcome everywhere and there have been several successful mixed marriages; but they remain determinedly Tibetan.

Admirable though the achievements of lay Tibetans have been, it is the attraction of Tibetan spirituality that has most greatly influenced people in the West. That feeling was greatly stimulated by the accessibility for the first time of many monks and lamas renowned for their sanctity and learning, and above all, of the Dalai Lama. During his frequent travels in Europe (including the U.S.S.R.), the U.S.A., and Japan and Mongolia, many thousands of men and women have experienced his tranquil, unaffected holiness and radiant humanity, and his intellectual exposition of profound Buddhist philosophy with penetrating simplicity and conviction. His exchange of views with leading churchmen all over the world, his enlightened leadership of his people in exile and avoidance of bitter political controversy have made him a well-known and much respected international figure.

The attraction of Tibetan thought and meditation techniques has led to the establishment in Europe and the U.S.A. of over a hundred centres for the teaching of Buddhist religious philos-

ophy and mysticism presided over by learned monks and lamas
from different doctrinal traditions. The teachers appear secure in
the belief that, from a somewhat superior spiritual base, they
have much to impart to the Western world; and although most of
the centres have prospered materially they have generally maintained a high standard of integrity and responsibility. In spite of a
fundamental conservatism, the minds of some of them must be
opening to ideas from the new world around them.

So the body of Tibetan exiles contains several different elements: monks and lamas, their numbers and quality fined down
by past persecution, preserving outside Tibet their traditions of
doctrine and monasticism, some conservatively, others with
more progressive views; laymen, including the main body of
villagers among whom the new generations are acquiring not
only technical skills but inevitably new ideas; enterprising busi-
nessmen who exemplify the Tibetan love of trade and travel, the
versatile and outspoken intelligentsia—all equally conscious of
being Tibetan. What creates that unity is still the common faith
even though it may be practised with varying degrees of
intensity.

Clearly there would be problems even now in integrating
these refugees of growing self-reliance and sophistication with
the Tibetans in Tibet who have been oppressed, blinkered and
regimented for many years and for whom it is a struggle to retain
their religion and culture. The longer the time of waiting the
greater the difficulty; but the refugees still keep the vision of
returning home while the people in Tibet live in hope of the
restoration of the Dalai Lama.

The Chinese are equally anxious for his return. Their recent
policy of liberalisation may suggest that with unresolved tension
in their relations with India and, more significantly, with the
U.S.S.R. they see the advantage of having the Tibetans, if not as
enthusiastic allies, at least as less discontented subjects. And they
may hope to give plausibility to their attempts to persuade the
Dalai Lama to come back and so rid themselves of a thorn in the
flesh and the embarrassment of the presence over the border of a
figure of world stature and impressive spiritual authority who

has eighty thousand exiled followers with articulate nationalistic opinions. The Dalai Lama has sometimes said that he hopes, sometimes that he believes, he will return; but his basic position is that he will not do so unless he is satisfied by some sort of plebiscite that his people are contented under the present regime. The Chinese, who insist that Tibet is part of China—though it became so only by violence in 1952—are unlikely to agree to any such test or, if he were to return, to accord to the Dalai Lama any function but that of a spiritual figurehead. Negotiations go on between his representatives and the Chinese but no progress is made; and there are hints that their policy of conciliation is wearing thin in the reported interruption of foreign visits to Tibet.

On the evidence from many different sources there is no doubt that thirty years of forcible Chinese occupation have brought on the Tibetan people much grievous suffering and hardship and the deprivation of their human rights. More than a small dose of liberalisation is needed from the Chinese to convince the Tibetans of their good intentions. Only if they could bring themselves to moderate their ingrained air of superiority and give not just contemptuous permission but at least the appearance of tolerant respect for the Tibetan practice of religion might they win respect in return and create an atmosphere that could allow nominal autonomy to be given a substantial form in which the Dalai Lama and his exiled followers could find a role and help to rebuild a peaceful and prosperous Tibet.

APPENDIX

1. *Treaty between Tibet and China* A.D. *821–822 (translation from the Tibetan text)*

The Great King of Tibet, the Miraculous Divine Lord, and the Great King of China, the Chinese Ruler Hwang-ti, being in the relationship of nephew and uncle, have conferred together for the alliance of their kingdoms. They have made and ratified a great agreement. Gods and men all know it and bear witness so that it may never be changed; and an account of the agreement has been engraved on this stone pillar to inform future ages and generations.

The Miraculous Divine Lord Thri-tsug De-tsen and the Chinese King Wên Wu Hsiao-te Wang-ti, nephew and uncle, seeking in their far-reaching wisdom to prevent all causes of harm to the welfare of their countries now or in the future, have extended their benevolence impartially over all. With the single desire of acting for the peace and benefit of all their subjects they have agreed on the high purpose of ensuring lasting good; and they have made this great treaty in order to fulfil their decision to restore the former ancient friendship and mutual regard and the old relationship of friendly neighbourliness.

Tibet and China shall abide by the frontiers of which they are now in occupation. All to the east is the country of Great China; and all to the west is, without question, the country of Great Tibet. Henceforth on neither side shall there be waging of war nor seizing of territory. If any person incurs suspicion he shall be arrested; his business shall be inquired into and he shall be escorted back.

Now that the two kingdoms have been allied by this great treaty it is necessary that messengers should once again be sent by the old route to maintain communications and carry the exchange of friendly messages regarding the harmonious relations between the Nephew and Uncle. According to the old custom, horses shall be changed at the foot of the Chiang Chun pass, the frontier between Tibet and China. At the Suiyung barrier the Chinese shall meet Tibetan envoys and provide them with all facilities from there onwards. At Ch'ing-shui the Tibetans shall meet Chinese envoys and provide all facilities. On both sides they shall be treated with customary honour and respect in conformity with the friendly relations between Nephew and Uncle.

Between the two countries no smoke nor dust shall be seen. There shall be no sudden alarms and the very word 'enemy' shall not be spoken. Even the frontier guards shall have no anxiety nor fear and shall enjoy land and bed at their ease. All shall live in peace and share the blessing of happiness for ten thousand years. The fame of this shall extend to all places reached by the sun and the moon.

This solemn agreement has established a great epoch when Tibetans shall be happy in the land of Tibet, and Chinese in the land of China. So that it may never be changed, the Three Precious Jewels of Religion, the Assembly of Saints, the Sun and Moon, Planets and Stars have been invoked as witnesses. An oath has been taken with solemn words and with the sacrifice of animals; and the agreement has been ratified.

If the parties do not act in accordance with this agreement or if they violate it, whichever it be, Tibet or China, nothing that the other party may do by way of retaliation shall be considered a breach of the treaty on their part.

The Kings and Ministers of Tibet and China have taken the prescribed oath to this effect and the agreement has been written in detail. The two Kings have affixed their seals. The Ministers specially empowered to execute the agreement have inscribed their signatures and copies have been deposited in the royal records of each party.

The treaty is carved in Tibetan and Chinese on one side of a stone pillar near the Jo-khang—the Cathedral of Lhasa. On another side is a historical introduction in Tibetan only; and on the other two sides are bilingual lists of the names of the ministers who witnessed it. The texts have been edited in *Ancient Historical Edicts at Lhasa* (H. E. Richardson. Vol. XIX of the Prize Publication Fund of the Royal Asiatic Society). The translation of the Tibetan text of the treaty proper is a revision of the somewhat clumsy, literal rendering given in the above-mentioned publication.

The king of Tibet named in the treaty is better known as Ralpachen (815–841); and the Chinese Emperor is Mu Tsung or the T'ang dynasty (821–825). The frontier appears to have been not far to the west of the Kansu-Shensi border.

Two translations of the Chinese text of the treaty can be seen in G. Timkowsky's *Travels of the Russian Mission through China*, etc. London 1827 and one by S. W. Bushell in *JRAS* 1880.

2. Treaty between Tibet and Bashahr, 1681

Professor L. Petech gives the best available information about this in his valuable article on 'The Tibetan-Ladakhi-Moghul War of 1681–1683' in the *Indian Historical Quarterly*, Vol. XXIII,

September 1947. At the time of that war there was an alliance and a brief general agreement about friendly relations and the exchange of envoys between Raja Kehari Singh of Bashahr and the Government of the Vth Dalai Lama.

3. Treaty between Tibet and Ladakh, 1683

This treaty terminated the war mentioned above. Its conditions are summarized by Professor Petech (op. cit.) and included the cession to Tibet of the Province of Ngari, commercial stipulations mainly connected with the important trade in wool, and the dispatch to Lhasa every second year of a sort of tribute mission. This liability was taken over by Kashmir when that State annexed Ladakh in 1842, and continued to be discharged down to 1950. The mission was known as the Lopchak. The frontier between Ladakh and Tibet was fixed at 'the Lhari stream at Demchok'.

4. Treaty between Tibet and Ladakh, 1842 (translation)

As on this auspicious day, the 2nd of Assuj, Sambhat 1899 [16th or 17th September A.D. 1842], we the officers of the Lhasa Government Kalon of Sokan and Bakshi Shajpuh, Commander of the Forces, and two officers on behalf of the most resplendent Sri Khalsaji Sahib, the asylum of the world, King Sher Singhji and Sri Maharaj Sahib Raja-i Rajagan Raja Sahib Bahadur Raja Gulab Singhji i.e., the Mukhtar-ud-Daula Diwan Hari Chand and the asylum of vizirs, Vizir Ratnun, in a meeting called together for the promotion of peace and unity, and by professions and vows of friendship, unity and sincerity of heart and by taking oaths like those of Kunjak Sahib, have arranged and agreed that relations of peace, friendship and unity between Sri Khalsaji and Sri Maharaj Sahib Bahadur Raja Gulab Singhji and the Emperor of China and the Lama Guru of Lhasa will henceforward remain firmly established for ever; and we declare in the presence of the Kunjak Sahib that on no account whatsoever will there be any deviation, difference or departure [from this agreement]. We shall neither at present nor in future have anything to do or interfere at all with the boundaries of Ladakh and its surroundings as fixed from ancient times and will allow the annual export of wool, shawls and tea by way of Ladakh according to old established custom.

Should any of the opponents of Sri Khalsaji and Sri Raja Sahib Bahadur at any time enter our territories, we shall not pay any heed to his words or allow him to remain in our country.

We shall offer no hindrance to traders of Ladakh who visit our territories. We shall not, even to the extent of a hair's breadth, act in contravention of the terms that we have agreed to above regarding firm friendship, unity and fixed boundaries of Ladakh and the keeping open of the route for wool, shawls and tea. We call Kunjak Sahib, Kairi Lassi, Zhoh Mahan, and Khushal Choh as witnesses to this treaty.

The agreement is quoted in Aitchison's *Treaties*, Vol. XIV, p. 15. The Tibetan signatories had been taken prisoner and it does not appear that any reference was made to Lhasa before the conclusion of the agreement. Not only the Dogra Raja of Jammoo, who had occupied Ladakh, but also his nominal overlord the Sikh ruler are cited as parties to the treaty. In fact, since the death of Ranjit Singh in 1839 the Maharaja of Jammoo had been virtually independent and proof of his position was seen in his refusal to support the Sikhs in their war against the British. Similarly, on the other side, the Chinese Emperor is mentioned as a party as well as the Dalai Lama.

Neither Sikhs nor Chinese took any part in the campaign in Ladakh and Tibet.

'The boundaries of Ladakh as fixed in ancient times' refer back to the treaty between Ladakh and Tibet in 1683. See No. 3 above.

5. Treaty between Tibet and Nepal, 1856 (translation)

Treaty of Peace, consisting of ten Articles, between the States of Gurkha and Tibet (Bhote), settled and concluded by us, the Chief Sardars, Bharadars, and Lamas of both Governments, whose signatures and seals are attached below. May God bear witness to it. We further agree that both States pay respect as always before to the Emperor of China and that the two States are to treat each other like brothers, for so long as their actions correspond with the spirit of this Treaty. May God not allow that State to prosper which may make war upon the other, unless the other's acts are contrary to this Treaty, in which case the State that declares war upon the other shall be exempt from all blame.

1. The Tibetan Government agrees to pay the sum of ten thousand Rupees annually in cash to the Gurkha Government.

2. The States of Gurkha and of Tibet have both respected the Emperor of China up to the present time. The country of Tibet is merely the shrine or place of worship of the Lama, for which reason the Gurkha Government will in future give all the assistance that may be in its power to the Government of Tibet, if the troops of any other 'Raja' invade that country.

3. The Government of Tibet agrees to discontinue the collection of all

duties that have hitherto been levied upon subjects of the Gurkha State, merchants and others trading with its country.

4. The Government of Tibet agrees to give up to the Gurkha Government all the Sikh prisoners now in captivity within its territories, and all the Gurkha Sipahis, and officers, and women who were captured in the war, also all the guns that were taken; and the Gurkha Government agrees to give up to the Government of Tibet all the Sipahis, also the ryots of Kerong, Kuti, Junga, Tagla Khar and Chewur Gumba, and all the arms and Yaks [chowrie cows] belonging to that country now in its possession, and on the final completion of this Treaty it will restore Tagla Khar, Chewur Gumba, Kerong, Junga, Kuti and Dhakling and will withdraw all the troops that may be on this side of the Bhairab Langar range.

5. A Bharadar on the part of the Gurkha Government (not merely a Naikia) will for the future reside at Lhasa.

6. The Gurkha Government, with the free consent of the Government of Tibet, will establish a trading factory at Lhasa, for the sale of all kinds of merchandise, from jewellery etc. etc. to articles of clothing and of food.

7. The Gurkha Bharadar residing at Lhasa will not interfere in the disputes of the subjects, merchants, traders, etc. etc. of the Government of Tibet, neither will the Tibetan Government interfere in any disputes between subjects of the Gurkha Government, Kashmiris of Nepal etc. etc., who may be residing within the jurisdiction of Lhasa, but whenever quarrels may occur between Gurkha and Tibetan subjects, the authorities of the two States will sit together and jointly adjudicate them; and all Amdani [fines etc.] will, if paid by subjects of Tibet, be taken by that Government, and if paid by Gurkha subjects, Kashmiris of Nepal etc., will be appropriated by the Gurkha Government.

8. Should any Gurkha subject commit a murder within the jurisdiction of that Government and take refuge in Tibet, he shall be surrendered by that country, and if any Tibetan subject who may have committed a murder there take refuge in the Gurkha country, he shall in like manner be given up to the Government of Tibet.

9. If the property of any Gurkha subjects and merchants be plundered by any subject of the Tibetan Government, the party who has stolen it shall be compelled by the Tibetan Government to restore it; should he not be able to do so at once, he shall be obliged by the Tibetan Bharadar to make some arrangement, and will be allowed a reasonable time to make it good. In like manner, if the property of any Tibetan subjects or merchants be plundered by any subject of the Gurkha Government, the party who has stolen it shall be compelled by the Gurkha authorities to restore it; should he not be able to do so at once, he shall be obliged by the Gurkha Government to make some arrangement and will be allowed a reasonable time to make it good.

10. All subjects of Tibet who may have joined the Gurkha cause during the war, and all subjects of the Gurkha Government who may have taken part

with the Tibetan Government, shall, after the completion of this Treaty be respected both in person and property, and shall not be injured by either Government.

Dated Sambhat 1912 Chaitra Badi 3rd (2nd day) Sombar; corresponding with 24th March 1856.

The treaty, apparently translated from the Nepalese text, is given in Aitchison's *Treaties*, Vol. XIV, pp. 49–50. A translation from the Tibetan is given in the Appendix to *Tibet: Past and Present* by Sir Charles Bell.

6. *The Convention of Chefoo (between the British Government and the Government of China), 1876*

Extract:

Her Majesty's Government having it in contemplation to send a mission of exploration next year, by way of Peking, through Kansuh and Kokonor, or by way of Szechuen to Thibet, and thence to India, the Tsungli Yamen, having due regard to the circumstances, will, when the time arrives, issue the necessary passports, and will address letters to the High Provincial Authorities and the Residents in Thibet. If the Mission should not be sent by these routes but should be proceeding across the Indian frontier to Thibet, the Tsungli Yamen, on receipt of a communication to that effect from the British Minister, will write to the Chinese Resident in Thibet, and the Resident, with due regard to the circumstances, will send officers to take care of the Mission, and passports for the Mission will be issued by the Tsungli Yamen, that its passage be not obstructed.

The above is a separate article. The main body of the Convention did not concern Tibet.

7. *Convention relating to Burmah and Thibet, July 24th 1886 (between the British Government and the Government of China)*

Extract:

Inasmuch as inquiry into the circumstances, by the Chinese Government, has shown the existence of many obstacles to the Mission to Thibet provided for in the separate article of the Chefoo Agreement, England consents to countermand the Mission forthwith. With regard to the desire of the British Government to consider arrangements for frontier trade between India and Thibet, it will be the duty of the Chinese Government, after careful inquiry into the circumstances, to adopt measures to exhort and encourage the people with a view to the promotion and development of trade. Should it be practicable, the Chinese Government shall then proceed carefully to consider trade regulations; but if insuperable obstacles should be found to exist, the British Government will not press the matter unduly.

The remainder of the Convention was concerned with the recognition of British supremacy in Burma and the above clause about Tibet appears to be in the nature of a concession to facilitate the principal object of the Convention.

8. *Convention of March 17th 1890 between Great Britain and China relating to Sikkim and Tibet (Ratifications exchanged at London, August 27th, 1890)*[1]

[English Text]

WHEREAS Her Majesty the Queen of the United Kingdom of Great Britain and Ireland, Empress of India, and His Majesty the Emperor of China, are sincerely desirous to maintain and perpetuate the relations of friendship and good understanding which now exist between their respective Empires; and whereas recent occurrences have tended towards a disturbance of the said relations, and it is desirable to clearly define and permanently settle certain matters connected with the boundary between Sikkim and Tibet, Her Britannic Majesty and His Majesty the Emperor of China have resolved to conclude a Convention on this subject, and have, for this purpose, named Plenipotentiaries, that is to say:

Her Majesty the Queen of Great Britain and Ireland, his Excellency the Most Honourable Henry Charles Keith Petty Fitzmaurice, G.M.S.I., G.C.M.G., G.M.I.E., Marquess of Lansdowne, Viceroy and Governor-General of India;

And His Majesty the Emperor of China, his Excellency Sheng Tai, Imperial Associate Resident in Tibet, Military Deputy Lieutenant-Governor;

Who, having met and communicated to each other their full powers, and finding these to be in proper form, have agreed upon the following Convention in eight Articles:—

I. The boundary of Sikkim and Tibet shall be the crest of the mountain-range separating the waters flowing into the Sikkim Teesta and its affluents from the waters flowing into the Tibetan Mochu and northwards into other rivers of Tibet. The line commences at Mount Gipmochi on the Bhutan frontier, and follows the above-mentioned water-parting to the point where it meets Nipal territory.

II. It is admitted that the British Government, whose Protectorate over the Sikkim State is hereby recognized, has direct and exclusive control over the internal administration and foreign relations of that State, and except through

---

[1] *British and Foreign State Papers*, 1889–1890, Vol. LXXXII, pp. 9–11.

and with the permission of the British Government neither the Ruler of the State nor any of its officers shall have official relations of any kind, formal or informal, with any other country.

III. The Government of Great Britain and Ireland and the Government of China engage reciprocally to respect the boundary as defined in Article I, and to prevent acts of aggression from their respective sides of the frontier.

IV. The question of providing increased facilities for trade across the Sikkim–Tibet frontier will hereafter be discussed with a view to a mutually satisfactory arrangement by the High Contracting Powers.

V. The question of pasturage on the Sikkim side of the frontier is reserved for further examination and future adjustment.

VI. The High Contracting Powers reserve for discussion and arrangement the method in which official communications between the British authorities in India and the authorities in Tibet shall be conducted.

VII. Two joint Commissioners shall, within six months from the ratification of this Convention, be appointed, one by the British Government in India, the other by the Chinese Resident in Tibet. The said Commissioners shall meet and discuss the questions which, by the last three preceding Articles, have been reserved.

VIII. The present Convention shall be ratified, and the ratifications shall be exchanged in London as soon as possible after the date of the signature thereof.

In witness whereof the respective negotiators have signed the same, and affixed thereunto the seals of their arms.

Done in quadruplicate at Calcutta, this 17th day of March, in the year of our Lord 1890, corresponding with the Chinese date, the 27th day of the second moon of the 16th year of Kuang Hsü.

LANSDOWNE.

Signature of the Chinese Plenipotentiary.

The Convention was signed at Calcutta. No Tibetan representative was present or took part in the negotiations.

9. *Regulations regarding Trade, Communication, and Pasturage, to be appended to the Convention between Great Britain and China of March 17, 1890, relative to Sikkim and Tibet. Signed at Darjeeling, December 5, 1893*[1]

1. A TRADE mart shall be established at Yatung on the Tibetan side of the frontier, and shall be open to all British subjects for purposes of trade from the 1st day of May, 1894. The Government of India shall be free to send officers to reside at Yatung to watch the conditions of British trade at that mart.

2. British subjects trading at Yatung shall be at liberty to travel freely to and fro between the frontier and Yatung, to reside at Yatung, and to rent

[1] *British and Foreign State Papers*, 1892–1893, Vol. LXXXV, pp. 1235–1237.

houses and godowns for their own accommodation, and the storage of their goods. The Chinese Government undertake that suitable buildings for the above purposes shall be provided for British subjects, and also that a special and fitting residence shall be provided for the officer or officers appointed by the Government of India under Regulation 1 to reside at Yatung. British subjects shall be at liberty to sell their goods to whomsoever they please, to purchase native commodities in kind or in money, to hire transport of any kind, and in general to conduct their business transactions in conformity with local usage, and without any vexatious restrictions. Such British subjects shall receive efficient protection for their persons and property. At Lang-jo and Ta-chun, between the frontier and Yatung, where rest-houses have been built by the Tibetan authorities, British subjects can break their journey in consideration of a daily rent.

3. Import and export trade in the following articles:—arms, ammunition, military stores, salt, liquors, and intoxicating or narcotic drugs, may, at the option of either Government, be entirely prohibited, or permitted only on such conditions as either Government, on their own side, may think fit to impose.

4. Goods, other than goods of the descriptions enumerated in Regulation 3, entering Tibet from British India, across the Sikkim–Tibet frontier, or *vice versa*, whatever their origin, shall be exempt from duty for a period of five years, commencing from the date of the opening of Yatung to trade; but after the expiration of this term, if found desirable, a tariff may be mutually agreed upon and enforced. Indian tea may be imported into Tibet at a rate of duty not exceeding that at which Chinese tea is imported into England, but trade in Indian tea shall not be engaged in during the five years for which other commodities are exempt.

5. All goods on arrival at Yatung, whether from British India or from Tibet, must be reported at the Custom Station there for examination, and the report must give full particulars of the description, quantity, and value of the goods.

6. In the event of trade disputes arising between British and Chinese or Tibetan subjects in Tibet, they shall be inquired into and settled in personal conference by the Political Officer for Sikkim and the Chinese Frontier Officer. The object of personal conference being to ascertain facts and do justice, where there is a divergence of views, the law of the country to which the defendant belongs shall guide.

7. Despatches from the Government of India to the Chinese Imperial Resident in Tibet shall be handed over by the Political Officer for Sikkim to the Chinese Frontier Officer, who will forward them by special courier.

Despatches from the Chinese Imperial Resident in Tibet to the Government of India will be handed over by the Chinese Frontier Officer to the Political Officer for Sikkim, who will forward them as quickly as possible.

8. Despatches between the Chinese and Indian officials must be treated with

due respect, and couriers will be assisted in passing to and fro by the officers of each Government.

9. After the expiration of one year from the date of the opening of Yatung, such Tibetans as continue to graze their cattle in Sikkim will be subject to such Regulations as the British Government may from time to time enact for the general conduct of grazing in Sikkim. Due notice will be given of such Regulations.

General Articles

1. In the event of disagreement between the Political Officer for Sikkim and the Chinese Frontier Officer, each official shall report the matter to his immediate superior, who in turn, if a settlement is not arrived at between them, shall refer such matter to their respective Governments for disposal.

2. After the lapse of five years from the date on which these Regulations shall come into force, and on six months' notice given by either party, these Regulations shall be subject to revision by Commissioners appointed on both sides for this purpose, who shall be empowered to decide on and adopt such amendments and extensions as experience shall prove to be desirable.

3. It having been stipulated that Joint Commissioners should be appointed by the British and Chinese Governments under Article VII of the Sikkim–Tibet Convention to meet and discuss, with a view to the final settlement of the questions reserved under Articles IV, V, and VI of the said Convention; and the Commissioners thus appointed having met and discussed the questions referred to, namely, trade, communication, and pasturage, have been further appointed to sign the Agreement in nine Regulations and three General Articles now arrived at, and to declare that the said nine Regulations and the three General Articles form part of the Convention itself.

In witness whereof the respective Commissioners have hereto subscribed their names.

Done in quadruplicate at Darjeeling, this 5th day of December, in the year 1893, corresponding with the Chinese date, the 28th day of the 10th moon of the 19th year of Kuang Hsu.

> A. W. PAUL, British Commissioner.
> HO CHANG-JUNG,
> JAMES H. HART, Chinese Commissioners.

A Tibetan Minister was present at the negotiations in Darjeeling but took no active part and did not sign the Regulations.

10. *Convention between Great Britain and Tibet. Signed at Lhasa, September 7th 1904*[1]

WHEREAS doubts and difficulties have arisen as to the meaning and validity of the Anglo-Chinese Convention of 1890, and the Trade Regulations of 1893,

---

[1] *British and Foreign State Papers*, 1904–1905, Vol. XCVIII, pp. 148–151.

and as to the liabilities of the Thibetan Government under these Agreements; and whereas recent occurrences have tended towards a disturbance of the relations of friendship and good understanding which have existed between the British Government and the Government of Thibet; and whereas it is desirable to restore peace and amicable relations, and to resolve and determine the doubts and difficulties as aforesaid, the said Governments have resolved to conclude a Convention with these objects, and the following Articles have been agreed upon by Colonel F. E. Younghusband, C.I.E., in virtue of full powers vested in him by His Britannic Majesty's Government, and on behalf of that said Government, and Lo-Sang Gyal-Tsen, the Ga-den Ti-Rimpoche, and the representatives of the Council, of the three monasteries Se-ra, Drepung, and Ga-den, and of the ecclesiastical and lay officials of the National Assembly on behalf of the Government of Thibet:—

I. The Government of Thibet engages to respect the Anglo-Chinese Convention of 1890, and to recognize the frontier between Sikkim and Thibet, as defined in Article I of the said Convention, and to erect boundary pillars accordingly.

II. The Thibetan Government undertakes to open forthwith trade marts to which all British and Thibetan subjects shall have free right of access at Gyangtse and Gartok, as well as at Yatung.

The Regulations applicable to the trade mart at Yatung, under the Anglo-Chinese Agreement of 1893, shall, subject to such amendments as may hereafter be agreed upon by common consent between the British and Thibetan Governments, apply to the marts above mentioned.

In addition to establishing trade marts at the places mentioned, the Thibetan Government undertakes to place no restrictions on the trade by existing routes, and to consider the question of establishing fresh trade marts under similar conditions if development of trade requires it.

III. The question of the amendment of the Regulations of 1893 is reserved for separate consideration, and the Thibetan Government undertakes to appoint fully authorized delegates to negotiate with representatives of the British Government as to the details of the amendments required.

IV. The Thibetan Government undertakes to levy no dues of any kind other than those provided for in the tariff to be mutually agreed upon.

V. The Thibetan Government undertakes to keep the roads to Gyangtse and Gartok from the frontier clear of all obstruction and in a state of repair suited to the needs of the trade, and to establish at Yatung, Gyangtse, and Gartok, and at each of the other trade marts that may hereafter be established, a Thibetan Agent who shall receive from the British Agent appointed to watch over British trade at the marts in question any letter which the latter may desire to send to the Thibetan or to the Chinese authorities. The Thibetan Agent shall also be responsible for the due delivery of such communications and for the transmission of replies.

VI. As an indemnity to the British Government for the expense incurred in the dispatch of armed troops to Lhasa, to exact reparation for breaches of Treaty obligations, and for the insults offered to and attacks upon the British Commissioner and his following and escort, the Thibetan Government engages to pay a sum of 500,000 *l.*—equivalent to 75 lakhs of rupees—to the British Government. The indemnity shall be payable at such place as the British Government may from time to time, after due notice, indicate, whether in Thibet or in the British districts of Darjeeling or Jalpaiguri, in seventy-five annual instalments of one lakh of rupees each on the 1st January in each year, beginning from the 1st January, 1906.

VII. As security for the payment of the above-mentioned indemnity, and for the fulfilment of the provisions relative to trade marts specified in Articles II, III, IV, and V, the British Government shall continue to occupy the Chumbi Valley until the indemnity has been paid, and until the trade marts have been effectively opened for three years, whichever date may be the later.

VIII. The Thibetan Government agrees to raze all forts and fortifications and remove all armaments which might impede the course of free communication between the British frontier and the towns of Gyangtse and Lhasa.

IX. The Government of Thibet engages that, without the previous consent of the British Government—

(*a*) No portion of Thibetan territory shall be ceded, sold, leased, mortgaged or otherwise given for occupation, to any Foreign Power;

(*b*) No such Power shall be permitted to intervene in Thibetan affairs;

(*c*) No Representatives or Agents of any Foreign Power shall be admitted to Thibet;

(*d*) No concessions for railways, roads, telegraphs, mining or other rights, shall be granted to any Foreign Power, or the subject of any Foreign Power. In the event of consent to such Concessions being granted, similar or equivalent Concessions shall be granted to the British Government;

(*e*) No Thibetan revenues, whether in kind or in cash, shall be pledged or assigned to any Foreign Power, or to the subject of any Foreign Power.

X. In witness whereof the negotiators have signed the same, and affixed thereunto the seals of their arms.

Done in quintuplicate at Lhasa, this 7th day of September, in the year of our Lord, 1904, corresponding with the Thibetan date, the 27th of the seventh month of the Wood Dragon year.

| (Thibet Frontier Commission.) (Seal of British Commissioner.) | F. E. YOUNGHUSBAND, Colonel, British Commissioner. | (Seal of the Dalai Lama affixed by the Ga-den Ti-Rimpoche.) |

| (Seal of Council.) | (Seal of Dre-pung Monastery.) | (Seal of Sera Monastery.) | (Seal of Ga-den Monastery.) | (Seal of National Assembly.) |

In proceeding to the signature of the Convention, dated this day, the representatives of Great Britain and Thibet declare that the English text shall be binding.

(Thibet Frontier Commission.)   F. E. YOUNGHUSBAND, Colonel, British Commissioner.   (Seal of the Dala Lama affixed by the Ga-den Ti-Rimpoche.)

(Seal of Council.)   (Seal of Dre-pung Monastery.)   (Seal of Sera Monastery.)   (Seal of Ga-den Monastery.)   (Seal of National Assembly.)

AMPTHILL,
Viceroy and Governor-General of India.

The Convention was ratified by the Viceroy and Governor-General of India in Council at Simla on the 11th day of November, 1904, subject to reduction of the indemnity to Rs. 25,00,000 and a declaration that British occupation of the Chumbi valley would cease after payment of three annual instalments of the indemnity, provided that the Tibetans had complied with the terms of the Convention in all other respects.

This was the first direct treaty between Great Britain and Tibet. The Chinese Amban at Lhasa was present at the negotiations and signing, but did not sign.

11. *Convention between Great Britain and China respecting Tibet. Signed at Peking, April 27 1906 (Ratifications exchanged at London July 23, 1906)*[1]

[Signed also in Chinese]

WHEREAS His Majesty the King of Great Britain and Ireland and of the British Dominions beyond the Seas, Emperor of India, and His Majesty the Emperor of China are sincerely desirous to maintain and perpetuate the relations of friendship and good understanding which now exist between their respective Empires;

And whereas the refusal of Tibet to recognise the validity of or to carry into full effect the provisions of the Anglo-Chinese Convention of March 17, 1890, and Regulations of December 5, 1893, placed the British Government under the necessity of taking steps to secure their rights and interests under the said Convention and Regulations;

And whereas a Convention of ten articles was signed at Lhasa on September 7, 1904, on behalf of Great Britain and Tibet, and was ratified by the Viceroy and Governor-General of India on behalf of Great Britain on November 11,

[1] *British and Foreign State Papers*, 1905-1906, Vol. XCIX, pp. 171-173.

1904, a declaration on behalf of Great Britain modifying its terms under certain conditions being appended thereto;

His Britannic Majesty and His Majesty the Emperor of China have resolved to conclude a Convention on this subject and have for this purpose named Plenipotentiaries, that is to say:—

His Majesty the King of Great Britain and Ireland:

Sir Ernest Mason Satow, Knight Grand Cross of the Most Distinguished Order of Saint Michael and Saint George, His said Majesty's Envoy Extraordinary and Minister Plenipotentiary to His Majesty the Emperor of China;

And His Majesty the Emperor of China:

His Excellency Tong Shoa-yi, His said Majesty's High Commissioner Plenipotentiary and a Vice-President of the Board of Foreign Affairs; who having communicated to each other their respective full powers and finding them to be in good and true form have agreed upon and concluded the following Convention in six articles:—

I. The Convention concluded on September 7, 1904, by Great Britain and Tibet, the texts of which in English and Chinese are attached to the present Convention as an annexe, is hereby confirmed, subject to the modification stated in the declaration appended thereto, and both of the High Contracting Parties engage to take at all times such steps as may be necessary to secure the due fulfilment of the terms specified therein.

II. The Government of Great Britain engages not to annex Tibetan territory or to interfere in the administration of Tibet. The Government of China also undertakes not to permit any other foreign state to interfere with the territory or internal administration of Tibet.

III. The Concessions which are mentioned in Article IX (d) of the Convention concluded on September 7th, 1904 by Great Britain and Tibet are denied to any state or to the subject of any state other than China, but it has been arranged with China that at the trade marts specified in Article II of the aforesaid Convention Great Britain shall be entitled to lay down telegraph lines connecting with India.

IV. The provisions of the Anglo-Chinese Convention of 1890 and Regulations of 1893 shall, subject to the terms of this present Convention and annexe thereto, remain in full force.

V. The English and Chinese texts of the present Convention have been carefully compared and found to correspond, but in the event of there being any difference of meaning between them the English text shall be authoritative.

VI. This Convention shall be ratified by the Sovereigns of both countries and ratifications shall be exchanged at London within three months after the date of signature by the Plenipotentiaries of both Powers.

In token whereof the respective Plenipotentiaries have signed and sealed this Convention, four copies in English and four in Chinese.

Done at Peking this twenty-seventh day of April, one thousand nine hundred

and six, being the fourth day of the fourth month of the thirty-second year
of the reign of Kuang-hsu.

ERNEST SATOW.
(Signature and Seal of the Chinese Plenipotentiary.)

Notes were also exchanged by which the Chinese undertook
not to employ any foreigners in Tibet.

The Tibetans took no part in this Convention and its terms
were never formally communicated to them.

12. *Convention between Great Britain and Russia relating to Persia,
Afghanistan and Tibet. Signed at St. Petersburg, August 31st 1907*

His Majesty the King of the United Kingdom of Great Britain and Ireland
and of the British Dominions beyond the Seas, Emperor of India, and His
Majesty the Emperor of All the Russias, animated by the sincere desire to
settle by mutual agreement different questions concerning the interests of their
States on the Continent of Asia, have determined to conclude Agreements
destined to prevent all cause of misunderstanding between Great Britain and
Russia in regard to the questions referred to, and have nominated for this purpose their respective Plenipotentiaries, to wit:

His Majesty the King of the United Kingdom of Great Britain and Ireland
and of the British Dominions beyond the Seas, Emperor of India, the Right
Honourable Sir Arthur Nicolson, His Majesty's Ambassador Extraordinary and
Plenipotentiary to His Majesty the Emperor of All the Russias;

His Majesty the Emperor of All the Russias, the Master of his Court Alexander Iswolsky, Minister for Foreign Affairs;

Who, having communicated to each other their full powers, found in good
and due form, have agreed on the following:—

Arrangement concerning Thibet

The Governments of Great Britain and Russia recognising the suzerain
rights of China in Thibet, and considering the fact that Great Britain, by
reason of her geographical position, has a special interest in the maintenance of
the *status quo* in the external relations of Thibet, have made the following
arrangement:—

ARTICLE I

The two High Contracting Parties engage to respect the territorial integrity
of Thibet and to abstain from all interference in the internal administration.

ARTICLE II

In conformity with the admitted principle of the suzerainty of China over
Thibet, Great Britain and Russia engage not to enter into negotiations with

Thibet except through the intermediary of the Chinese Government. This engagement does not exclude the direct relations between British Commercial Agents and the Thibetan authorities provided for in Article V of the Convention between Great Britain and Thibet of the 7th September 1904, and confirmed by the Convention between Great Britain and China of the 27th April 1906; nor does it modify the engagements entered into by Great Britain and China in Article I of the said Convention of 1906.

It is clearly understood that Buddhists, subjects of Great Britain or of Russia, may enter into direct relations on strictly religious matters with the Dalai Lama and the other representatives of Buddhism in Thibet; the Governments of Great Britain and Russia engage, as far as they are concerned, not to allow those relations to infringe the stipulations of the present arrangement.

ARTICLE III

The British and Russian Governments respectively engage not to send Representatives to Lhasa.

ARTICLE IV

The two High Contracting Parties engage neither to seek nor to obtain, whether for themselves or their subjects, any Concessions for railways, roads, telegraphs, and mines, or other rights in Thibet.

ARTICLE V

The two Governments agree that no part of the revenues of Thibet, whether in kind or in cash, shall be pledged or assigned to Great Britain or Russia or to any of their subjects.

Annexe to the arrangement between Great Britain and Russia concerning Thibet.

Great Britain reaffirms the declaration, signed by His Excellency the Viceroy and Governor-General of India and appended to the ratification of the Convention of the 7th September 1904, to the effect that the occupation of the Chumbi Valley by British forces shall cease after the payment of three annual instalments of the indemnity of 25,00,000 rupees, provided that the trade marts mentioned in Article II of that Convention have been effectively opened for three years, and that in the meantime the Thibetan authorities have faithfully complied in all respects with the terms of the said Convention of 1904. It is clearly understood that if the occupation of the Chumbi Valley by the British forces has, for any reason, not been terminated at the time anticipated in the above Declaration, the British and Russian Governments will enter upon a friendly exchange of views on this subject.

The present Convention shall be ratified, and the ratification exchanged at St. Petersburgh as soon as possible.

In witness whereof the respective Plenipotentiaries have signed the present Convention and affixed thereto their seals.

Done in duplicate at St. Petersburgh, the 18th (31st) August 1907.

The Tibetans were never informed about the provisions of this treaty.

13. *Agreement between Great Britain, China and Tibet amending Trade Regulations in Tibet, of December 5, 1893. Signed at Calcutta, April 20, 1908 (Ratifications exchanged at Peking, October 14, 1908)*[1]

TIBET TRADE REGULATIONS

Preamble

WHEREAS by Article I of the Convention between Great Britain and China on the 27th April, 1906, that is the 4th day of the 4th moon of the 32nd year of Kwang Hsu, it was provided that both the High Contracting Parties should engage to take at all times such steps as might be necessary to secure the due fulfilment of the terms specified in the Lhasa Convention of the 7th September, 1904, between Great Britain and Tibet, the text of which in English and Chinese was attached as an Annexe to the above-named Convention;

And whereas it was stipulated in Article III of the said Lhasa Convention that the question of the amendment of the Tibet Trade Regulations which were signed by the British and Chinese Commissioners on the 5th day of December, 1893 should be reserved for separate consideration, and whereas the amendment of these Regulations is now necessary;

His Majesty the King of the United Kingdom of Great Britain and Ireland and of the British Dominions beyond the Seas, Emperor of India, and His Majesty the Emperor of the Chinese Empire have for this purpose named as their Plenipotentiaries, that is to say:

His Majesty the King of Great Britain and Ireland and of the British Dominions beyond the Seas, Emperor of India: Mr. E. C. Wilton, C.M.G.;

His Majesty the Emperor of the Chinese Empire: His Majesty's Special Commissioner Chang Yin Tang;

And the High Authorities of Tibet have named as their fully authorized representative to act under the directions of Chang Tachen and take part in the negotiations, the Tsarong Shape, Wang Chuk Gyalpo.

And whereas Mr. E. C. Wilton and Chang Tachen have communicated to each other since their respective full powers and have found them to be in good and true form and have found the authorization of the Tibetan Delegate to be also in good and true form, the following amended Regulations have been agreed upon:—

1. The Trade Regulations of 1893 shall remain in force in so far as they are not inconsistent with these Regulations.

2. The following places shall form, and be included within, the boundaries of the Gyantse mart:—

[1] *British and Foreign State Papers*, 1907–1908, Vol. CI, pp. 170–175.

(*a*) The line begins at the Chumig Dangsang (Chhu-Mig-Dangs-Sangs) north-east of the Gyantse Fort, and thence it runs in a curved line, passing behind the Pekor Chode (Dpal-Hkhor-Choos-Sde), down to Chag-Dong-Gang (Phyag-Gdong-Sgang); thence passing straight over the Nyan Chu, it reaches the Zamsa (Zam-Srag).

(*b*) From the Zamsa the line continues to run, in a south-eastern direction, round to Lachi-To (Gla-Dkyii-Stod), embracing all the farms on its way, viz., the Lahong, the Hogtso (Hog-Mtsho), the Tong-Chung-Shi (Grong-Chhung-Gshis), and the Rabgang (Rab-Sgang), &c.

(*c*) From Lachi-To the line runs to the Yutog (Gyu-Thog), and thence runs straight, passing through the whole area of Gamkar-Shi (Ragal-Mkhar-Gshis), to Chumig Dangsang.

As difficulty is experienced in obtaining suitable houses and godowns at some of the marts, it is agreed that British subjects may also lease lands for the building of houses and godowns at the marts, the locality for such building sites to be marked out specially at each mart by the Chinese and Tibetan authorities in consultation with the British Trade Agent. The British Trade Agents and British subjects shall not build houses and godowns except in such localities, and this arrangement shall not be held to prejudice in any way the administration of the Chinese and Tibetan local authorities over such localities, or the right of British subjects to rent houses and godowns outside such localities for their own accommodation and the storage of their goods.

British subjects desiring to lease building sites shall apply through the British Trade Agent to the Municipal Office at the mart for a permit to lease. The amount of rent, or the period or conditions of the lease, shall then be settled in a friendly way by the lessee and the owner themselves. In the event of a disagreement between the owner and lessee as to the amount of rent or the period or condition of the lease, the case will be settled by the Chinese and Tibetan Authorities, in consultation with the British Trade Agent. After the lease is settled, the sites shall be verified by the Chinese and Tibetan Officers of the Municipal Office conjointly with the British Trade Agent. No building is to be commenced by the lessee on a site before the municipal office has issued him a permit to build, but it is agreed that there shall be no vexatious delays in the issue of such permit.

3. The administration of the trade marts shall remain with the Tibetan Officers, under the Chinese Officers' supervision and directions.

The Trade Agents at the marts and Frontier Officers shall be of suitable rank, and shall hold personal intercourse and correspondence one with another on terms of mutual respect and friendly treatment.

Questions which cannot be decided by agreement between the Trade Agents and the Local Authorities shall be referred for settlement to the Government of India and the Tibetan High Authorities at Lhasa. The purport of a reference by the Government of India will be communicated to the Chinese Imperial

Resident at Lhasa. Questions which cannot be decided by agreement between the Government of India and the Tibetan High Authorities at Lhasa shall, in accordance with the terms of Article I of the Peking Convention of 1906, be referred for settlement to the Governments of Great Britain and China.

4. In the event of disputes arising at the marts between British subjects and persons of Chinese and Tibetan nationalities, they shall be inquired into and settled in personal conferences between the British Trade Agent at the nearest mart and the Chinese and Tibetan Authorities of the Judicial Court at the mart, the object of personal conference being to ascertain facts and to do justice. Where there is a divergence of view the law of the country to which the defendant belongs shall guide. In any of such mixed cases, the Officer or Officers of the defendant's nationality shall preside at the trial, the Officer or Officers of the plaintiff's country merely attending to watch the course of the trial.

All questions in regard to rights, whether of property or person, arising between British subjects, shall be subject to the jurisdiction of the British Authorities.

British subjects who may commit any crime at the marts or on the routes to the marts shall be handed over by the local authorities to the British Trade Agent at the mart nearest to the scene of offence, to be tried and punished according to the laws of India, but such British subjects shall not be subjected by the local authorities to any ill-usage in excess of necessary restraint.

Chinese and Tibetan subjects, who may be guilty of any criminal act towards British subjects at the marts or on the routes thereto, shall be arrested and punished by the Chinese and Tibetan Authorities according to law.

Justice shall be equitably and impartially administered on both sides.

Should it happen that Chinese or Tibetan subjects bring a criminal complaint against a British subject before the British Trade Agent, the Chinese or Tibetan Authorities shall have the right to send a representative, or representatives, to watch the course of trial in the British Trade Agent's Court. Similarly, in cases in which a British subject has reason to complain of a Chinese or Tibetan subject in the Judicial Court at the mart, the British Trade Agent shall have the right to send a representative to the Judicial Court to watch the course of trial.

5. The Tibetan Authorities, in obedience to the instructions of the Peking Government, having a strong desire to reform the judicial system of Tibet, and to bring it into accord with that of Western nations, Great Britain agrees to relinquish her rights of extra-territoriality in Tibet, whenever such rights are relinquished in China, and when she is satisfied that the state of the Tibetan laws and the arrangements for their administration and other considerations warrant her in so doing.

6. After the withdrawal of the British troops, all the rest-houses, eleven in number, built by Great Britain upon the routes leading from the Indian frontier to Gyantse, shall be taken over at original cost by China and rented to

the Government of India at a fair rate. One-half of each rest-house will be reserved for the use of the British officials employed on the inspection and maintenance of the telegraph lines from the marts to the Indian frontier and for the storage of their materials, but the rest-houses shall otherwise be available for occupation by British, Chinese, and Tibetan officers of respectability who may proceed to and from the marts.

Great Britain is prepared to consider the transfer to China of the telegraph lines from the Indian frontier to Gyantse when the telegraph lines from China reach that mart, and in the meantime Chinese and Tibetan messages will be duly received and transmitted by the line constructed by the Government of India.

In the meantime China shall be responsible for the due protection of the telegraph lines from the marts to the Indian frontier, and it is agreed that all persons damaging the lines or interfering in any way with them or with the officials engaged in the inspection or maintenance thereof shall at once be severely punished by the local authorities.

7. In law suits involving cases of debt on account of loans, commercial failure, and bankruptcy, the authorities concerned shall grant a hearing and take steps necessary to enforce payment; but, if the debtor plead poverty and be without means, the authorities concerned shall not be held responsible for the said debts, nor shall any public or official property be distrained upon in order to satisfy these debts.

8. The British Trade Agents at the various trade marts now or hereafter to be established in Tibet may make arrangements for the carriage and transmission of their posts to and from the frontier of India. The couriers employed in conveying these posts shall receive all possible assistance from the local authorities whose districts they traverse and shall be accorded the same protection as the persons employed in carrying the despatches of the Tibetan Authorities. When efficient arrangements have been made by China in Tibet for a postal service, the question of the abolition of the Trade Agents' couriers will be taken into consideration by Great Britain and China. No restrictions whatever shall be placed on the employment by British officers and traders of Chinese and Tibetan subjects in any lawful capacity. The persons so employed shall not be exposed to any kind of molestation or suffer any loss of civil rights to which they may be entitled as Tibetan subjects, but they shall not be exempted from all lawful taxation. If they be guilty of any criminal act, they shall be dealt with by the local authorities according to law without any attempt on the part of their employer to screen or conceal them.

9. British officers and subjects, as well as goods, proceeding to the trade marts, must adhere to the trade routes from the frontier of India. They shall not, without permission, proceed beyond the marts, or to Gartok from Yatung and Gyantse, or from Gartok to Yatung and Gyantse, by any route through the interior of Tibet, but natives of the Indian frontier, who have already by usage traded and resided in Tibet, elsewhere than at the marts shall be at liberty to

continue their trade, in accordance with the existing practice, but when so trading or residing they shall remain, as heretofore, amenable to the local jurisdiction.

10. In cases where officials or traders, *en route* to and from India or Tibet, are robbed of treasure or merchandise, public or private, they shall forthwith report to the Police officers, who shall take immediate measures to arrest the robbers and hand them to the Local Authorities. The Local Authorities shall bring them to instant trial, and shall also recover and restore the stolen property. But if the robbers flee to places out of the jurisdiction and influence of Tibet, and cannot be arrested, the Police and the Local Authorities shall not be held responsible for such losses.

11. For public safety, tanks or stores of kerosene oil or any other combustible or dangerous articles in bulk must be placed far away from inhabited places at the marts.

British or Indian merchants wishing to build such tanks or stores may not do so until, as provided in Regulation 2, they have made application for a suitable site.

12. British subjects shall be at liberty to deal in kind or in money, to sell their goods to whomsoever they please, to purchase native commodities from whomsoever they please, to hire transport of any kind, and to conduct in general their business transactions in conformity with local usage and without any vexatious restrictions or oppressive exactions whatever.

It being the duty of the Police and Local Authorities to afford efficient protection at all times to the persons and property of the British subjects at the marts, and along the routes to the marts, China engages to arrange effective police measures at the marts and along the routes to the marts. On due fulfilment of these arrangements, Great Britain undertakes to withdraw the Trade Agents' guards at the marts and to station no troops in Tibet, so as to remove all cause for suspicion and disturbance among the inhabitants. The Chinese Authorities will not prevent the British Trade Agents holding personal intercourse and correspondence with the Tibetan officers and people.

Tibetan subjects trading, travelling, or residing in India shall receive equal advantages to those accorded by this Regulation to British subjects in Tibet.

13. The present Regulations shall be in force for a period of ten years reckoned from the date of signature by the two Plenipotentiaries as well as by the Tibetan Delegate; but if no demand for revision be made by either side within six months after the end of the first ten years, then the Regulations shall remain in force for another ten years from the end of the first ten years; and so it shall be at the end of each successive ten years.

14. The English, Chinese, and Tibetan texts of the present Regulations have been carefully compared, and, in the event of any question arising as to the interpretation of these Regulations, the sense as expressed in the English text shall be held to be the correct sense.

15. The ratifications of the present Regulations under the hand of His Majesty the King of Great Britain and Ireland, and of His Majesty the Emperor of the Chinese Empire, respectively, shall be exchanged at London and Peking within six months from the date of signature.

In witness whereof the two Plenipotentiaries and the Tibetan Delegate have signed and sealed the present Regulations.

Done in quadruplicate at Calcutta this 20th day of April, in the year of our Lord 1908, corresponding with the Chinese date, the 20th day of the 3rd moon of the 34th year of Kuang-hsu.

E. C. WILTON,
British Commissioner.

Signature of
CHANG YIN TANG,
Chinese Special Commissioner.

Signature of
WANG CHUK GYALPO,
Tibetan Delegate.

In spite of the intention expressed in Article II of the 1904 Convention, the new Regulations were in fact negotiated by the Chinese Commissioner. The Tibetan representative took no active part but merely signed the regulations.

14. *Treaty between Tibet and Mongolia. January 1913*
   [*Said to have been signed at Urga in January 1913*]

Whereas Mongolia and Tibet, having freed themselves from the Manchu dynasty and separated themselves from China, have become independent States, and whereas the two States have always professed one and the same religion, and to the end that their ancient mutual friendships may be strengthened: on the part of the Government of the Sovereign of the Mongolian people—Nikta Biliktu Da Lama Rabdan, acting Minister of Foreign Affairs and Assistant Minister-General and Manlai Caatyr Bei Tzu Damdinsurun; on the part of the Dalai Lama, Ruler of Tibet—Gujir Tsanshib Kanchen Lubsan-Agwan, Donir Agwan Choinzin Tschichamtso, manager of the bank, and Gendun-Galsan, secretary, have agreed on the following:—

ARTICLE I

The Dalai Lama, Sovereign of Tibet, approves of and acknowledges the formation of an independent Mongolian State, and the proclamation on the 9th day of the 11th month of the year of the Pig, of the master of the Yellow Faith Je-tsun Dampa Lama as the Sovereign of the land.

ARTICLE 2

The Sovereign of the Mongolian people Je-tsun Dampa Lama approves and acknowledges the formation of an independent State and the proclamation of the Dalai Lama as Sovereign of Tibet.

ARTICLE 3

Both States shall take measures, after mutual consideration, for the prosperity of the Buddhist faith.

ARTICLE 4

Both States, the Mongolian and the Tibetan, shall henceforth, for all time, afford each other aid against dangers from without and from within.

ARTICLE 5

Both States, each on its own territory, shall afford mutual aid to their subjects, travelling officially and privately on religious or on State business.

ARTICLE 6

Both States, the Mongolian and the Tibetan, shall, as formerly, carry on mutual trade in the produce of their lands—in goods, cattle &c., and likewise open industrial institutions.

ARTICLE 7

Henceforth transactions on credit shall be allowed only with the knowledge and permission of official institutions; without such permission no claims shall be examined by Government Institutions.

Should such agreements have been entered into before the conclusion of the present treaty, and should the parties thereto be unable to settle matters amicably, while the loss suffered is great, the payment of such debts may be enforced by the said institutions, but in no case shall the debts concern the *Shabinars* and *Hoshuns*.

ARTICLE 8

Should it be necessary to supplement the articles of this treaty, the Mongolian and Tibetan Governments shall appoint special Plenipotentiaries, who shall come to an Agreement according to the circumstances then existing.

ARTICLE 9

The present treaty shall come into force on the date of the signature thereof.

Plenipotentiaries of the Mongolian Government: Acting Ministers of Foreign Affairs Biliktu Da Lama Rabdan and Assistant Minister-General and Manlai Caatyr Bei Tzu Damdinsurun.

Plenipotentiaries of the Dalai Lama, Sovereign of Tibet: Gujir Tsanshib Kanchen Lubsan Agwan, Donir Agwan Choinzin Tschichamtso, manager of the Bank of Tibet, and Gendun-Galsan, secretary.

According to the Mongolian chronology, on the 4th day of the 12th month of the second year of 'Him who is exalted by all'.

According to the chronology of Tibet, in the year of the Water-Mouse, on the same month and day.

The validity of the above agreement was never clearly established. See Bell, *Tibet: Past and Present*, pp. 150, 151.

15. *India–Tibet Frontier 1914. Exchange of notes between the British and Tibetan Plenipotentiaries*

To
> Lönchen Shatra, Tibetan Plenipotentiary.

In February last you accepted the India–Tibet frontier from the Isu Razi Pass to the Bhutan frontier, as given in the map (two sheets), of which two copies are herewith attached, subject to the confirmation of your government and the following conditions:—

(a) The Tibetan ownership in private estates on the British side of the frontier will not be disturbed.

(b) If the sacred places of Tso Karpo and Tsari Sarpa fall within a days march of the British side of the frontier, they will be included in Tibetan territory and the frontier modified accordingly.

I understand that your Government have now agreed to this frontier subject to the above two conditions. I shall be glad to learn definitely from you that this is the case.

You wished to know whether certain dues now collected by the Tibetan Government at Tsöna Jong and in Kongbu and Kham from the Monpas and Lopas for articles sold may still be collected. Mr. Bell has informed you that such details will be settled in a friendly spirit, when you have furnished him the further information, which you have promised.

The final settlement of this India–Tibet frontier will help to prevent causes of future dispute and thus cannot fail to be of great advantage to both Governments.

A. H. McMAHON,
Delhi 24th March 1914.   British Plenipotentiary.

The map referred to in this and the succeeding note has been published for the first time in *An Atlas of the Northern Frontier of India,* issued on 15 January 1960 by the Ministry of External Affairs of the Government of India.

[*Translation*]

To

Sir Henry McMahon,
British Plenipotentiary to the China–Tibet Conference.

As it was feared that there might be friction in future unless the boundary between India and Tibet is clearly defined, I submitted the map, which you sent to me in February last, to the Tibetan Government at Lhasa for orders. I have now received orders from Lhasa, and I accordingly agree to the boundary as marked in red in the two copies of the maps signed by you subject to the condition mentioned in your letter, dated 24th March, sent to me through Mr. Bell. I have signed and sealed the two copies of the maps. I have kept one copy here and return herewith the other.

Sent on the 29th day of the 1st month of the Wood-Tiger year (25th March 1914) by Lönchen Shatra, the Tibetan Plenipotentiary.

Seal of Lönchen Shatra.

16. *Convention between Great Britain, China, and Tibet. Simla 1914*[1]

His Majesty the King of the United Kingdom of Great Britain and Ireland and of the British Dominions beyond the Seas, Emperor of India, His Excellency the President of the Republic of China, and His Holiness the Dalai Lama of Tibet, being sincerely desirous to settle by mutual agreement various questions concerning the interests of their several States on the Continent of Asia, and further to regulate the relations of their several Governments, have resolved to conclude a Convention on this subject and have nominated for this purpose their respective Plenipotentiaries, that is to say:

His Majesty the King of the United Kingdom of Great Britain and Ireland and of the British Dominions beyond the Seas, Emperor of India, Sir Arthur Henry McMahon, Knight Grand Cross of the Royal Victorian Order, Knight Commander of the Most Eminent Order of the Indian Empire, Companion of the Most Exalted Order of the Star of India, Secretary to the Government of India, Foreign and Political Department;

His Excellency the President of the Republic of China, Monsieur Ivan Chen, Officer of the Order of the Chia Ho;

His Holiness the Dalai Lama of Tibet, Lönchen Ga-den Shatra Pal-jor Dorje; who having communicated to each other their respective full powers

[1] Whereas the Simla Convention itself after being initialled by the Chinese Plenipotentiary was not signed or ratified by the Chinese Government, it was accepted as binding by the two other parties as between themselves.

and finding them to be in good and due form have agreed upon and concluded the following Convention in eleven Articles:—

ARTICLE I

The Conventions specified in the Schedule to the present Convention shall, except in so far as they may have been modified by, or may be inconsistent with or repugnant to, any of the provisions of the present Convention, continue to be binding upon the High Contracting Parties.

ARTICLE 2

The Governments of Great Britain and China recognising that Tibet is under the suzerainty of China, and recognising also the autonomy of Outer Tibet, engage to respect the territorial integrity of the country, and to abstain from interference in the administration of Outer Tibet (including the selection and installation of the Dalai Lama), which shall remain in the hands of the Tibetan Government at Lhasa.

The Government of China engages not to convert Tibet into a Chinese province. The Government of Great Britain engages not to annex Tibet or any portion of it.

ARTICLE 3

Recognising the special interest of Great Britain, in virtue of the geographical position of Tibet, in the existence of an effective Tibetan Government, and in the maintenance of peace and order in the neighbourhood of the frontiers of India and adjoining States, the Government of China engages, except as provided in Article 4 of this Convention, not to send troops into Outer Tibet, nor to station civil or military officers, nor to establish Chinese colonies in the country. Should any such troops or officials remain in Outer Tibet at the date of the signature of this Convention, they shall be withdrawn within a period not exceeding three months.

The Government of Great Britain engages not to station military or civil officers in Tibet (except as provided in the Convention of September 7, 1904, between Great Britain and Tibet) nor troops (except the Agents' escorts), nor to establish colonies in that country.

ARTICLE 4

The foregoing Article shall not be held to preclude the continuance of the arrangement by which, in the past, a Chinese high official with suitable escort has been maintained at Lhasa, but it is hereby provided that the said escort shall in no circumstances exceed 300 men.

ARTICLE 5

The Governments of China and Tibet engage that they will not enter into any negotiations or agreements regarding Tibet with one another, or with any other Power, excepting such negotiations and agreements between Great Britain and Tibet as are provided for by the Convention of September 7, 1904, between Great Britain and Tibet and the Convention of April 27, 1906, between Great Britain and China.

ARTICLE 6

Article III of the Convention of April 27, 1906, between Great Britain and China is hereby cancelled, and it is understood that in Article IX(d) of the Convention of September 7, 1904, between Great Britain and Tibet the term 'Foreign Power' does not include China.

Not less favourable treatment shall be accorded to British commerce than to the commerce of China or the most favoured nation.

ARTICLE 7

(a) The Tibet Trade Regulations of 1893 and 1908 are hereby cancelled.

(b) The Tibetan Government engages to negotiate with the British Government new Trade Regulations for Outer Tibet to give effect to Articles II, IV and V of the Convention of September 7, 1904, between Great Britain and Tibet without delay; provided always that such Regulations shall in no way modify the present Convention except with the consent of the Chinese Government.

ARTICLE 8

The British Agent who resides at Gyantse may visit Lhasa with his escort whenever it is necessary to consult with the Tibetan Government regarding matters arising out of the Convention of September 7, 1904, between Great Britain and Tibet, which it has been found impossible to settle at Gyantse by correspondence or otherwise.

ARTICLE 9

For the purpose of the present Convention the borders of Tibet, and the boundary between Outer and Inner Tibet, shall be as shown in red and blue respectively on the map attached hereto.[1]

Nothing in the present Convention shall be held to prejudice the existing rights of the Tibetan Government in Inner Tibet, which include the power to select and appoint the high priests of monasteries and to retain full control in all matters affecting religious institutions.

ARTICLE 10

The English, Chinese and Tibetan texts of the present Convention have been carefully examined and found to correspond, but in the event of there being any difference of meaning between them the English text shall be authoritative.

[1] Published for the first time, by the Government of India in *An Atlas of the Northern Frontier of India*, 15 January 1960.

ARTICLE II

The present Convention will take effect from the date of signature.

In token whereof the respective Plenipotentiaries have signed and sealed this Convention, three copies in English, three in Chinese and three in Tibetan. Done at Simla this third day of July, A.D., one thousand nine hundred and fourteen, corresponding with the Chinese date, the third day of the seventh month of the third year of the Republic, and the Tibetan date, the tenth day of the fifth month of the Wood-Tiger year.

Initial[1] of the Lönchen Shatra.	(Initialled) A.H.M.
Seal of the Lönchen Shatra.	Seal of the British Plenipotentiary.

Schedule

1. Convention between Great Britain and China relating to Sikkim and Tibet, signed at Calcutta the 17th March 1890.

2. Convention between Great Britain and Tibet, signed at Lhasa the 7th September 1904.

3. Convention between Great Britain and China respecting Tibet, signed at Peking the 27th April 1906.

The notes exchanged are to the following effect:—

1. It is understood by the High Contracting Parties that Tibet forms part of Chinese territory.

2. After the selection and installation of the Dalai Lama by the Tibetan Government, the latter will notify the installation to the Chinese Government whose representative at Lhasa will then formally communicate to His Holiness the titles consistent with his dignity, which have been conferred by the Chinese Government.

3. It is also understood that the selection and appointment of all officers in Outer Tibet will rest with the Tibetan Government.

4. Outer Tibet shall not be represented in the Chinese Parliament or in any other similar body.

5. It is understood that the escorts attached to the British Trade Agencies in Tibet shall not exceed seventy-five per centum of the escort of the Chinese Representative at Lhasa.

6. The Government of China is hereby released from its engagements under Article III of the Convention of March 17, 1890, between Great Britain and China to prevent acts of aggression from the Tibetan side of the Tibet–Sikkim frontier.

7. The Chinese high official referred to in Article 4 will be free to enter Tibet as soon as the terms of Article 3 have been fulfilled to the satisfaction of

---

[1] Owing to the impossibility of writing initials in Tibetan, the mark of the Lonchen at this place is his signature.

representatives of the three signatories to this Convention, who will investigate and report without delay.

Initial of the Lönchen Shatra.   (Initialled) A.H.M.

Seal of the Lönchen Shatra.   Seal of the British Plenipotentiary.

On the withdrawal of the Chinese, a Declaration was signed by the plenipotentiaries of Britain and Tibet declaring that the Convention was to be binding on the Governments of Britain and Tibet and agreeing that so long as the Chinese Government withheld its signature it would be debarred from the enjoyment of privileges accruing thereunder.

17. *Anglo-Tibetan Trade Regulations—3rd of July 1914*

Whereas by Article 7 of the Convention concluded between the Governments of Great Britain, China and Tibet on the third day of July, A.D. 1914, the Trade Regulations of 1893 and 1908 were cancelled and the Tibetan Government engaged to negotiate with the British Government new Trade Regulations for Outer Tibet to give effect to Articles II, IV and V of the Convention of 1904;

His Majesty the King of the United Kingdom of Great Britain and Ireland, and of the British Dominions beyond the Seas, Emperor of India, and His Holiness the Dalai Lama of Tibet have for this purpose named as their Plenipotentiaries, that is to say:

His Majesty the King of Great Britain and Ireland and of the British Dominions beyond the Seas, Emperor of India, Sir A. H. McMahon, G.C.V.O., K.C.I.E., C.S.I.:

His Holiness the Dalai Lama of Tibet, Lönchen Ga-den Shatra Pal-jor Dorje;

And whereas Sir A. H. McMahon and Lönchen Ga-den Shatra Pal-jor Dorje have communicated to each other since their respective full powers and have found them to be in good and true form, the following Regulations have been agreed upon:—

I. The area falling within a radius of three miles from the British Trade Agency site will be considered as the area of such Trade Mart.

It is agreed that British subjects may lease lands for the building of houses and godowns at the Marts. This arrangement shall not be held to prejudice the right of British subjects to rent houses and godowns outside the Marts for their own accommodation and the storage of their goods. British subjects desiring to lease building sites shall apply through the British Trade Agent to the Tibetan Trade Agent. In consultation with the British Trade Agent the Tibetan Trade Agent will assign such or other suitable building sites without unnecessary delay. They shall fix the terms of the leases in conformity with the existing laws and rates.

II. The administration of the Trade Marts shall remain with the Tibetan Authorities, with the exception of the British Trade Agency sites and compounds of the rest-houses, which will be under the exclusive control of the British Trade Agents.

The Trade Agents at the Marts and Frontier Officers shall be of suitable rank, and shall hold personal intercourse and correspondence with one another on terms of mutual respect and friendly treatment.

III. In the event of disputes arising at the Marts or on the routes to the Marts between British subjects and subjects of other nationalities, they shall be enquired into and settled in personal conference between the British and Tibetan Trade Agents at the nearest Mart. Where there is a divergence of view the law of the country to which the defendant belongs shall guide.

All questions in regard to rights, whether of property or person, arising between British subjects, shall be subject to the jurisdiction of the British Authorities.

British subjects, who may commit any crime at the Marts or on the routes to the Marts, shall be handed over by the Local Authorities to the British Trade Agent at the Mart nearest to the scene of the offence, to be tried and punished according to the laws of India, but such British subjects shall not be subjected by the Local Authorities to any ill-usage in excess of necessary restraint.

Tibetan subjects, who may be guilty of any criminal act towards British subjects, shall be arrested and punished by the Tibetan Authorities according to law.

Should it happen that a Tibetan subject or subjects bring a criminal complaint against a British subject or subjects before the British Trade Agent, the Tibetan Authorities shall have the right to send a representative or representatives of suitable rank to attend the trial in the British Trade Agent's Court. Similarly in cases in which a British subject or subjects have reason to complain against a Tibetan subject or subjects, the British Trade Agent shall have the right to send a representative or representatives to the Tibetan Trade Agent's Court to attend the trial.

IV. The Government of India shall retain the right to maintain the telegraph lines from the Indian frontier to the Marts. Tibetan messages will be duly received and transmitted by these lines. The Tibetan Authorities shall be responsible for the due protection of the telegraph lines from the Marts to the Indian frontier, and it is agreed that all persons damaging the lines or interfering with them in any way or with the officials engaged in the inspection or maintenance thereof shall at once be severely punished.

V. The British Trade Agents at the various Trade Marts now or hereafter to be established in Tibet may make arrangements for the carriage and transport of their posts to and from the frontier of India. The couriers employed in conveying these posts shall receive all possible assistance from the Local Authorities whose districts they traverse, and shall be accorded the same protection and facilities as the persons employed in carrying the despatches of the Tibetan Government.

No restrictions whatever shall be placed on the employment by British officers and traders of Tibetan subjects in any lawful capacity. The persons so employed shall not be exposed to any kind of molestation or suffer any loss of civil rights, to which they may be entitled as Tibetan subjects, but they shall not be exempted from lawful taxation. If they be guilty of any criminal act, they shall be dealt with by the Local Authorities according to law without any attempt on the part of their employer to screen them.

VI. No rights of monopoly as regards commerce or industry shall be granted to any official or private company, institution, or individual in Tibet. It is of course understood that companies and individuals, who have already received such monopolies from the Tibetan Government previous to the conclusions of this agreement, shall retain their rights and privileges until the expiry of the period fixed.

VII. British subjects shall be at liberty to deal in kind or in money, to sell their goods to whomsoever they please, to hire transport of any kind, and to conduct in general their business transactions in conformity with local usage and without any vexations, restrictions or oppressive exactions whatever. The Tibetan Authorities will not hinder the British Trade Agents or other British subjects from holding personal intercourse or correspondence with the inhabitants of the country.

It being the duty of the Police and the Local Authorities to afford efficient protection at all times to the persons and property of the British subjects at the Marts and along the routes to the Marts, Tibet engages to arrange effective Police measures at the Marts and along the routes to the Marts.

VIII. Import and export in the following Articles:—

arms, ammunition, military stores, liquors and intoxicating or narcotic drugs.

may at the option of either Government be entirely prohibited, or permitted only on such conditions as either Government on their own side may think fit to impose.

IX. The present Regulations shall be in force for a period of ten years reckoned from the date of signature by the two Plenipotentiaries; but, if no demand for revision be made on either side within six months after the end of the first ten years the Regulations shall remain in force for another ten years from the end of the first ten years; and so it shall be at the end of each successive ten years.

X. The English and Tibetan texts of the present Regulations have been carefully compared, but in the event of there being any difference of meaning between them the English text shall be authoritative.

XI. The present Regulations shall come into force from the date of signature. Done at Simla this third day of July, A.D. one thousand nine hundred and fourteen, corresponding with the Tibetan date, the tenth day of the fifth month of the Wood-Tiger year.

Seal of the Dalai Lama.	A. HENRY MCMAHON, British Plenipotentiary.
Signature of the Lönchen Shatra.	Seal of the British Plenipotentiary.
Seal of the Lönchen Shatra.	

Seal of the	Seal of the	Seal of the	Seal of the
Drepung	Sera	Gaden	National
Monastery.	Monastery.	Monastery.	Assembly.

Negotiated and signed only by the British and Tibetan plenipotentiaries.

18. *Agreement on Measures for the Peaceful Liberation of Tibet (17-point Agreement of May 23, 1951)*

The Tibetan nationality is one of the nationalities with a long history within the boundaries of China and, like many other nationalities, it has done its glorious duty in the course of the creation and development of the great Motherland. But, over the last 100 years or more, imperialist forces penetrated into China and in consequence also penetrated into the Tibetan region and carried out all kinds of deceptions and provocations. Like previous reactionary Governments, the Kuomintang reactionary Government continued to carry out a policy of oppression and sowing dissension among the nationalities, causing division and disunity among the Tibetan people. The local government of Tibet did not oppose the imperialist deception and provocation and adopted an unpatriotic attitude towards the great Motherland. Under such conditions the Tibetan nationality and people were plunged into the depths of enslavement and sufferings. In 1949 basic victory was achieved on a nation-wide scale in the Chinese people's war of liberation; the common domestic enemy of all nationalities—the Kuomintang reactionary Government—was overthrown and the common foreign enemy of all nationalities—the aggressive imperialist forces—was driven out. On this basis the founding of the People's Republic of China (CPR) and of the Chinese People's Government (CPG) was announced.

In accordance with the Common Programme passed by the Chinese People's Political Consultative Conference (CPPCC), the CPG declared that all nationalities within the boundaries of the CPR are equal and that they shall establish unity and mutual aid and oppose imperialism and their own public enemies, so that the CPR will become a big family of fraternity and co-operation, composed of all its nationalities. Within the big family of all nationalities of the CPR, national regional autonomy shall be exercised in areas where national minorities are concentrated and all national minorities shall have freedom to develop their spoken and written languages and to preserve or reform their customs, habits and religious beliefs, and the CPG shall assist all national minorities to develop their political, economic, cultural and educational construction work. Since then, all nationalities within the country—with the exception of those in the areas of Tibet and Taiwan—have gained liberation. Under the unified leadership of the CPG and the direct leadership of higher levels of people's governments, all national minorities have fully enjoyed the right of national equality and have exercised, or are exercising, national regional autonomy.

In order that the influences of aggressive imperialist forces in Tibet might be successfully eliminated, the unification of the territory and sovereignty of the CPR accomplished, and national defence safeguarded; in order that the Tibetan nationality and people might be freed and return to the big family of the CPR to enjoy the same rights of national equality as all other nationalities in the country and develop their political, economic, cultural and educational work, the CPG, when it ordered the People's Liberation Army (PLA) to march into Tibet, notified the local government of Tibet to send delegates to the central authorities to conduct talks for the conclusion of an agreement on measures for the peaceful liberation of Tibet. In the latter part of April 1951 the delegates with full powers of the local government of Tibet arrived in Peking. The CPG appointed representatives with full powers to conduct talks on a friendly basis with the delegates with full powers of the local government of Tibet. As a result of the talks both parties agreed to establish this agreement and ensure that it be carried into effect.

(1) The Tibetan people shall unite and drive out imperialist aggressive forces from Tibet; the Tibetan people shall return to the big family of the Motherland—the People's Republic of China.

(2) The local government of Tibet shall actively assist the PLA to enter Tibet and consolidate the national defences.

(3) In accordance with the policy towards nationalities laid down in the Common Programme of the CPPCC, the Tibetan people have the right of exercising national regional autonomy under the unified leadership of the CPG.

(4) The central authorities will not alter the existing political system in Tibet. The central authorities also will not alter the established status, functions and powers of the Dalai Lama. Officials of various ranks shall hold office as usual.

(5) The established status, functions and powers of the Panchen Ngoerhtehni shall be maintained.

(6) By the established status, functions and powers of the Dalai Lama and of the Panchen Ngoerhtehni are meant the status, functions and powers of the

thirteenth Dalai Lama and of the ninth Panchen Ngoerhtehni when they were in friendly and amicable relations with each other.

(7) The policy of freedom of religious belief laid down in the Common Programme of the CPPCC shall be carried out. The religious beliefs, customs and habits of the Tibetan people shall be respected and lama monasteries shall be protected. The central authorities will not effect a change in the income of the monasteries.

(8) Tibetan troops shall be reorganised step by step into the PLA and become a part of the national defence forces of the CPR.

(9) The spoken and written language and school education of the Tibetan nationality shall be developed step by step in accordance with the actual conditions in Tibet.

(10) Tibetan agriculture, livestock-raising, industry and commerce shall be developed step by step and the people's livelihood shall be improved step by step in accordance with the actual conditions in Tibet.

(11) In matters related to various reforms in Tibet, there will be no compulsion on the part of the central authorities. The local government of Tibet should carry out reforms of its own accord, and, when the people raise demands for reform, they shall be settled by means of consultation with the leading personnel of Tibet.

(12) In so far as former pro-imperialist and pro-Kuomintang officials resolutely sever relations with imperialism and the Kuomintang and do not engage in sabotage or resistance, they may continue to hold office irrespective of their past.

(13) The PLA entering Tibet shall abide by all the above-mentioned policies and shall also be fair in all buying and selling and shall not arbitrarily take a needle or thread from the people.

(14) The CPG shall have centralised handling of all external affairs of the area of Tibet; and there will be peaceful co-existence with neighbouring countries and establishment and development of fair commercial and trading relations with them on the basis of equality, mutual benefit and mutual respect for territory and sovereignty.

(15) In order to ensure the implementation of this agreement, the CPG shall set up a Military and Administrative Committee and a Military Area HQ in Tibet and—apart from the personnel sent there by the CPG—shall absorb as many local Tibetan personnel as possible to take part in the work. Local Tibetan personnel taking part in the Military and Administrative Committee may include patriotic elements from the local government of Tibet, various districts and various principal monasteries; the name-list shall be set forth after consultation between the representatives designated by the CPG and various quarters concerned and shall be submitted to the CPG for appointment.

(16) Funds needed by the Military and Administrative Committee, the Military Area HQ and the PLA entering Tibet shall be provided by the CPG.

The local government of Tibet should assist the PLA in the purchase and transport of food, fodder and other daily necessities.

(17) This agreement shall come into force immediately after signature and seals are affixed to it.

Signed and sealed by delegates of the CPG with full powers: Chief Delegate —Li Wei-Han (Chairman of the Commission of Nationalities Affairs); Delegates—Chang Ching-wu, Chang Kuo-hua, Sun Chih-yuan. Delegates with full powers of the local government of Tibet: Chief Delegate—Kaloon Ngabou Ngawang Jigme (Ngabo Shape); Delegates—Dazasak Khemey Sonam Wangdi, Khentrung Thupten Tenthar, Khenchung Thupten Lekmuun, Rimshi Samposey Tenzin Thundup. Peking, 23rd May, 1951.

19. Sino-Indian Agreement, 29th April 1954

AGREEMENT

Between

THE REPUBLIC OF INDIA AND THE PEOPLE'S REPUBLIC OF CHINA ON TRADE AND INTERCOURSE

Between

TIBET REGION OF CHINA AND INDIA

The Government of the Republic of India and the Central People's Government of the People's Republic of China.

Being desirous of promoting trade and cultural intercourse between Tibet Region of China and India and of facilitating pilgrimage and travel by the peoples of China and India.

Have resolved to enter into the present Agreement based on the following principles:

(1) mutual respect for each other's territorial integrity and sovereignty,
(2) mutual non-aggression,
(3) mutual non-interference in each other's internal affairs,
(4) equality and mutual benefit, and
(5) peaceful co-existence.

And for this purpose have appointed as their respective Plenipotentiaries:

The Government of the Republic of India, H. E. Nedyam Raghavan, Ambassador Extraordinary and Plenipotentiary of India accredited to the People's Republic of China; the Central People's Government of the People's Republic of China, H. E. Chang Han-fu, Vice-Minister of Foreign Affairs of the Central People's Government, who, having examined each other's credentials and finding them in good and due form, have agreed upon the following:—

ARTICLE I

The High Contracting Parties mutually agree to establish Trade Agencies:

(1) The Government of India agrees that the Government of China may establish Trade Agencies at New Delhi, Calcutta and Kalimpong.

(2) The Government of China agrees that the Government of India may establish Trade Agencies at Yatung, Gyantse and Gartok.

The Trade Agencies of both Parties shall be accorded the same status and same treatment. The Trade Agents of both Parties shall enjoy freedom from arrest while exercising their functions, and shall enjoy in respect of themselves, their wives and children who are dependent on them for livelihood freedom from search.

The Trade Agencies of both Parties shall enjoy the privileges and immunities for couriers, mail-bags and communications in code.

ARTICLE II

The High Contracting Parties agree that traders of both countries known to be customarily and specifically engaged in trade between Tibet Region of China and India may trade at the following places:

(1) The Government of China agrees to specify (1) Yatung, (2) Gyantse and (3) Phari as markets for trade. The Government of India agrees that trade may be carried on in India, including places like (1) Kalimpong, (2) Siliguri and (3) Calcutta, according to customary practice.

(2) The Government of China agrees to specify (1) Gartok, (2) Pulanchung (Taklakot), (3) Gyanima-Khargo, (4) Gyanima-Chakra, (5) Ramura, (6) Dongbra, (7) Puling-Sumdo, (8) Nabra, (9) Shangtse and (10) Tashigong as markets for trade; the Government of India agrees that in future, when in accordance with the development and need of trade between the Ari District of Tibet Region of China and India, it has become necessary to specify markets for trade in the corresponding district in India adjacent to the Ari District of Tibet Region of China, it will be prepared to consider on the basis of equality and reciprocity to do so.

ARTICLE III

The High Contracting Parties agree that pilgrimage by religious believers of the two countries shall be carried on in accordance with the following provisions:—

(1) Pilgrims from India of Lamaist, Hindu and Buddhist faiths may visit Kang Rimpoche (Kailas) and Mavam Tso (Manasarovar) in Tibet Region of China in accordance with custom.

(2) Pilgrims from Tibet Region of China of Lamaist and Buddhist faiths may visit Banaras, Sarnath, Gaya and Sanchi in India in accordance with custom.

(3) Pilgrims customarily visiting Lhasa may continue to do so in accordance with custom.

ARTICLE IV

Traders and pilgrims of both countries may travel by the following passes and route:

(1) Shipki La pass, (2) Mana pass, (3) Niti pass, (4) Kungri Bingri pass, (5) Darma pass, and (6) Lipu Lekh pass.

Also, the customary route leading to Tashigong along the valley of the Shangatsangpu (Indus) River may continue to be traversed in accordance with custom.

ARTICLE V

For travelling across the border, the High Contracting Parties agree that diplomatic personnel, officials and nationals of the two countries shall hold passports issued by their own respective countries and visaed by the other Party except as provided in Paragraphs 1, 2, 3 and 4 of this Article.

(1) Traders of both countries known to be customarily and specifically engaged in trade between Tibet Region of China and India, their wives and children who are dependent on them for livelihood and their attendants will be allowed entry for purposes of trade into India or Tibet Region of China, as the case may be, in accordance with custom on the production of certificates duly issued by the local government of their own country or by its duly authorised agents and examined by the border check-posts of the other Party.

(2) Inhabitants of the border districts of the two countries who cross the border to carry on petty trade or to visit friends and relatives may proceed to the border districts of the other Party as they have customarily done heretofore and need not be restricted to the passes and route specified in Article IV above and shall not be required to hold passports, visas or permits.

(3) Porters and mule-team drivers of the two countries who cross the border to perform necessary transportation services need not hold passports issued by their own country, but shall only hold certificates good for a definite period of time (three months, half a year or one year) duly issued by the local government of their own country or by its duly authorised agents and produce them for registration at the border checkposts of the other Party.

(4) Pilgrims of both countries need not carry documents of certification but shall register at the border checkposts of the other Party and receive a permit for pilgrimage.

(5) Notwithstanding the provisions of the foregoing paragraphs of this Article, either Government may refuse entry to any particular person.

(6) Persons who enter the territory of the other Party in accordance with the foregoing paragraphs of this Article may stay within its territory only after complying with the procedures specified by the other Party.

ARTICLE VI

The present Agreement shall come into effect upon ratification by both Governments and shall remain in force for eight (8) years. Extension of the present Agreement may be negotiated by the two Parties if either Party requests for it six (6) months prior to the expiry of the Agreement and the request is agreed to by the other Party.

Done in duplicate in Peking on the twenty-ninth day of April, 1954, in the Hindi, Chinese and English languages, all texts being equally valid.

(Sd.) NEDYAM RAGHAVAN,
Plenipotentiary of the
Government of the
Republic of India.

(Sd.) CHANG HAN-FU,
Plenipotentiary of the Central
People's Government, People's
Republic of China.

Notes Exchanged

NOTE

Peking, April 29, 1954

YOUR EXCELLENCY MR. VICE-FOREIGN MINISTER,

In the course of our discussions regarding the Agreement on Trade and Intercourse Between the Tibet Region of China and India, which has been happily concluded today, the Delegation of the Government of the Republic of India and the Delegation of the Government of the People's Republic of China agreed that certain matters be regulated by an exchange of Notes. In pursuance of this understanding, it is hereby agreed between the two Governments as follows:—

(1) The Government of India will be pleased to withdraw completely within six (6) months from date of exchange of the present notes the military escorts now stationed at Yatung and Gyantse in Tibet Region of China. The Government of China will render facilities and assistance in such withdrawal.

(2) The Government of India will be pleased to hand over to the Government of China at a reasonable price the postal, telegraph and public telephone services together with their equipment operated by the Government of India in Tibet Region of China. The concrete measures in this regard will be decided upon through further negotiations between the Indian Embassy in China and the Foreign Ministry of China, which shall start immediately after the exchange of the present notes.

(3) The Government of India will be pleased to hand over to the Government of China at a reasonable price the twelve (12) rest houses of the

Government of India in Tibet Region of China. The concrete measures in this regard will be decided upon through further negotiations between the Indian Embassy in China and the Foreign Ministry of China, which shall start immediately after the exchange of the present notes. The Government of China agrees that they shall continue as rest houses.

(4) The Government of China agrees that all buildings within the compound walls of the Trade Agencies of the Government of India at Yatung and Gyantse in Tibet Region of China may be retained by the Government of India. The Government of India may continue to lease the land within its Agency compound walls from the Chinese side. And the Government of India agrees that the Trade Agencies of the Government of China at Kalimpong and Calcutta may lease lands from the Indian side for the use of the Agencies and construct buildings thereon. The Government of China will render every possible assistance for housing the Indian Trade Agency at Gartok. The Government of India will also render every possible assistance for housing the Chinese Trade Agency at New Delhi.

(5) The Government of India will be pleased to return to the Government of China all lands used or occupied by the Government of India other than the lands within its Trade Agency compound walls at Yatung.

If there are godowns and buildings of the Government of India on the above-mentioned lands used or occupied and to be returned by the Government of India and if Indian traders have stores, godowns or buildings on the above-mentioned lands so that there is a need to continue leasing lands, the Government of China agrees to sign contracts with the Government of India or Indian traders, as the case may be, for leasing to them those parts of the land occupied by the said godowns, buildings or stores and pertaining thereto.

(6) The Trade Agents of both Parties may, in accordance with the laws and regulations of the local governments, have access to their nationals involved in civil or criminal cases.

(7) The Trade Agents and traders of both countries may hire employees in the locality.

(8) The hospitals of the India Trade Agencies at Gyantse and Yatung will continue to serve personnel of the Indian Trade Agencies.

(9) Each Government shall protect the person and property of the traders and pilgrims of the other country.

(10) The Government of China agrees, so far as possible, to construct rest houses for the use of pilgrims along the route from Pulan-chung (Taklakot) to Kang Rimpoche (Kailas) and Mavam Tso (Manasarovar); and the Government of India agrees to place all possible facilities in India at the disposal of pilgrims.

(11) Traders and pilgrims of both countries shall have the facility of hiring means of transportation at normal and reasonable rates.

(12) The three Trade Agencies of each Party may function throughout the year.

(13) Traders of each country may rent buildings and godowns in accordance with local regulations in places under the jurisdiction of the other Party.

(14) Traders of both countries may carry on normal trade in accordance with local regulations at places as provided in Article II of the Agreement.

(15) Disputes between traders of both countries over debts and claims shall be handled in accordance with local laws and regulations.

On behalf of the Government of the Republic of India I hereby agree that the present Note along with Your Excellency's reply shall become an agreement between our two Governments which shall come into force upon the exchange of the present Notes.

I avail myself of this opportunity to express to Your Excellency Mr. Vice-Foreign Minister, the assurances of my highest consideration.

(Sd.) N. RAGHAVAN,
Ambassador Extraordinary and Pleni-potentiary of the Republic of India.

His Excellency Mr. Chang Han-fu,
Vice-Minister of Foreign Affairs,
Central People's Government,
People's Republic of China.

20. *Trade Agreement (Agreement between the Republic of India and the People's Republic of China, 14 October 1954)*

The Government of the Republic of India and the Central People's Government of the People's Republic of China, animated by the common desire to develop trade between the two countries and to strengthen further the friendship that already exists between the Governments and the peoples of India and China have, on the basis of equality and mutual benefit, reached agreements as follows:—

ARTICLE I

The two contracting parties being desirous of adopting all appropriate measures for the expansion of trade between the two countries agree to give the fullest consideration to all suggestions for the promotion of such trade.

ARTICLE II

The two contracting parties agree that all commercial transactions between the two countries shall be carried out in accordance with the Import, Export and Foreign Exchange Regulations in force from time to time in their respective countries.

ARTICLE III

The two contracting parties agree to accord, subject to the laws and regulations of the two countries for the time being in force, facilities for the import and export of the commodities mentioned in the attached Schedules 'A' and 'B'.

ARTICLE IV

The present Agreement will not preclude the two contracting parties from facilitating trade in commodities not mentioned in the attached Schedules 'A' and 'B'.

ARTICLE V

The Trade between the Republic of India and the Tibet Region of the People's Republic of China will be conducted in accordance with the provisions of the Agreement between the Republic of India and the People's Republic of China on Trade and Intercourse between India and the Tibet Region of China signed in Peking on the 29th April 1954.

ARTICLE VI

The Government of the Republic of India agree that on request by the Government of the People's Republic of China, they will subject to the regulations in force, accord reasonable facilities for the entry into the Port of Calcutta and subsequent movement to the Tibet Region of the People's Republic of China, of such commercial goods as cannot be obtained in India. These facilities will be accorded only to goods of Chinese origin.

ARTICLE VII

All commercial and non-commercial payments between the Republic of India and the People's Republic of China may be effected in Indian rupees or in pounds sterling as may be mutually convenient. For the purpose of facilitating such payments, the People's Bank of China will open one or more account(s) with one or more commercial bank(s) in India authorised to deal in Foreign Exchange to be called account(s) 'A'. In addition, the People's Bank of China will, if necessary, open another account with the Reserve Bank of India to be called account 'B'. All payments between the two countries will be made through account(s) 'A'. Account 'B' will be used only for replenishing the balance(s) in account(s) 'A' whenever necessary. Payments to be made by residents of India to residents of the People's Republic of China will be effected by crediting the amounts of such payments to the above-mentioned account(s) 'A'. Payments to be made to residents of India by residents of the People's Republic of China will be effected by debiting the said account(s) 'A'. The account(s) 'A' will be replenished as and when necessary by one of the following methods, namely:—

(i) by transfer of funds from another account 'A' of the People's Bank of China with another commercial bank, or from account 'B' with the Reserve Bank of India;

(ii) by sale of sterling to the bank concerned. Account 'B' will be replenished by either sale of sterling to the Reserve Bank of India or by transfer of funds from account(s) 'A'.

2. Article VII of this Agreement covers the following payments:—

    (i) Payments for the commodities imported or exported under the present Agreement;

    (ii) Payments connected with commercial transactions and covering insurance, freight (in case of shipments of goods by the ships of either country), port charges, storage and forwarding expenses and bunkering;

    (iii) Payments for distribution of films, for incomes and expenses of cultural performances and other exhibitions;

    (iv) Payments of expenses on account of tours of delegations of commercial, cultural, social or official nature;

    (v) Payments for the maintenance of the Embassy, Consulates and Trade Agencies of the Republic of India in China and for the maintenance of the Embassy, Consulates and Trade Agencies of the People's Republic of China in India;

    (vi) Other non-commercial payments on which agreement is reached between the Reserve Bank of India and the People's Bank of China.

3. Any balances on the credit side of the account(s) 'A' or account 'B' maintained by the People's Bank of China will be convertible on demand into sterling at any time at the usual Banks' selling rate for sterling as fixed from time to time by the Indian Exchange Banks' Association. The above mentioned balances will be convertible into sterling even after the expiry of this Agreement.

4. Payments for Border Trade between the Republic of India and the People's Republic of China, however, will be settled according to the customary practice.

ARTICLE VIII

The two contracting parties agree to consult with each other on questions that may arise in the course of the implementation of the present Agreement.

ARTICLE IX

This Agreement will come into force from the date of its signature and will remain valid for a period of two years.

This Agreement can be extended or renewed by negotiation between the two contracting parties to be commenced three months prior to its expiry.

Done in duplicate in New Delhi on the fourteenth Day of October 1954, in the Hindi, Chinese and English languages, all texts being equally authentic.

(Sd.) KUNG YUAN,	(Sd.) H. V. R. IENGAR,
On behalf of the Government of the People's Republic of China.	On behalf of the Government of the Republic of India.

Schedules of Goods for Export not reproduced.

United Nations General Assembly

Fourteenth Session

Eight hundred and thirty-fourth Plenary Meeting
October 21st 1959

The Question of Tibet: Draft Resolution submitted by the Federation of Malaya and Ireland.

The General Assembly,

Recalling the principles regarding fundamental human rights and freedoms set out in the Charter of the United Nations and in the Universal Declaration of Human Rights adopted by the General Assembly on December 10th 1948,

Considering that the fundamental human rights and freedoms to which the Tibetan people, like all others, are entitled include the right to civil and religious liberty for all without distinction,

Mindful also of the distinctive cultural and religious heritage of the people of Tibet and of the autonomy which they have traditionally enjoyed,

Gravely concerned at reports, including the official statements of His Holiness the Dalai Lama, to the effect that the fundamental human rights and freedoms of the people of Tibet have been forcibly denied to them,

Deploring the effect of these events in increasing international tensions and embittering relations between peoples at a time when earnest and positive efforts are being made by responsible leaders to reduce tension and improve international relations,

1. Affirms its belief that respect for the principles of the Charter and of the Universal Declaration of Human Rights is essential for the evolution of a peaceful world order based on the rule of law,

2. Calls for respect for the fundamental human rights of the Tibetan people and for their distinctive cultural and religious life.

Voting by roll call:

In favour: Federation of Malaya, Greece, Guatemala, Haiti, Honduras, Iceland, Iran, Ireland, Israel, Italy, Japan, Jordan, Laos, Liberia, Luxembourg, Mexico, Netherlands, New Zealand, Nicaragua, Norway, Pakistan, Panama, Paraguay, Peru, Philippines, Sweden, Thailand, Tunisia, Turkey, United States of America, Uruguay, Venezuela, Argentina, Australia, Austria, Bolivia, Brazil, Canada, Chile, China, Colombia, Cuba, Denmark, Ecuador, El Salvador.

Against: Hungary, Poland, Romania, Ukrainian Soviet Socialist Republic, Union of Soviet Socialist Republics, Albania, Bulgaria, Byelorussian S.S.R., Czechoslovakia.

Abstaining: Finland, France, Ghana, India, Indonesia, Iraq, Lebanon, Libya, Morocco, Nepal, Portugal, Saudi Arabia, Spain, Sudan, Union of South Africa, United Arab Republic, United Kingdom of Great Britain and Northern Ireland, Yemen, Yugoslavia, Afghanistan, Belgium, Burma, Cambodia, Ceylon, Dominican Republic, Ethiopia.

The draft resolution was adopted by 45 votes to 9 with 26 abstentions.

The vote of Costa Rica, whose delegate was absent, was later recorded in favour of the resolution.

CHRONOLOGICAL TABLE

This table is intended to give a general synopsis of the rulers of Tibet and China and also of the Regents and Panchen Lamas of Tibet. Mongolia is included for the sake of showing only the most important figures there who from time to time influenced the history of Tibet or China.

Dates marked ★ are dubious or controversial. An explanation of the doubts or uncertainties is a task for a more detailed work.

Tibetan names are given in a phonetic rendering and some are in an abbreviated form but one which is readily intelligible to Tibetans. Vowels in Tibetan are pronounced approximately as in Italian.

To save space and because the details of contemporary Tibetan leaders are unknown, the names of the Chinese Emperors of the Five Dynasties and the early Sung Emperors have been omitted. Emperors of the T'ang, Sung, and Ming dynasties are identified by their dynastic titles (miao hao); those of the Yuan dynasty by one of their Mongolian names; and those of the Ch'ing by their regnal titles (nier nao) which appear to be commonly used in popular histories.

TIBET	MONGOLIA	CHINA
'THE CHÖ-GYE': 'RELIGIOUS KINGS'		THE T'ANG DYNASTY
A.D.		A.D.
c.618★ Song-tsen Gam-po, b. 605★		Kao Tsu 618
		T'ai Tsung 627
649 Mang-song Mang-tsen, b. .646★		Kao Tsung 650
676 Dü-song Mang-po-je		
		Chung Tsung 684
		Jui Tsung
		Wu Hao (Empress)
704 Tri-de Tsug-ten		Chung Tsung 705
		Jui Tsung 710
		Hüan Tsung 713
754 Tri-song De-tsen, b. 742		Su Tsung 756
		Tai Tsung 763
		Tê Tsung 780
797★ Mu-ne Tsen-po		Shun Tsung 805
800★ Tri-de Song-tsen (Se-na-lek)		Hien Tsung 806
815 Tri-tsug De-tsen (Ral-pa-chen)		Mu Tsung 821
		King Tsung 825
		Wên Tsung 827

304

838* Lang Darma, d. 842

Break-up of
the Tibetan Kingdom
into numerous
lay and monastic principalities
e.g. Yarlung, Ngari, Purang,
Tshal, Sakya, etc.

Wu Tsung	842
Süan Tsung	847
I Tsung	860
Hi Tsung	874
Chao Tsung	884
Chao Süan Ti	895
End of the T'ang Dynasty	905

THE FIVE DYNASTIES 907

THE SUNG DYNASTY 960

MONGOL KHAKANS

Chingis, 1162–1227

Ming Tsung	1195
	1203

Ogotai, d. 1241
Kuyuk

	1229
	1246

Mongka

	1251

Kublai

	1260
Tu Tsung	1260
Kung Ti	1265
Twan Tsung	1275
Ti Ping	1276
	1278

THE YUAN DYNASTY

Kublai 1279

Timur 1295

ASCENDANCY OF SAKYA

1207 Tibetan Chiefs submit to Chingis Khan

1249 Sakya Pandita made Viceroy of Tibet for the Mongols

1253 Phagpa succeeds as Viceroy
1261 Phagpa given the title 'Tisri'

1280 Rinchen Tisri
1282 Dharmapalarakshita Tisri
128 Yeshe Rinchen Tisri
1295 Tragpa Öser Tisri

305

CHRONOLOGICAL TABLE—Continued

TIBET	MONGOLIA	CHINA
1303 Rinchen Gyantsen Tisri		
1304 Dorje Pal Tisri		
		1307 Kuluk
		1311 Buyantu
1313 Sangye Pal Tisri		
1316 Kunga Lotro Tisri		
		1320 Gegen
		1324 Yesun Timur
1327 Kunga Lekpa Chungne Tisri		
		1328 Kushala
		1329 Togh Timur
1330 Kunga Gyantsen Tisri, d. 1358		
		1332 Rinchenpal
		1333 Toghon Timur, d. 1370
THE SECOND KINGDOM		**THE MING DYNASTY**
1350* Chang-chub Gyantsen of Pagmotru takes power		
1364 Sakya Gyantsen		
1368 Resumption of Tibetan independence		1368 T'ai Tsu
	1371 Ayushitala s.o. Toghon Timur	
1373 Trakpa Rinchen		
	1378 Toguz Timur, d. 1388	
1381 Sonam Tralepa		
1386 Trakpa Chang-chub		
HIERARCHS OF THE GELUGPA SECT		
Tsong-Khapa (Lobzang Trakpa) founder of the sect, 1357–1419		
		1399 Hwei Ti
Gedün Truppa, 1st Dalai Lama, 1391–1475		1403 Ch'êng Tsu (Yung Lo)
		1425 Jên Tsung
		1426 Süan Tsung
	Essen, Oirat leader, usurped power, c. 1435–1455	1436 Ying Tsung
1443 Trakpa Chungne		
		1450 Tai Tsung
		1457 King Ti
		Ying Tsung
1465* Sangye Gyantsen Pal Zangpo		1465 Hien Tsung

1481	Dön-yö Dorje of *Rimpung* takes power	Gedun Gyatso, IInd Dalai Lama, 1475–1542		Dayan, 29th descendant o Chingis, 1470–1543, regained power	Hiao Tsung	1488
					Wu Tsung	1506
					She Tsung	1522
1522*	Ngawang Namgye			Altan, grandson of Dayan, in power 1543–1583	Muh Tsung	1567
1550*	Töndup Tseten	Sonam Gyatso, 1543–1588, IIIrd Dalai Lama given the title by Altan Khan in 1578[1]			Shên Tsung	1573
1565	Karma Tseten of *Tsang* takes power					
1582	Lhawang Dorje *fl.*	Yönten Gyatso, IVth Dalai Lama, 1589–1617 great grandson of Altan Khan			Kwang Tsung	1620
1603	Phüntso Namgye *fl.*				Hi Tsung	1621
1621	Karma Ten-Kyong, *d.* 1642	Ngawang Lobzang Gyatso, Vth Dalai Lama, 1617–1682		Gusri, Qośot leader, acquires power in Kokonor region	Chwang Lieh Ti	1628

A.D.	THE DALAI LAMAS	'KINGS' OF TIBET	PANCHEN LAMAS		THE MANCHU CH'ING DYNASTY	A.D.
1642	V Ngawang Lobzang Gyatso, 1617–1682	Gusri	I Chokyi Gyaltsen, 1570–1662			
					Shun Chih	1644
1655		Dayan Khan				
					K'ang Hsi	1661
1663			II Lobzang Yeshe, *d.* 1737			
1668		Tenzin Dalai Khan				
				Galden Dzungar		1676
1679	(Sangye Gyatso, Regent, *d.* 1705)					
1683	VI Tsang-yang Gyatso, *d.* 1706					
1696		Tenzin Wangchuk Khan				
1697		Lhabzang Khan, *d.* 1717		Tsewang Rabten		1697
1708	VII Kezang Gyatso, *d.* 1757					

[1] Sonam Gyatso is properly the first Dalai Lama, but the title is customarily given to his two predecessors also.

CHRONOLOGICAL TABLE—*Continued*

	TIBET	MONGOLIA	CHINA	
1720	Overlordship of Ch'ing Emperors of China established		Yung Ch'êng	1722 / 1727
1728	Phola Sonam Tobgye	Galden Tsering		
1738	III Lobzang Palden Yeshe, *d.* 1780		Chi'en Lung	1735
1747	Gyurmé Namgyal, *d.* 1750	Tsewang Dorje Namgyel		1745
1757	REGENTS / Demo Rimpoche I	Lama Dargye / Dawa Achi / Amursana, *d.* 1757		1750 / 1753 / 1755
1758	VIII Jampel Gyatso, *d.* 1804			
1777	Tsomoling Nomenkhan I to 1784			
1781	IV Tempé Nyima, *d.* 1854			
1791	Tatsa Rimpoche I		Chia Ch'ing	1796
1806	IX Luntok Gyatso, *d.* 1815			
1810	Demo Rimpoche II			
1816	X Tshultrim Gyatso, *d.* 1837		Tao Kwang	1820
1819	Tsomoling Nomenkhan II			
1820				
1838	XI Khedrup Gyatso, *d.* 1856			
			THE CH'ING DYNASTY	
1844	Panchen Lama Tempé Nyima, for 8 months			
1845	Reting Hutuktu I to 1862		Hsien Fêng	1850
1855	V Chokyi Trakpa, Tenpai Wangchuk *d.* 1882			
1856	XII Trinle Gyatso, *d.* 1875		T'ung Chih	1861

Date	Tibetan Government / Dalai Lamas	Regents / Ganden Tripa	Panchen Lamas	China
1862		Shatra Lönchen to 1864		Regency of Empress Tz'ŭ Hsi from 1861
1864		Ganden Tripa Lobzang		to 1875
1875		Khenrab Wangchuk to 1875		Kwang Hsü 1875
1876	XIII Thupten Gyatso, *d.* 1933	Tatsa Rimpoche II to 1886		
1883				
1886		Demo Rimpoche III to 1895		
1895	XIII Dalai Lama takes power	Ganden Tripa Lobzang Gyantsen		Regency of Empress Tz'ŭ Hsi from 1898 to 1908
1904	(Dalai Lama in	Ganden Tripa Tsomoling Rimpoche to 1913		
1908	flight and exile			Hsüan T'ung 1908
1910	from Tibet)			Revolution. End of Ch'ing Dynasty 1911
				REPUBLIC
1912	Resumption of Tibetan independence			Yuan Shih-k'ai to 1916 1912
1913	XIII Dalai Lama returns to Tibet			
				Chiang Kai-shek 1928
1933		Reting Hutuktu II to 1947		
1935	XIV Tenzin Gyatso			
1938			VI Chökyi Nyima, *d.* 1937	
1947		Taktra Rimpoche to 1950	VII Chökyi Gyaltsen	
				COMMUNIST 'PEOPLE'S REPUBLIC'
1951	Tibet annexed to Communist China			Mao Tse-tung 1949
1959	XIV Dalai Lama takes refuge in India. Tibetan Government dissolved by Communist Chinese Government			

ADDENDA

CHAPTER I

The greater part of this chapter has no relevance to present conditions under the Chinese Communist regime.

page 3. The Chinese have redrawn the map of Tibet, which they call Hsitsang, and show it only to the west of approximately Long. 92° 15′ E. Former Tibetan territory to the east of that line is now shown as falling within Hsikang.

page 6. The population of Tibet ("Hsitsang") was reported in 1982 to be 1,700,000.

p. 7, line 25. Lhasa now consists of the old Tibetan city with a population of 50,000 and a new, entirely separate, Chinese city of 70,000.

page 9, line 6. Good barley can be found at elevations of 15,000 feet.

page 18, lines 8-11. The division of the administrative service into monk and lay branches was instituted in 1792.

CHAPTER II

page 30, lines 5-7. Recently published photographic copies of MSS from Tun huang (*Choix de Documents de Touen houang,* Paris, 1978, 1979) throw light on the well-organized frontier administration in which for some sixty years the Tibetans employed educated local Chinese as officials.

page 33, line 20. A Tibetan princedom of some importance, founded c. 950 by Pan lo chi, possibly a descendant of the former Tibetan royal family, continued in the neighbourhood of the Kokonor until the Mongol conquest in 1227.

page 35, lines 9-11. The Yuan emperors sweetened the relationship with Tibet by very large gifts of money and valuables.

CHAPTER III

p. 45, lines 6-7. A mural painting in the Cathedral of Lhasa is stated by the Chinese to show the Lama making obeisance to the Emperor; it is clear from the gesture that he is preaching religion to him.

page 46, line 19. There appears to be no truth in the story that Sangye Gyatso was the son of the Dalai Lama. He was, incidentally, mainly responsible for the new Potala buildings.

page 47, lines 2-4. The evidence is that Sangye Gyatso did in fact conceal the death of the Vth Dalai Lama and the discovery of his successor for fourteen years from all but a very few trusted persons. The Emperor did, however, suspect the truth.

page 49, line 28. A blot on the Chinese behaviour was the spectacularly cruel execution of Lhabzang's Tibetan opponent, Tagtsepa.

page 50, line 12. In his Geographical Edict dated 1721 the Emperor more correctly says that it was only in that year (1721) that Tibet could be inscribed in a map of the Chinese empire.

page 52. Phola Teji was known to his contemporaries as Pholhanas, from the name of his estate.

page 53, lines 34, 35. The VIIth Dalai Lama (1708–1757) exempted the estates of the Panchen Lama from taxation. The VIIIth (1758–1804) revoked that exemption. The XIIIth (1876–1933) increased the taxation.

CHAPTER V

page 75, lines 24-26. Passports granted by the Chinese to French missionaries on the eastern frontier of Tibet were rejected by the Tibetans in 1865. Similar passports given to Przhevalsky, Gill and Count Szechenyi between 1874 and 1878 were also rejected. In 1879 the Tibetans formally announced their intention to exclude all foreigners from their country.

page 76, line 22. The Dalai Lama on his accession issued a decree virtually amounting to a declaration of independence (Tada, *The XIIth Dalai Lama,* Tokyo, 1965).

page 77. The Chinese Amban at Lhasa told the Foreign Secretary to the Indian Government that he was only a guest, not master, at Lhasa (P. Mehra, *The Younghusband Expedition,* London, 1968, p. 74).

CHAPTER VI

page 98, last line. Morley was "determined to depose from its usurped position of independent power" the Government of India of which he was deeply suspicious.

page 103, lines 26-27. Curzon in 1900 disliked the word "suzerainty" which had caused trouble in the Transvaal and was "of vague extent and doubtful application." It was to cause more trouble in connection with the Simla Convention of 1914. With regard to its interpretation one may consider the treaty of 1899 about Kuwait, regarded as under Turkish suzerainty but British protection; and the treaty of Kiakhta, 1914, between China and Russia about Mongolia described as autonomous under Chinese suzerainty but Russian protection.

CHAPTER VII

page 107, line 8. The note of 17 August 1912 referred to existing treaty relations between the U.K. and Tibet.

page 117, lines 1-6. In reporting to his government on the frontier proposals Ivan Chen referred only to the Sino-Tibetan frontier east and north of the Tila La; he said nothing about the Indo-Tibetan frontier.

page 119. A Japanese military officer Yajima Yasujiro, who was in Tibet from 1910 to 1917, was employed to train Tibetan troops.

CHAPTER VIII

page 128, lines 1-4. The Mongols had similar fears that the Panchen would come to reinstate the Jetsundamba Lama with the help of a Chinese army.

page 131, line 21. The party brought a letter from Dorjiev who is said to have warned the Dalai Lama privately against them.

CHAPTER IX

page 139, line 6. Lungshar swiftly brought about the downfall of his rival Kunphel La: see Shakabpa, *Tibet* pp. 274-276 for an eyewitness account of these dramatic events and the rising in Kham by Kunphel La's supporter, Tobgye Pangdatshang.

page 142, line 18. The Tibetans asked for the return of Dege and Nyarong.

page 146, line 26. After the Panchen Lama's death a faction of his followers tried to set up a shadow government in Kham but were brought to heel by the Governor of Sichuan.

page 148, lines 7-8. It has been suggested that Gould's account in *The Jewel in the Lotus* implies that he tricked the Tibetan Government into this arrangement. That is not true. The presence of the British Mission was valuable to the Tibetans in their continuing negotiations with the Panchen Lama and gave them the means of communicating with the Chinese Government through the British Ambassador in China in such a way that receipt of their message could not be denied. The idea of a journey by Gould to meet the Panchen had been found unacceptable; and Gould's health made it necessary for him to leave Lhasa. The leading members of the Tibetan Government had been consulted privately and had readily agreed well before Gould's last formal meeting with the Cabinet. This decision avoided the question of the permanency of the mission which neither Whitehall nor the Government of India wanted to contemplate. Shakabpa (*Tibet*, p. 281) is incorrect in saying that Gould asked for permission to establish a mission with similar rights to the Chinese. No such request was ever made.

CHAPTER X

page 155. The XIIIth Dalai Lama had set up such a bureau in 1910 but it had ceased to function.

page 162, line 7. Lots were cast whether or not to resist by force.

page 163, line 35. United States policy, originally depending on the 'Open Door', was unwilling to acknowledge Tibet, Mongolia and Manchuria as anything but part of China, and so 'open'. The position later stated, in 1960, by Mr Herter was that 'The historical position of the U.S.A. was to consider Tibet autonomous under the suzerainty of China yet had always stood for the principle of self-determination'.

page 165, line 10. Eden records (*The Reckoning*, p. 425) that at the Cairo summit in 1943 he had to be firm against Wang Chung-hui's attempt to get him to recognize their old claims on Tibet.

page 166, line 10. Li Tieh-tseng, p. 190, reports a statement in 1945 by Chiang Kai-shek offering increased autonomy to Tibet.

CHAPTER XI

page 174, line 15. The message was sent direct to Delhi as I declined to transmit it in those terms.

CHAPTER XII

page 183, last paragraph. Incorrect. The force travelled by a pass further to the east. The same mistake appears on page 229, line 9.

page 187, line 3. I was informed in 1961 by Tibetan officials that the U.S.A. had offered them arms if they intended to resist.

page 200, line 21. According to private information Chou En-lai and Liu Kai-ming discussed the 1951 treaty with the Dalai Lama near Mukden in 1955 and modified some of its provisions.

page 204, line 21. These measures were announced by the Chinese Administrator Chang Ching-wu at a great meeting at Lhasa but he declined a request to commit them to writing.

CHAPTER XIII

page 220, line 15. The USSR later changed its tune and in 1967 referred to the Tibetan fight for freedom and independence in 1959. China was also accused of genocide in Tibet. In 1950 a spokesman stated that the USSR was willing to help Tibet, if asked.

CHAPTER XIV

page 232, line 1. This was also a turning point in Sino-Soviet relations when Soviet criticism of Chinese action on the Indian frontier caused resentment in China.

page 234. Add at end:

The tension was broken in October 1962 when Chinese troops attacked and severely defeated Indian forces defending the eastern end of the McMahon Line. There was a simultaneous attack on Indian positions in the Ladakh sector. Nehru appealed to the U.S.A. for support and the U.S. 6th and 7th fleets were alerted and moved towards the Bay of Bengal. The Chinese eventually withdrew, taking many Indian prisoners-of-war to detention in Tibet. Former positions were gradually restored leaving controversy about the origin of the fighting and further years of bitter diplomatic exchanges about minor border incidents from Ladakh to Sikkim, and other provocations. Only by 1982 were there signs of detente and an attempt to find a solution of the differences.

APPENDIX

page 261. Treaty between Tibet and Ladakh, 1842. The translation appears to be the work of a Ladakhi Muslim. The copy of the treaty in the Tibetan archives, which is translated in Shakabpa's *Tibet,* p. 327, makes no mention of the Emperor of China.

page 302. In December 1960 a similar resolution was put on the agenda of the General Assembly by 49 votes to 13 but was not debated until the following year when it was passed by 56 votes to 11. The terms, which included mention of the right to self-determination, are quoted in *My Land and My People,* by H.H. the Dalai Lama, pp. 246–247. Another resolution on the same lines was passed by 43 votes to 26 in the General Assembly in December 1966. There has been no further resolution since then.

SELECT SOURCES AND BIBLIOGRAPHY

Abbreviations: *ICJ*—International Commission of Jurists. *JRAS—Journal of the Royal Asiatic Society. JRCAS—Journal of the Royal Central Asian Society.*

I THE TIBETAN BACKGROUND

BELL, SIR CHARLES, *Tibet: Past and Present.* Oxford 1924.
    The People of Tibet. Oxford 1928.
    The Religion of Tibet. Oxford 1931.
    Portrait of the Dalai Lama. London 1942.
    Grammar of Colloquial Tibetan. Calcutta 1919.
MACDONALD, D. *Twenty Years in Tibet.* London 1932.
    The Land of the Lama. London 1928.
HEDIN, SVEN. *Transhimalaya.* London 1909–1913.
BUXTON, L. H. D. *Peoples of Asia.* London 1925.
HADDON, A. C. *Races of Man.* London 1909.
HANNAH, H. B. *Grammar of the Tibetan Language.* Calcutta 1912.
TUCCI, G. *Tibetan Painted Scrolls.* Rome 1949.
SNELLGROVE, D. L. *Buddhist Himalaya.* Oxford 1957.
WADDELL, L. A. *Lamaism, the Buddhism of Tibet.* 2nd edn. Cambridge 1934.
WESSELS, C. J. (S.J.) *Early Jesuit Travellers in Central Asia.* The Hague 1924.
FILIPPI, F. DE. *Desideri. An Account of Tibet.* Broadway Travellers, London 1937.
PALLIS, M. *Peaks and Lamas.* London 1939.

II THE RELIGIOUS KINGS TO THE RULE OF THE DALAI LAMAS: 630–1642

BUSHELL, S. W. 'Early History of Tibet from Chinese Sources'. *Journal of the Royal Asiatic Society* 1880.
BACOT, J., THOMAS, F. W., and TOUSSAINT, C. *Documents de Touen Houang relatifs à l'Histoire du Tibet.* Paris 1946.
PETECH, L. *A Study on the Chronicles of Ladakh.* Calcutta 1939.
LI, TIEH-TSENG. *The Historical Status of Tibet.* New York 1956.
RICHARDSON, H. E. *Ancient Historical Edicts at Lhasa.* London 1952.
TUCCI, G. *Tibetan Painted Scrolls.*
GROUSSET, R. *L'Empire des Steppes.* Paris 1948.
DAS, S. C. 'A Short History of the House of Phagdu'. *JRAS (Bengal)* Aug. 1905.
    'Tibet Under her Last Kings'. Ibid. June 1905.
CRONIN, V. *The Wise Man from the West.* London 1958.
ROCKHILL, W. W. *The Dalai Lamas of Lhasa.* Leyden 1910.
FAIRBANK, J. K., and TENG, S. Y. 'On the Ch'ing Tributary System'. *Harvard Journal of Asiatic Studies* June 1941.

III MANCHU PROTECTORATE IN TIBET: 1720–1792

PETECH, L. *China and Tibet in the Early XVIII Century.* Leyden 1950.
PARKER, E. H. 'Manchu Relations with Tibet'. *JRAS* 1885.
GROUSSET, R. *The Rise and Splendour of the Chinese Empire.* London 1952.
LI, TIEH-TSENG. op. cit.

ROCKHILL, W. W. op. cit.
WADDELL, L. A. op. cit.
SNELLGROVE, D. L. op. cit.

The Emperor K'ang Hsi's edict of 1720 has been translated from the Chinese text by Rockhill in *JRAS* 1891 and by M. Jamétel in *L'Épigraphie Chinoise au Tibet*, Peking/Paris 1880. The writer is preparing a translation from the Tibetan text at Lhasa.

IV TIBET'S DOORS CLOSE: 1792

WESSELS, C. J. op. cit.
FILIPPI, F. DE. op. cit.
MARKHAM, SIR CLEMENTS. *Narrative of the mission of G. Bogle to Tibet, and the journey of J. Manning to Lhasa, with Notes and Lives*. London 1879.
TURNER, S. *An Account of an Embassy to the Court of the Teshoo Lama*. London 1800.
CAMMANN, S. *Trade Through the Himalayas*. Princeton and London 1951.
LAMB, A. 'Tibet in Anglo-Chinese Relations'. *Journal of the Royal Central Asian Society* 1957/58.
    'Britain and Chinese Central Asia'. *The Road to Lhasa*. London 1960.
RICHARDSON, H. E. 'The Karmapa Sect'. *JRAS* 1958/59.
LI. op. cit.
ROCKHILL. op. cit.
HUC, FR. E. *Travels in Tartary, Thibet and China (1844-48)*. London 1879.

Use has also been made of the Tibetan text of inscriptions of the Ch'ing period from Lhasa, not all of which have been published.

V THE WEST BREAKS IN

AITCHISON, SIR CHARLES. *A Collection of Treaties, Engagements, and Sanads relating to India and Neighbouring Countries*, Vols. XII and XIV. Calcutta 1929–1931.
MACKENZIE, SIR ALEXANDER. *History of Relations with the Hill Tribes of the N.E. Frontier of Bengal*. Calcutta 1884.
HOLDICH, SIR THOMAS. *Tibet the Mysterious*. London 1908.
SANDBERG, G. *The Exploration of Tibet*. Calcutta 1904.
LAMB, A. "Britain and Chinese Central Asia". op. cit.
DAVIS, SIR JOHN. *Chinese Miscellanies*. London 1865.
BELL, SIR CHARLES. *Tibet: Past and Present* and *Portrait of the Dalai Lama*.
LI, T-T. op. cit.
PARES, SIR BERNARD. *History of Russia*. London 1955.
GROUSSET, R. *L'Empire des Steppes*.
HODGSON, B. H. *Essays on the Languages, Literature and Religion of Nepal and Tibet*. London 1874.
MARKHAM. op. cit.
TURNER, S. op. cit.
TSYBIKOV, G. T. 'Lhasa and Central Tibet'. *Journal of the Smithsonian Institution*. Washington 1904.

Cambridge History of India, Vol. VI. Cambridge 1932.
RONALDSHAY, LORD. *Life of Lord Curzon*. London 1927.
KAWAGUCHI, EKAI. *Three Years in Tibet*. Madras 1909.
LANDON, P. *Lhasa*. London 1905.
LAMB, A. 'Some Notes on Russian Intrigue in Tibet'. *JRAS* 1959.
H.M.G. Papers Relating to Tibet 1904/05: Cd 1920, 2054 2370.
YOUNGHUSBAND, SIR FRANCIS. *India and Tibet*. London 1910.
FLEMING, P. *Bayonets to Lhasa*. London 1961.
WADDELL, L. A. *Lhasa and its Mysteries*. London 1905.
CANDLER, E. *The Unveiling of Lhasa*. London 1905.

VI RESTORATION OF TIBET'S INDEPENDENCE: 1912

BELL; LANDON; LI; WADDELL; YOUNGHUSBAND. op. cit.
TEICHMAN, SIR ERIC. *Travels of a Consular Officer in Eastern Tibet*. Cambridge 1922.

VII THE SIMLA CONVENTION: 1914

LI; TEICHMAN. op. cit.
GOULD, SIR BASIL. *The Jewel in the Lotus*. London 1957.
ANON. *The Boundary Question between China and Tibet*. Peking 1940.

VIII CLOSER TIES WITH BRITAIN: 1920–1933

BELL; LI. op. cit.
CHAPMAN, F. S. *Lhasa the Holy City*. London 1940.

IX INTERREGNUM: 1933–1940

BELL; GOULD; CHAPMAN; LI. op. cit.
SHEN, T. L. and LIU, S. C. *Tibet and the Tibetans*. Stanford and London 1952.

From the time of Gould's mission to Lhasa as well as for some facts relating to earlier periods the writer has drawn largely on his own experience in Tibet, India, and China, supplemented by personal inquiries from leading Tibetan officials at Lhasa and elsewhere.

X NEUTRALITY PRESERVED: 1940–1946

BELL; GOULD; LI; SHEN and LIU. op. cit.
International Commission of Jurists. *The Question of Tibet and the Rule of Law* Geneva 1959.
HOPKINSON, A. J. 'The Position of Tibet'. *JRCAS*, July 1950.
HARRER, H. *Seven Years in Tibet*. London 1953.

XI WINDS OF CHANGE

LI; SHEN and LIU; HARRER. op. cit.
Government of India. White Papers I (7 September 1959). Notes Exchanged between the Governments of India and China. 1954–1959: also II (4 November 1959) and III (29 February 1960).
The Indian Press.

XII COMMUNIST OCCUPATION OF TIBET

LI; HARRER; I.C.J. op. cit. British and Indian Press.

FORD, R. *Captured in Tibet*. London 1957.

MEHRA, P. L. 'India, China and Tibet, 1950–1954'. *Indian Quarterly* Jan. 1956.

XIII THE TIBETAN RISING

British and Indian Press. Five articles by H. HARRER in the *Daily Mail*, 11–15 May 1959.

Government of India White Papers; I.C.J. report. op. cit.

SEN, CHANAKYA. *Tibet Disappears*. London 1960.

MORAES, F. *The Revolt in Tibet*. New York 1960.

Published records of the 124th meeting of the General Committee and the 826th and 831st to 834th Plenary Meetings of the General Assembly of the United Nations 1959.

XIV DISPUTE BETWEEN INDIA AND CHINA ON THE FRONTIER OF TIBET

Government of India White Papers; British and Indian Press. SEN; MORAES. op. cit.

BAILEY, F. M. *No Passport for Tibet*. London 1957.

China—Tibet—Assam. London 1945.

CAROE, SIR OLAF. 'The Geography and Ethnics of India's Northern Frontiers'. *The Geographical Journal*. September 1960.

XV TIBETANS IN EXILE

International Commission of Jurists. *Tibet and the People's Republic of China*. Geneva August 1960.

XVI EPILOGUE

DAWA NORBU. *Red Star over Tibet*. London 1974.

GINSBURGS, G. and MATHOS, M. *Communist China and Tibet*. The Hague 1974.

Information Office of H. H. The Dalai Lama. *Tibetans in Exile*, Dharamsala 1981.

SHAKABPA, W. D. *Tibet*. New Haven and London 1967. *Tibetan Review*, monthly, New Delhi.

INDEX

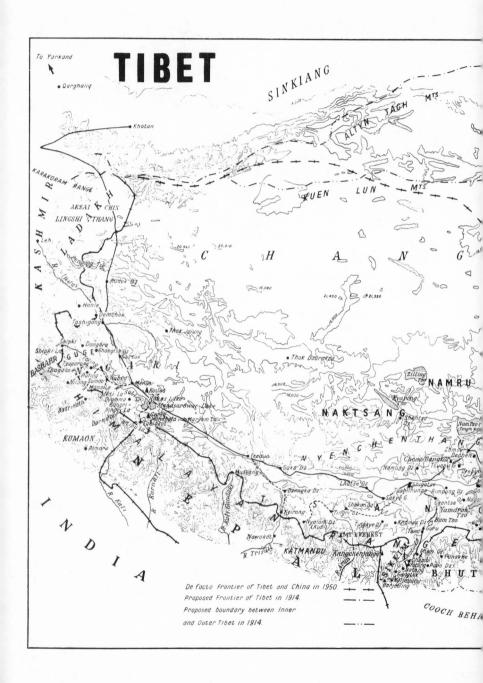

TIBET

De facto Frontier of Tibet and China in 1950
Proposed Frontier of Tibet in 1914.
Proposed boundary between Inner
and Outer Tibet in 1914.

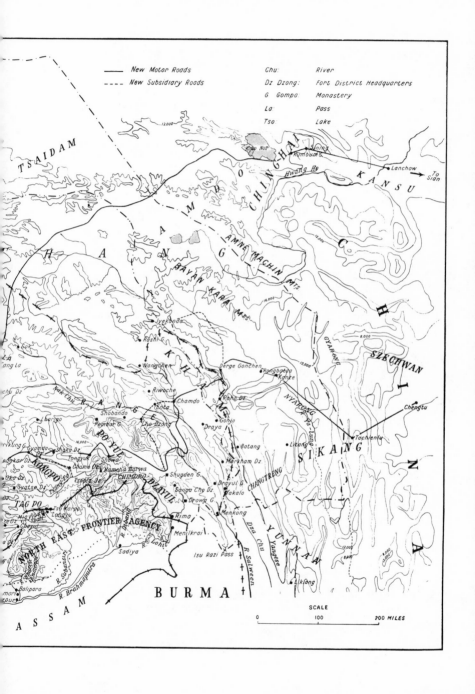

New Motor Roads
New Subsidiary Roads

Chu: River
Dz Dzong: Fort District Headquarters
G Gompa: Monastery
La: Pass
Tso: Lake

TSAIDAM

CHINGHAI

KANSU

Koko Nor
Kumbum G.
Sining
Lanchow
To Sian

Hwang Ho

12,000

AMNE MACHIN Mts.

BAYAN KARA Mts.

C H A N G   T A N G

CHE

12,000

8,000

GYARONG

SZECHWAN

Jyekundo
Nangchen
Rashi G.

Derge Gonchen
Kongbotsa
Kanze

NYARONG

12,000

Chengtu

Riwoche
Chamdo
Kota
Shobando
Pembar G.
Cho Dzong
Iberigo

K H A M

Baho Dz.
Gonjo
Draya

Tachienlu

Likiang
Batang

SIKANG

Yalung

Markham Dz.

CHANGTRENG

Draya

POYUL

Shaka Dz.
Tongyuk
Showa
Chame Dz.
Tsegang

Namcha Barwa
CHIMDRO DZAYUL
Espera J.

Shugden G.
Drayul G.
Yakalo
Drowa G.
Menkong

YUNNAN

KONGPO

TAG PO
Tso Karpo
Lobdza

Rima

Dza Chu

Likiang

12,000

8,000

Menilkrai

R. Salween

R. Yangtse

NORTH EAST FRONTIER AGENCY

Chayul

Sadiya

Isu Razi Pass

Balipara
R. Brahmaputra

A S S A M

B U R M A

SCALE
0   100   200 MILES